Second Language Teaching and Learning with Technology: Views of Emergent Researchers

Edited by Sylvie Thouësny and Linda Bradley

Published by Research-publishing.net
Dublin, Ireland
info@research-publishing.net

Second Language Teaching and Learning with Technology: Views of Emergent Researchers
Edited by Sylvie Thouësny and Linda Bradley

© 2011 by research-publishing.net
Research-publishing.net is a not-for-profit association

All articles in this book are licensed under a Creative Commons Attribution-Noncommercial-No Derivative Works 3.0 Unported License. You are free to share, copy, distribute and transmit the work under the following conditions:
- Attribution: You must attribute the work in the manner specified by the publisher.
- Noncommercial: You may not use this work for commercial purposes.
- No Derivative Works: You may not alter, transform, or build upon this work.

Research-publishing.net has no responsibility for the persistence or accuracy of URLs for external or third-party Internet websites referred to in this publication, and does not guarantee that any content on such websites is, or will remain, accurate or appropriate. Moreover, research-publishing.net does not take any responsibility for the content of the pages written by the authors of this book. The authors have recognised that the work described was not published before (except in the form of an abstract or as part of a published lecture, or thesis), or that it is not under consideration for publication elsewhere. While the advice and information in this book are believed to be true and accurate on the date of its going to press, neither the authors, the editors, nor the publisher can accept any legal responsibility for any errors or omissions that may be made. The publisher makes no warranty, expressed or implied, with respect to the material contained herein.

Trademark notice: Product or corporate names may be trademarks or registered trademarks, and are used only for identification and explanation without intent to infringe.

The print on demand version is an exact printed copy of the original eBook project which can be found at http://www.research-publishing.net.

Typeset by research-publishing.net
Cover design by Raphaël Savina (raphael@savina.net)
- Fonts used are licensed under a SIL Open Font License.
- Cantarell, designer Dave Crossland; Old Standard TT, designer Alexey Kryukov.

ISBN13: 978-1-908416-00-1 (eBook)
ISBN13: 978-1-908416-01-8 (print on demand)

British Library Cataloguing-in-Publication Data.
A cataloguing record for this book is available from the British Library.

Table of Contents

Notes on Contributors iv

Acknowledgements ix

Foreword x

Introduction on Views of Emergent Researchers in L2 Teaching and Learning with Technology
Sylvie Thouësny and Linda Bradley 1

Personal Learning Environments in Higher Education Language Courses: An Informal and Learner-Centred Approach
Ilona Laakkonen 9

QuickAssist: Reading and Learning Vocabulary Independently with the Help of CALL and NLP Technologies
Peter Wood 29

Self-Assessment and Tutor Assessment in Online Language Learning Materials: InGenio FCE Online Course and Tester
Ana Sevilla-Pavón, Antonio Martínez-Sáez, and José Macario de Siqueira 45

Mobile-Assisted Language Learning: Designing for Your Students
Agnieszka Palalas 71

Table of Contents

**A Design for Intercultural Exchange –
An Analysis of Engineering Students' Interaction
with English Majors in a Poetry Blog**
Linda Bradley, Berner Lindström, Hans Rystedt, and Magnus Gustafsson.......95

**Developing Sociolinguistic Competence
through Intercultural Online Exchange**
Mathy Ritchie...................123

**Second Language Learning by Exchanging Cultural
Contexts through the Mobile Group Blog**
Yinjuan Shao...................143

**Dynamically Assessing Written Language: To what Extent
Do Learners of French Language Accept Mediation?**
Sylvie Thouësny...................169

**Computer-Mediated Negotiated Interactions:
How is Meaning Negotiated in Discussion
Boards, Text Chat and Videoconferencing?**
Cédric Sarré...................189

Name Index...................211

Notes on Contributors

Editors

Sylvie Thouësny is a Ph.D. student at Dublin City University, Ireland. Her current research focuses on language learner variability and language learner modeling to assist second language teachers in the provision of strategic and effective feedback adapted to each individual. This field of research mainly draws on disciplines such as applied linguistics, human computer interaction, natural language processing, intelligent computer-assisted language learning, and dynamic assessment.

Linda Bradley is a Ph.D. student and lecturer at the Centre for Language and Communication, Chalmers University of Technology, Sweden. Her research interest is language learning and technology, investigating students' interaction, communication and linguistic production in online environments within higher education. Her publications focus on student collaboration and intercultural learning on web based tools such as wikis and blogs. In addition, she has a general interest in self-directed learning on emergent mobile devices.

Reading Committee

Françoise Blin has been working in CALL since the late eighties. She holds a PhD in Educational Technology from the Open University, UK. Her more recent work focuses on the applications of Activity Theory to CALL research, design, and practice. She is Vice-President of EUROCALL, co-editor of ReCALL (with June Thompson), and deputy editor of Alsic (Apprentissage des Langues et Systèmes de Communication). She is currently Associate Dean for Learning Innovation in the Faculty of Humanities and Social Sciences at Dublin City University, Ireland.

Ana Gimeno-Sanz, Ph.D. in English Philology, is Associate Professor in English Language in the Department of Applied Linguistics, Universidad Politécnica de Valencia, Spain. She is Head of the CAMILLE Research Group, devoted to research and development in CALL. She is currently President of the European Association for Computer-Assisted Language Learning (EUROCALL). She serves on several journals' academic advisory panels, including ReCALL (CUP) and the CALL Journal (Taylor & Francis) and is editor of EUROCALL's online journal, The EUROCALL Review.

Agnes Kukulska-Hulme is Professor of Learning Technology and Communication in the Institute of Educational Technology at The Open University, UK, where she leads the Next Generation Distance Learning research programme. She is President of the International Association for Mobile Learning and a member of the Editorial Board of the International Journal of Mobile and Blended Learning. She has been working in mobile learning research since 2001, leading numerous projects investigating learning innovation, self-directed learning and informal mobile language learning.

Meei-Ling Liaw is Professor in the Department of English at National Taichung University, Taiwan, and adjunct faculty in the Global Program of College of New Jersey, U.S.A. In 2001 she was a Fulbright Scholar conducting research at U.C. Berkeley and in 2008 at U.C. Irvine. Her research interests include using computer technology to facilitate EFL learning as well as reading and writing instruction. Her recent publications focus on using telecollaboration for intercultural learning. In addition to telecollaborative projects, currently she is conducting projects funded by the National Science Council in Taiwan on English language education policies.

Hans Paulussen is a senior researcher at the University of Leuven (K.U.Leuven KULAK, Belgium). He is involved in computational linguistic projects on computer-assisted language learning, corpus compilation, tagging and parsing. He was main corpus developer of the Dutch Parallel Corpus and coordinates the technical part of the compilation and exploitation of the learner corpus of French (LCF).

Peppi Taalas has expertise in (language) learning technologies, new learning cultures and professional staff development programmes. She has been active in the development of the Finnish virtual university and similar strategic initiatives. Currently she is involved in various research and development projects that deal with the changing notions of teaching and learning practices, literacy pedagogies and the ways in which teachers create and design learning activities that include multimodal aspects of learning and learning materials. She is the director of the Language Centre at the University of Jyväskylä.

Monica Ward's research interests include computer-assisted language learning (CALL) for Minority and Endangered Languages (e.g., Irish and Nawat) and the integration of natural language processing (NLP) techniques in CALL. The use of Software Engineering techniques in CALL draws on both industry and academic experience. Other areas of interest are CALL in non-traditional contexts (e.g., primary schools) and CALL normalisation and deployment; getting real people, outside of universities, to actually use CALL resources is not an easy task.

Authors

Ilona Laakkonen, MA, is a researcher at the Centre for Applied Language Studies, University of Jyväskylä. Her interests are in developing and researching multimodal pedagogies and new environments for language teaching and learning. For her Ph.D. she is exploring the concept and implementation of personal learning environments (PLE). She has also created online learning materials and taught students in the principles of online corpora and data-driven learning. Common for these interests is the learner-centred approach to teaching and learning of languages.

José Macário de Siqueira graduated in Computer Engineering from the University of Campinas (UNICAMP), Brazil, in 2003 and is currently completing his doctoral thesis at the Department of Applied Linguistics (Universidad Politécnica de Valencia, Spain) within the "Languages & Technology" Ph.D. programme. He is a researcher of the CAMILLE Research Group and has published several papers on Computer-Assisted Language Learning (CALL) and software development in specialised journals.

Notes on Contributors

Antonio Martínez-Sáez graduated in English Studies and in Translation and Interpreting Studies from the Universidad de Valencia (Spain) and is currently completing his doctoral thesis at the Department of Applied Linguistics (Universidad Politécnica de Valencia) within the "Languages & Technology" Ph.D. programme. He holds a four year research grant awarded by the Valencian Regional Government and is part of the CAMILLE Research Group. He has been involved in several research projects, attended national and international conferences and published several articles and reviews on computer assisted language learning and testing.

Agnieszka Palalas is a Doctoral Candidate at Athabasca University, currently working as Lead Researcher/Curriculum Specialist at George Brown College, Toronto, Canada. In her research of mobile learning, Agnieszka has combined her expertise of instructional design and computer technologies with 20 years of experience as a language instructor. Agnieszka holds a Master's Degree in DE (Instructional Design, Program Development & Educational Technologies), Advanced Graduate Diploma in DE (Technology) and in Programming, as well as a degree in Linguistics and TESL.

Mathy Ritchie has recently obtained her Ph.D. in Educational Studies from the University of Victoria. She is currently teaching French as a second language and teacher training courses at Simon Fraser University in Burnaby, British Columbia. In her work, she aims to connect French learners with Francophones in different ways to enrich their learning experience and give them opportunities to develop specific competences. Her research addresses computer-mediated communication, sociolinguistic and cultural competences, second language acquisition, and teacher education.

Cédric Sarré teaches ESP classes at Orléans University (France) and specialises in ESP course development, aimed at science students, with a particular emphasis on network-based telecollaborative work. His research interests are Second Language Acquisition (SLA) and Network-Based Language Teaching (NBLT). He has just completed a Ph.D. on the development of interactional competence in network-based telecollaborative language learning settings.

Notes on Contributors

Ana Sevilla-Pavón graduated in Modern Languages (English and French) from the Universidad de Valencia (Spain) and is currently completing her doctoral thesis at the Department of Applied Linguistics (Universidad Politécnica de Valencia) within the "Languages & Technology" Ph.D. programme. She holds a four year research grant awarded by the Valencian Regional Government and is currently a researcher of the CAMILLE Research Group. She has been involved in several research projects, published several research papers and participated in a number of national and international conferences on computer-assisted language learning and testing.

Yinjuan Shao has gained a doctorate in Learning Sciences and Technology from the University of Nottingham, UK. She is a Research Fellow at Nanyang Technological University in Singapore. Her interests include second language learning with emerging technology, game-based learning, learning in virtual reality, and mobile technology in learning and teaching, with special concern for mobile learning in and out of school, across formal and informal settings.

Peter Wood came to the University of Waterloo, ON, Canada to do a Ph.D. in German after having worked as a language teacher at various institutions and in different settings. Now he teaches German and Linguistics at the University of Saskatchewan. His main research interests are CALL, Computational Linguistics, Formal Linguistics and Second Language Acquisition.

Proofreaders

Cathy Fowley is a Ph.D. candidate in Dublin City University; she has recently submitted her dissertation, entitled "Publishing the Confidential: an ethnographic study of young Irish bloggers", where she analyses the relationship between authors, readers and technology, as well as the management of privacy in young people's blogs. Her research interests are Internet research, digital literacy, young people and the internet, older people and the internet, Internet ethics, and life-writing.

Neasa Ní Chiaráin is a postgraduate student in the Centre for Language and Communication Studies at Trinity College, Dublin, Ireland. Her main research interest is in SLA/FLA and she is specialising in CALL. She is at present investigating the potential application of text-to-speech technology in language teaching/learning, with specific reference to the Irish language. She is also interested in the acquisition of French and German as second languages.

Acknowledgements

This book project has indeed been a very rewarding experience. It has been a pleasure to meet everyone participating in this book and to have the opportunity to work collaboratively over the Internet. This is an eBook that will be openly accessible online and the process of getting there is also reflected in the fact that we have only met online.

First of all, we would like to thank all young researchers who have contributed with expertise in their area of study. This has resulted in nine chapters dealing with current topics of relevance for the field of CALL. We are very grateful to for having seven senior researchers as blind reviewers to guide the writers with relevant comments and to certify that the content is communicated in the best possible way. A special mention should also be made to Graham Davies for valuable input concerning topics to include in the introductory phase of this project. We are also very happy for the great effort that our two proofreaders have put into scrutinising the texts. Lastly, we would like to express our gratitude to family, friends, and colleagues for their support and encouragement throughout this project.

Sylvie Thouësny and Linda Bradley

Foreword

Only through research can a field be established as an academic discipline. Computer-assisted language learning (CALL) has come of age and nobody will now disagree that the field has become, in its own right, a very significant area within applied linguistics. As pointed out in the 2010 version of EUROCALL's[*] Research Policy Statement, "[r]esearch in CALL has been carried out for more than thirty years, and has now reached a significant level of volume and maturity. It is a truly international discipline and has led to notable improvements in the teaching and learning of languages in secondary and higher education institutions worldwide". This eBook is certainly an extremely good example of international research in CALL as all of its authors cover an impressive number of countries worldwide. And this, I think, is one of the most important attributes of CALL, the fact that research is conducted in a truly international fashion where researchers and practitioners alike collaborate incessantly to keep up with the constantly evolving technologies or, should we say, to ensure that these endlessly evolving technologies are exploited to the utmost advantage of language learning and teaching and to introduce improvements in language acquisition.

The scope of the research issues dealt with in the papers included in this eBook is also an illustrative sample of how CALL is evolving and a good example of the paths that the field is now taking. From well-established web-based learning environments to mobile learning, through current web 2.0 applications such as blogs, which foster intercultural contexts and/or diverse means of computer-mediated interaction. Although the authors are all emergent researchers, the maturity of their work is a mirror of the maturity of the field and an illustration of the ongoing development that CALL is experiencing. All of the papers have something in common: the research is intended so that others may gain understanding and also to broaden the insights in order to improve the language learning experience.

---

*European Association for Computer-Assisted Language Learning (EUROCALL)

---

x

One of the major achievements of this eBook is precisely the fact that it has emerged to give light to research in CALL that has stemmed from emergent researchers; that is, keen and devoted scholars whose work and know-how are undeniably necessary for the field to continue progressing and, very especially for it to nurture the very essence that sustains it, i.e., language learning and teaching and its many pedagogical practices.

I'd sincerely like to congratulate the editors of this eBook, Linda Bradley and Sylvie Thouësny for their resolution in undertaking this endeavour which will no doubt be an example of good practice for the CALL community at large.

Prof. Ana Gimeno-Sanz
President of the European Association
for Computer Assisted Language Learning
Universidad Politécnica de Valencia, Spain

Reference

EUROCALL Research Policy Statement. (2010). Retrieved from http://www.eurocall-languages.org/research/research_policy.html

Introduction on Views of Emergent Researchers in L2 Teaching and Learning with Technology

Sylvie Thouësny and Linda Bradley*

Abstract

Although technology has become embedded in our everyday life, researchers and practitioners constantly strive to find ways of incorporating technology in education, with language learning being one of those fields (Garrett, 2009). Numerous publications on this subject are available, mostly on condition that one is affiliated with a university, and that this university subscribes to a broad spectrum of publications. With the aim of widening free access research publications, we have elaborated a peer-reviewed eBook published under a Creative Commons licence which provides not only protection but also freedom for authors and editors. Young researchers from a variety of countries participated with a chapter of their ongoing projects. The themes approached within these projects represent topical areas of language learning and teaching, and technology within collaborative, personal and virtual learning environments. After providing an overview of the steps taken to develop this eBook project, this chapter gives a brief account of the innovative applications of technology in second language teaching and learning found in the eBook.

Keywords: language learning and teaching, technology, open access publication, eBook, creative commons licence, peer-reviewing.

---

*Dublin City University, Ireland, and Chalmers University of Technology, Sweden, respectively.
e-mails: sylvie.thouesny@icall-research.net, linda.bradley@chalmers.se

How to cite this chapter: Thouësny, S., & Bradley, L. (2011). Introduction on views of emergent researchers in L2 teaching and learning with technology. In S. Thouësny & L. Bradley (Eds.), *Second language teaching and learning with technology: views of emergent researchers* (pp. 1-8). Dublin: Research-publishing.net.

Chapter 1

1. Introduction

The field of computer-assisted language learning (CALL) is expanding. Since Burns' (1979) doctoral dissertation, arguably recognised as the first study on the impact of computer-assisted instruction on learner uptake (Hawisher & Selfe, 2007), CALL has "evolved at a remarkable rate" (Levy & Stockwell, 2006, p. 1). The term CALL, as opposed to other acronyms, such as CAI (computer-assisted instruction), or TELL (technology-enhanced language learning), is preferred in this publication mostly "because of its now well-established presence in the discourse surrounding the topic", and because of its focus on "the technology itself" (Hubbard & Levy, 2006, p. 9).

Defined as "the search for and study of applications of the computer in language teaching and learning" (Levy, 1997, p. 1), CALL, and more precisely technology in CALL, has been widely used to promote learning, assess learners' language, and collect data for all kinds of investigation. As mentioned by Hernández-Ramos (2005), the effects of technology used by teachers and students should not be merely defined as questions of access, but instead be further regarded as questions of (a) availability in terms of appropriateness of software and technical support, and (b) integration in terms of a person's training. In other words, the effect of technology use should support teachers' productivity and students' accomplishments with regard to language learning.

Learners may have access to technology in educational settings in two distinct ways: learning from and learning with technology (Reeves, 1998, p. 1). While the former implies a relative passivity from the learner, the latter infers an active participation (Hill, Wiley, Miller Nelson, & Han, 2004). More specifically, a learning from technology approach generally considers computers as tutors, and takes various forms to deliver the instructional material to the learner, such as computer-assisted instruction (Ringstaff & Kelley, 2002). On the other hand, learners, in a learning with technology method, are "no longer solely taking the information, [but are also] contributing to the knowledge base" (Hill et al., 2004, p. 443). Computers connected to the Internet are, therefore, regarded as tools or "resource to help [students] develop higher order thinking, creativity, research skills, and so on", thus promoting social interaction and learning (Ringstaff & Kelley, 2002, p. 2).

Recent forms of CALL research where the web is involved has implied moving into more interactive environments where learners are active participants (Davies, 2007). For CALL there is a great value in investigating the increasing number of Internet-based technologies that are in constant flux, developing further understanding of the impact of these technologies in relation to learning processes. From exploring what such technology can do, there is also a need to investigate how the Internet can support teaching and learning processes and why (Hill et al., 2004). At the present time, existing research frequently highlights the use of technology as rewarding for both learners and teachers in second language learning classrooms. Yet, there are issues to consider. Although technology has become embedded in our everyday life, incorporating technology in education is a challenging endeavour.

2. The eBook project

The idea behind this eBook project was targeting young researchers, having just completed, or nearly completed their Ph.D., with a research focus on language learning by means of Internet technology and web-based computer applications. The two editors who started this project are Ph.D. students. Also part of the idea was making the eBook easily accessible for anyone on the Internet. Since the eBook deals with research studies of web-based language learning, the nature of the content embraces the openness of the Internet. This is why it is digital rights management free and accessible online, free of charge.

In order to verify a high quality of all chapters, there has been a reading committee consisting of seven prominent senior CALL researchers together with the two editors. As mentioned by Bucholtz (2010), "scholars who opt out of peer review don't get the chance to sharpen and refine their work in response to the critical evaluations of specialist readers, and thus they may not be spurred to produce the best research of which they are capable" (p. 89). The work process has consisted of several stages from the original selection of approved abstracts by invited Ph.D. student writers, to at least two versions of blind reviewing of the full chapters, to ensure highly qualitative scholarly work.

Our aim with this eBook is to present innovative applications of technology in second language teaching and learning, as well as to explore the transformation of the different techniques to different theoretical frameworks. It has also been desired to have a representation of researchers from different parts of the world as contributors. When the reviewing process was finished, there were nine selected chapters from seven different countries: Canada, Finland, France, Ireland, Spain, Sweden, and Singapore. Thus, the chapters of this eBook consist of the work of eleven young researchers within the field of netbased language learning. These nine chapters all deal with topical areas of internet-based CALL.

3. Contributors to this eBook

Each chapter in this volume presents current projects within web-based language learning performed by young researchers. There are different aspects brought up revolving around self-learning, online interaction and negotiation.

Chapter 2. Ilona Laakkonen with *Personal Learning Environments in Higher Education Language Courses: An Informal and Learner-Centred Approach* discusses the use of personal learning environments (PLE) based on Web 2.0 applications for language courses in higher education. As a technological approach, the PLE can be seen as a response to institutionally controlled learning systems dominating the educational field. Student PLEs are individually tailored learning spaces placing the control of the learning tools and processes in the hands of the learners to design. The F-SHAPE project is presented where a PLE is integrated in higher education language courses.

Chapter 3. Peter Wood with *QuickAssist: Reading and Learning Vocabulary Independently with the Help of CALL and NLP Technologies* brings up the concept of independent learning in foreign language instruction and takes a critical look at available tutorial CALL software. He describes the development of a natural language processing (NLP) technology that can be used to promote independent language learning and reports of his findings of a user study.

Chapter 4. Ana Sevilla-Pavón, Antonio Martínez-Sáez, and José Macario de Siqueira with *Self-assessment and Tutor Assessment in Online Language Learning Materials: InGenio FCE Online Course and Tester* address different modalities of assessment processes of the basic skills of reading, writing, listening and speaking tested by the Cambridge First Certificate in English Examination. They explore ways in which a content manager and courseware delivery platform contribute to the effectiveness and efficiency of the assessment of those skills.

Chapter 5. Agnieszka Palalas with *Mobile-Assisted Language Learning: Designing for Your Students* reports on a design-based research study seeking to enhance ESL students' aural skills by means of mobile devices through integrating mobile-assisted language learning (MALL). The design of the MALL solution evolved from a set of podcasts to a suite of learning tools which enable access to a networked community of practice and other resources required for the completion of language tasks.

Chapter 6. Linda Bradley with *A Design for Intercultural Exchange – An Analysis of Engineering Students' Interaction with English Majors in a Poetry Blog* investigates student interaction over a blog in a cross-cultural student exchange between native speakers and non-native speakers of English in higher education analysing and interpreting poetry. In the blog posts, the students' cultural voices are seen, offering a meeting between very contrasting groups from different disciplines, nationalities and language backgrounds. In such an environment, there are a number of features at play, where language and translation issues are prominent parts.

Chapter 7. Mathy Ritchie with *Developing Sociolinguistic Competence through Intercultural Online Exchange* explores conditions for the development of sociolinguistic competence of second language learners in a computer-mediated communication intercultural exchange such as in the form of text-based chats and discussion forum. Non-native speakers were exposed to stylistic variation and made minor changes in their use of sociolinguistic elements, showing that they developed sensitivity to the vernacular style used by native-speakers.

Chapter 8. Yinjuan Shao with *Second Language Learning by Exchanging Cultural Contexts through the Mobile Group Blog* demonstrates the use of mobile group blogging among Chinese learners of English. Recording and sharing learners' experiences in the target culture are helping learners who are far away from the target language surroundings to enhance the understandings of 'real' language use in 'real' culture. Results show a spontaneous shift from using native language to second language in the target culture, how students' learning motivation and language efficacy has been improved.

Chapter 9. Sylvie Thouësny with *Dynamically Assessing Written Language: To what Extent Do Learners of French Language Accept Mediation?* addresses the area of dynamic assessment and investigates how learners of French respond to assistance when correcting their texts. The learners were asked to correct themselves with and without assistance by means of a computer-based application. Results not only show that learners' acceptance of mediation is unsystematic, but also demonstrate that learners may refuse and argue the mediation offered.

Chapter 10. Cédric Sarré with *Computer-Mediated Negotiated Interactions: How is Meaning Negotiated in Discussion Boards, Text Chat and Videoconferencing?* investigates voice-based computer-mediated communication (CMC) in second language acquisition compared with other text-based CMC modes. The aim was to investigate the three modes of discussion board, text chat, and videoconferencing, to see how negotiated interaction was fostered as well as the influence of task type on interaction. Overall, videoconferencing was conducive to more negotiation of meaning than the other two modes. Also, discussion board interactions did not generate any corrective feedback.

References

Bucholtz, M. (2010). In the profession: peer review in academic publishing. *Journal of English Linguistics*, 38(1), 88-93. doi:10.1177/0075424209356851

Burns, H. L. J. (1979). *Stimulating rhetorical invention in English composition through computer-assisted instruction*. Unpublished doctoral dissertation. University of Texas, Austin, Texas.

Davies, G. (2007). *Computer assisted language learning: where are we and where are we going?* Retrieved from http://www.camsoftpartners.co.uk/docs/UCALL_Keynote.htm

Garrett, N. (2009). Technology in the service of language learning: trends and issues, republication from The Modern Language Journal, 75, 1991, 74–101. *The Modern Language Journal*, 93(s1), 697-718. doi:10.1111/j.1540-4781.2009.00968.x

Hawisher, G. E., & Selfe, C. L. (2007). On computers and writing. In R. Andrews & C. A. Haythornthwaite (Eds.), *The SAGE handbook of e-learning research* (pp. 73-96). Thousand Oaks, California: SAGE Publications. Retrieved from http://sage-ereference.com/hdbk_elearningrsch/Article_n3.html

Hernández-Ramos, P. (2005). If not here, where? Understanding teachers' use of technology in Silicon Valley schools. *Journal of Research on Technology in Education*, 38(1), 39-64.

Hill, J. R., Wiley, D., Miller Nelson, L., & Han, S. (2004). Exploring research on Internet-based learning: from infrastructure to interactions. In D. H. Jonassen (Ed.), *Handbook of research for educational communications and technology* (2nd ed., pp. 433-460). New Jersey: Lawrence Erlbaum associates.

Hubbard, P., & Levy, M. (2006). The scope of CALL education. In P. Hubbard & M. Levy (Eds.), *Teacher education in CALL* (pp. 3-20). Amsterdam: John Benjamins Publishing Company.

Levy, M. (1997). *Computer assisted language learning: context and conceptualization*. Oxford: Oxford University Press.

Levy, M., & Stockwell, G. (2006). *CALL dimensions: options and issues in computer-assisted language learning*. Mahwah, New Jersey: Lawrence Erlbaum Associates.

Chapter 1

Reeves, T. C. (1998). The Impact of media and technology in schools: a research report prepared for The Bertelsmann Foundation. *The Bertelsmann Foundation*, 1-44. Retrieved from http://it.coe.uga.edu/~treeves/edit6900/BertelsmannReeves98.pdf

Ringstaff, C., & Kelley, L. (2002). The learning return on our educational technology investment: a review of findings from research. *WestEd*, 1-30. Retrieved from http://tinyurl.com/clkd9b

Website

Creative Commons Licence: http://creativecommons.org/licenses/by-nc-nd/3.0/legalcode

Personal Learning Environments in Higher Education Language Courses: An Informal and Learner-Centred Approach

Ilona Laakkonen[*]

Abstract

The chapter discusses the potential of personal learning environments (PLE) based on Web 2.0 applications for language courses in higher education (HE). This novel approach to the use of information and communication technologies (ICT) in education involves learners in the design of learning environments, tools and processes. The chapter begins with an introduction to the concept of PLEs and identifies drivers behind its increasing popularity. It discusses the multiple ways in which the concept has been understood and applied, and demonstrates the manner in which its principles resonate with developments in the field of computer-assisted language learning (CALL). The chapter will present the F-SHAPE project. This is a project which is being carried out in the University of Jyväskylä Language Centre and which investigates the integration of elements of the PLE concept into higher education language courses through cooperation with researchers, teachers, administrators and students. The application of a highly constructivist and learner-centred approach in the context of formal education is not without problems. Opportunities and challenges that will manifest themselves through this approach will be considered from the perspective of pedagogy, technology, students, and teachers.

Keywords: personal learning environment (PLE), learner-based approach, higher education, multimodal pedagogies, design-based research (DBR).

---

[*]University of Jyväskylä, Finland. e-mail: ilona.laakkonen@jyu.fi

How to cite this chapter: Laakkonen, I. (2011). Personal learning environments in higher education language courses: an informal and learner-centred approach. In S. Thouësny & L. Bradley (Eds.), *Second language teaching and learning with technology: views of emergent researchers* (pp. 9-28). Dublin: Research-publishing.net.

Chapter 2

1. Introduction

This chapter discusses the potential of personal learning environments as a solution to meet the challenges faced when designing learning and integrating technology for language courses in higher education today. With the proliferation of the Internet, Web 2.0 applications, social networks and gaming, students are involved in highly engaging activities in their everyday lives. They use the vast web-based knowledge resources to read and write, sometimes in foreign languages, but chiefly in the Internet Lingua Franca which is English. As Thorne and Reinhardt (2008) point out, "emerging literacies associated with digital media are highly relevant to their current and future lives as language users" (p. 560). Lankshear and Knobel (2007) suggest that youth in the developed world share a whole new mindset that is different from the traditional, industrialist mindset, and is characterised by a sense of existence and spatiality that extends to the virtual space. This "post-industrial mindset" also incorporates much of what has been said about Web 2.0 in terms of collaboration, production and participation. One of the major tasks faced by today's world is that of bridging the "new" mindset of digital insiders and the "old" mindset on which models of education are still based.

A significant argument in the current pedagogical debate relates to our understanding of formal education. If we hold the view that the purpose of formal education is to equip students with life skills as opposed to focusing on test performance, then our understanding of *what* should be learned and, perhaps, *how* learning should take place will alter. For example, Barab and Roth (2006, p. 3) support the view of Lave (1988) that learners should be engaged in rich learning situations where learning has a direct *functional value* which enhances learner's understanding of the real world, as opposed to the content being acquired with the aim of exchanging it for a test score (having *exchange value*). Combined with the growing emphasis on informal learning, this idea strengthens the perception of learning as a life-long and life-wide process that exceeds the boundaries of educational institutions. In the context of language learning, this means placing greater emphasis on the development of the learning competencies and resources of the individual learner, and designing learning environments in which language is not detached from the context of its use.

The PLE can be seen as one possible solution towards meeting the goals of education in the knowledge society: students need to be equipped with skills that enable them to actively seek information and construct knowledge, participate in the world, maintain learning throughout their lives and embrace continuous change. As a technological approach, the PLE can be seen as a response to the shortcomings of institutionally controlled learning management systems (LMSs) that dominate the educational field; student PLEs are individually tailored learning spaces that place control of the learning tools and processes in the hands of the learners. For language learning, there is great potential, as the PLE approach encourages interactivity and fosters the creation of learner communities combining informal and formal learning on the one hand, and providing the possibility to track and transfer learning between courses, subjects, and educational institutes, on the other. In essence, the PLE approach encourages students to become active agents in the design of their own learning.

The chapter focuses on the potential of the PLE approach through its integration into language courses at the University of Jyväskylä Language Centre. It begins by discussing the drivers behind the development of PLEs as well as exploring current understanding of learning environments. The concept is then contextualised by illustrating some recent developments in the field of computer-assisted language learning. The aims and scope of the F-SHAPE project are presented in the final section. As part of the F-SHAPE project, PLE practices are developed and integrated into language courses through close cooperation with researchers, teachers, administrators and students. The possibilities and constraints of the implementation will be considered from the perspective of pedagogy, technology, students, and teachers.

2. Drivers for PLE: Web 2.0 and new understandings of learning

The emergence and proliferation of the Internet and social media technologies play a double role in educational change in that they pose both new demands and new possibilities not previously experienced. This section of the

Chapter 2

chapter links the background of the PLE ideology to recent developments in 21st century learning, Web 2.0 technologies, and learner-centred approaches in CALL.

2.1. Learning as a social and participatory activity

The social aspect of learning has long been recognised, combining as it does collaborative knowledge building and interaction. This notion has been enhanced by the development and proliferation of social media. Another aspect of learning, however, concerns the role assigned to the learner in the learning process. This entails a participatory rather than an acquisitional metaphor for learning, (Sfard, 1998). The participatory metaphor for learning is reflected in the development of ICTs by Sykes, Oskoz and Thorne (2008) who argue that Web 2.0 changes the position of the learner from consumer to producer and creator, and his/her role in the educational community to that of co-builder and contributor.

There is a significant gap between the way in which students engage with new media and ICTs in their daily lives and the way in which school practices rely mainly on print media (Luukka et al., 2008, cf. The Two Mindsets by Lankshear & Knobel, 2007). Commensurate with the rise of networked information and the Internet, the volume of information available has increased to a level that a key ability required from future professionals is related to seeking, evaluating and managing information and knowledge. The formal education setting can no longer be regarded as the only place of worth in which knowledge resides. In today's world vast quantities of information are available to those who possess the skills and motivation to go in search of it. This means that, as opposed to focusing on content knowledge alone, education must focus instead on providing the skills and competencies necessary for learning, constructing knowledge and managing information. As a consequence of this, learners can no longer play the role of passive recipients of information, but rather should assume a new role as active participants in the process of developing their own expertise through selecting, deconstructing, building and creating knowledge and new meanings together with their interlocutors.

The possibilities for education created by the development of social technologies are well documented by Solomon and Schrum (2007), who state that Web 2.0 signals "a transition from isolation to interconnectedness" for its users, as it promotes a number of ways in which multiple users can participate and collaborate in writing, editing, commenting and creating (p. 13). The use of Web 2.0 and the adoption of its practices are still at a very preliminary stage in the educational domain, and their potential in the context of implications for learning are, as yet, largely untapped.

2.2. 21st century learning environments

The ideology behind the PLE is reflected in current thinking relating to 21st century learning and learning environments. The Partnership for 21st Century Skills (2009) regards 21st century learning environments as "support systems that organise the condition in which humans learn best –systems that accommodate the unique learning needs of every learner and support the positive human relationships needed for effective learning" (p. 3). Furthermore, 21st century learning must take place in contexts that "promote interaction and a sense of community [that] enable formal and informal learning" (Cornell, 2002, in Partnership for 21st Century Skills, 2009). The concept of the PLE is supported by the theories posited in 21st century learning as it is tailored to the individual's learning needs and incorporates a strong social aspect.

2.3. Web 2.0 and personal learning environments

Felix (2003) claims that the paradigm shift in pedagogy towards constructivism was already occurring in the absence of technology, but that multimodal and networked technologies enhanced its appeal. Learner-centred, personalised views of learning have long been in existence and have also been boosted by the inherent changes in the nature of the web which have altered the approach to the use and development of technologies.

The concept of Web 2.0 and PLEs is intertwined. Downes (2007) posits that the values of Web 2.0 and the concept of PLEs are essentially as one, namely "the fostering of social networks and communities, the emphasis on creation rather than consumption, and the decentralisation of content and control" (p. 19). Worthwhile web applications, which are an essential element of student PLEs, facilitate the arrangement of learning resources and tools and the creation of learning networks, while at the same time encouraging communication and the publication of both the process and the outcome of the learning experience.

The pedagogical aims of the PLE are based on the ideas of constructivist and socio-cultural theories of learning, but it is claimed that a whole new theory of learning, such as the concept of connectivism (Siemens, 2004), is demanded in the highly networked world in which PLEs currently exist. By conceiving of the PLE first and foremost as an ideology that places emphasis on learning rather than on teaching, and that promotes learner responsibility and control, the concept is closely bound up with the larger field of educational and pedagogical change. This means that the motivation for research and development around the concept of the PLE is primarily pedagogical, rather than technological, even though much of what it encompasses is related to or results from the development of ICTs.

2.4. Web 2.0 and learner-centredness in CALL

CALL practitioners have readily embraced possibilities of Web 2.0 for language and literacy studies. Sykes et al. (2008) envisage emerging technologies being used in the near-future to create meaningful context by adding "real world relevance" to facilitate L2 communication in the classroom. Wikis are already being used to facilitate joint content creation; blogs serve as arenas of self-expression and "enhanced readership" (Sykes et al., 2008, p. 532). Social networks such as Facebook and MySpace allow students to network, interact and share. Social bookmarking sites serve a platform for organising content and for building and sharing knowledge. These tools provide opportunities for networking with people who share similar interests, people joining to form communities of practice (see e.g., Wenger, 1998), and people interacting within an affinity space (Gee, 2004).

Kenning (2007) posits that the motivation for ICT integration into language education is significant because of the inherent role ICT plays in everyday communication. This is not confined to equipping learners with transferable skills such as electronic literacy, but entails "the fact that language, in today's world, tends to be experienced as mediated communication" (Kenning, 2007, p. 158). She quotes Warschauer and Healey (1998), who state that "the ability to read, write, and communicate effectively over computer networks will be essential for success in almost every sphere of life" (p. 64). Kenning (2007) calls for embedding language learning in social practices, not only for the sake of motivation and relevance, but "in order to capitalise on student experience in the world outside" (p. 159).

In their review of design practices in CALL, Levy and Stockwell (2006) identify learner-centredness as a core element in the design of CALL materials and learning environments. As research in CALL has perhaps previously concentrated around a single technology within the bounds of a single theoretical or pedagogical orientation, the design process today is far more complex and often involves the application of various theoretical approaches and the inclusion of complementary technologies. As Levy and Stockwell (2006) put it, "[p]rincipal among these [issues that come to the fore] is perhaps the multidimensional nature of the design process as developers try to weave together elements of theory, pedagogy, technology, and best practice, often drawn from a number of different fields or disciplines" (p. 27).

As a general principle of design in CALL, understanding the learners' experiences and expectations of technology use is common practice. However, it is noteworthy that teachers continue to be seen as the lead designers of the learning process with learners being treated as mere bystanders. Learner needs and experiences are considered, but learners do not have a contributive role in the actual design process. The PLE framework changes this by involving learners in the actual design of learning materials and structures through selecting tools and applications, work modes and resources. Within the PLE approach, the role of the student alters from that of participant to contributor in the overall process.

Chapter 2

3. Approaches to personal learning environments

Heretofore, pedagogy has been put forward as the main motivation for the development of PLEs. A large proportion of the work on PLEs, however, is motivated by interests in developing new technologies. This section describes pedagogical and technological approaches to PLEs, and summarises the values they have in common. The binary of ownership and control is then discussed, followed by some examples of PLE implementation.

3.1. PLE: a pedagogical or a technological concept?

Definitions of PLEs vary depending on the viewpoint of the authors regarding technology and pedagogy. Attwell (2007) describes the PLE first and foremost as an ideational concept that meets many of the challenges educational systems face today. Attwell (2008) elaborates by stating that the PLE represents a new approach towards developing e-learning tools: PLEs are no longer tightly integrated in a virtual learning environment (VLE) but are combined into a flexible entity that can be selected and adapted according to the needs of the individual learner. This definition of a PLE emphasises the philosophical and ideological aspects of the concept over a specific technological solution, and it is particularly fruitful when the interest is in developing practices and pedagogies around the concept.

An alternative approach to the PLE is a more technological one. PLEs can be seen as a response to the shortcomings of the institutionally controlled learning management systems (LMSs). LMSs have typically been designed with an administrative focus, as opposed to a pedagogical one. Van Harmelen (2008) sees PLEs as part of a "learning ecosystem" (p. 35), comprising the computer-based parts of the ecology. In his view, the ecosystem consists of resources available to the learner: people (peers, teachers), print materials, computational materials (including the Internet), and various other resources (such as pen and paper). A student PLE would comprise the computer-based parts of the ecology, including desktop programs, browsers, and mobile devices. However, this view has its dangers: instead of integrating technology into learning, it builds up artificial boundaries between ICTs and traditional, print-based tools, keeping the work on the computer separate from the work in the classroom.

3.2. Reconciling the binaries of ownership and control

The pedagogical and technological approaches to PLEs are not difficult to reconcile, as they share much in common: the consideration of personal and social aspects of learning, the preference for open and free technologies, and a focus on the learner and the learning process. A more relevant consideration is the extent to which learner-control and ownership can be realised in the context of formal education. Inspired by the PLE ideology, traditional LMSs and platforms have been developed to support both social and personalised aspects of learning. However, these solutions can be criticised, as an environment that is managed by the educational organisation contradicts the inherent principle of the PLE belonging to the students.

Peña-López and Adell (2010) and Laakkonen and Juntunen (2009) bring a conciliatory perspective to PLEs. They regard PLEs as personal devices or systems, which can incorporate institutional resources and tools. The educational institutions, in turn, have to be "PLE-able, they have to rethink themselves, be more flexible, more open, and adapt to the new learning realities" (Peña-López & Adell, 2010). Wheeler (2010) proposes a hybrid approach to PLEs, arguing that students need structure and support when adopting Web 2.0 tools and building their learning environments.

3.3. Some solutions for PLEs

In its simplest form, a PLE is a loose collection of tools from which learners can choose in order to organise their learning. The collection may be presented in the form of an image, for instance, which demonstrates the tools and resources that can be used for learning, helps identify the functions for which the tools are used, and thus enhances learners' awareness of the way in which they learn best, and of the contexts in which their learning takes place. For example, a student PLE for an English as a foreign language (EFL) course may look like Elena's mindmap, in which she has grouped the tools and resources around the concepts of Cultural Competence, Language Competence, People & Places, and Information, and then into subsections such as Informal/Formal and Listening, Speaking, Reading and Writing. There are as many ways to map a PLE as there are learners, and a collection PLE diagrams can be found in the EdTechPost wiki. The process of learners constructing their own learning environment involves not only tracking their learning process, but also familiarising themselves with the tools available, and the possibilities for their use.

Guth (2009) investigates the use of PLEs as part of language courses. She describes a research project set up to study the potential of social software for teaching EFL using an action research approach. Similar to design-based research, action research assumes a cyclic process, in which practices and tools are adapted and readapted after collecting feedback and data during the process. Guth's students built their PLEs using personal blogs. The blogs were complemented with a feed reader and a social bookmarking site. Student-centredness was achieved in that no teacher-produced materials were used and students were charged with the responsibility of finding resources to support their own learning. It was envisaged that as the learning community would grow, resources would develop into shared learning materials.

Drexler (2010) proposes a model of a networked student. In her study the primary goal of the PLE was to replace the traditional textbook. She made use of customisable web pages (e.g., Symbaloo, PageFlakes, iGoogle, NetVibes) to pull together information from various sources: social bookmarking sites, news readers, blogs, podcasts and digital notebooks.

4. Integrating the PLE approach in HE language courses

This part describes the F-SHAPE project, in which university level language courses are developed based on the PLE approach. After a general introduction to the research project, followed by an examination of the research context, it then focuses on the principles and practices of PLE implementation.

4.1. The F-SHAPE project

The F-SHAPE (Future Space for Shared and Personal Learning and Working) is a research and development project with a focus on flexible learning solutions to fit the needs of adult learners and work life. The project explores the boundaries of various different learning spaces: virtual spaces, personal and shared space, as well as informal and formal learning contexts. The concept of PLE is used as an alternative to traditional approaches to learning environments: the F-SHAPE project seeks to develop learning concepts, solutions and environments that respect the needs of the individual learner, while still acknowledging the interests of the organisation and supporting collaborative and community-based aspects of learning (The F-SHAPE project website 2009).

The project follows the principles of design-based research (DBR), (see Reinking & Bradley, 2007). DBR involves a goal-oriented, pragmatic and iterative view of research and proposes a strategy for developing learning practices through empirical research. One of the contexts for research is the University of Jyväskylä Language Centre, in which new solutions for preparing students with skills needed for work life and for lifelong language learning are developed as a joint venture by researchers, teachers, students and administrators.

4.2. The University of Jyväskylä Language Centre as a context

Much of the work on PLEs from the pedagogical point of view has been driven by the interest of individual teachers (e.g., Drexler, 2010; Guth, 2009). In the context of the Language Centre, the aim is to integrate the PLE ideology on a broader, organisational level. Essential prerequisites for this type of development include the close involvement of the director, guaranteed administrative support, and adequate resourcing for teachers in terms of time allotted for the project. The operational culture of the organisation is a factor of key importance.

Chapter 2

The University of Jyväskylä Language Centre offers an excellent context for developing the PLE concept and for exploring the pedagogies and practices which stem from it. The unit has a long tradition of research and development, and its staff enjoys a high level of collegiality. Many of the goals of the PLE approach already constitute part of the teaching philosophy of the Language Centre. Multiliteracy, ICT skills, and transferable, life-long, independent learning skills are cited as points of focus in the teaching of academic English language and communications skills (see the Language Centre website). The general teaching goal of the unit is to create effective and convincing communicators, employing a multimodal approach to teaching. This approach links meaningful communication to real life situations, supports individual and peer processes, and encourages creativity and self-regulation. In the Finnish HE system, language and communication courses constitute a compulsory element of all degree programmes and students are drawn from a range of academic fields and backgrounds.

4.3. The project in practice

In the F-SHAPE project at the Language Centre, principles of PLE are integrated into regular language courses, with the aim of equipping students with the competencies needed for the world of work and for lifelong language learning. The process of PLE implementation is initiated through meetings and discussions with the teachers involved in the project. For each individual course the "PLEisation" is conducted in close cooperation with the teacher. Resources, goals and tools are identified so that course aims and evaluation, opportunities for learners to develop their PLEs and for teachers to apply learner-centredness and learner-initiation to work modes can be achieved.

In order to develop PLEs, learners need support and structure. These are provided jointly by researchers and teachers. The first step is that learners are encouraged to collect the tools they already use for language learning, and to identify the potential for language learning opportunities in the technologies and applications they use in their everyday lives. These tools and practices are then evaluated and adopted for use on the course. Introduction of additional tools and training in the use of tools for learning may be necessary.

During and after each course, feedback and information concerning experiences of the process are gathered and evaluated and subsequently adapted to better meet the initial goals. This information informs the practices adopted in subsequent courses.

From the technological perspective, what is required is a solution that would facilitate:

- the creation of personal spaces with different levels of publicity; in these spaces students can collect the resources they need, access tools, and make visible the process and contents of learning;

- sharing and collaboration, building a joint library of resources and tools, collaborating for knowledge construction and creativity;

- networking with peers and with larger communities; to find people who share similar interests and work in associated fields.

The solution can consist of a set of Web 2.0 applications, and it can make use of the LMS offered by the organisation when applicable. This type of approach is akin to the model of PLE presented by Wheeler (2010). In the current study, the PLE in formal context should be built around learners' needs and should capitalise on the tools and practices employed by them in their everyday lives. The resources and requirements offered by the institution should not be ignored, as they provide valuable tools for the development of the PLE, such as computers, mobile devices, applications, desktop programs, and technical support.

5. PLE: opportunities and challenges

There are both opportunities and challenges that need to be considered when implementing the highly ideological concept of the PLE in the context of formal education. Here we discuss the opportunities and challenges with reference to students, teachers, pedagogy, and technology respectively, and propose some solutions based on observations made during the F-SHAPE project.

5.1. Students

Implementing the PLE means taking a step towards self-regulated learning and learner autonomy (Atwell, 2007). Warschauer (2000) reports that motivation is strongly increased when learners find the activities they engage in socially and culturally relevant (p. 52). Autonomy and self-direction are closely related to learner motivation through self-determination theory and attribution theory. According to Deci, Vallerand, Pelletier and Ryan (1991, in Benson, 2001, p. 69), intrinsic motivation leads to effective learning, and it is promoted by settings where the locus of control is with the learner. As there is a relationship between intrinsic motivation and self-directedness, taking control of the learning may help learners to develop motivational patterns that lead to more effective learning results (Benson, 2001). In the field of Attribution theory, Benson (2001) quotes Dickinson (1995, p. 172) who states that learners who believe that they have control over their own learning tend to be more successful.

Taking responsibility for their own learning requires of learners the ability and skills necessary to identify complex, real-life problems, and to construct knowledge in order to solve them. Some of the students may not be familiar with suitable web applications and consequently significant effort may be required in order to become proficient in their use. Moreover, many of the teachers involved in the project have reported on their previous experiments with learner autonomy and expressed their concerns, as many students seem reluctant to accept responsibility for their learning. A key question here is how to encourage teachers and engage students in self-directedness when it is a question of delayed rewards. In the F-SHAPE project we are exploring solutions in theories of gaming and learning (Gee, 2003) through fostering creativity and play in order to support language learning.

5.2. Teachers

The PLE approach (like learner-centred approaches in general) requires of teachers the adoption of a new role as coaches, or facilitators in the process of learning. They are faced with the challenge of balancing learner autonomy and structure, personal choice and general evaluation criteria (McLoughlin & Lee, 2009). Teachers may be concerned due to inadequate proficiency with regard to the usage of tools employed by their students. This is not necessary, however. What is required is that teachers have a general understanding of technologies suitable for learning, but the mastery of individual applications is not essential. When teachers are new to social media and learner-centred design, they need time, resources and pedagogical support from the institution in which they work. The administrative support from the Language Centre motivates the teachers involved in the project and provides them with the time resources to rethink their courses and to develop pedagogical practices. In addition, close cooperation with researchers who have knowledge of Web 2.0 applications and learner-centred pedagogy will encourage the teachers during the process.

5.3. Pedagogy

There are several pedagogical challenges related to the creation of PLEs in a formal context. The most salient is perhaps the intrinsic paradox of applying an apparently informal approach in the context of formal education with set learning goals, standard forms of assessment and prevalent practices of 'teacher-centred' modes of work. Changing practices and modes of production require a thorough reconsideration and modification of assessment: if the learner holds the control over the learning process, teachers have to develop alternative types of assessment. To make full use of many Web 2.0 technologies, the learning resulting from and manifested in the creation of collaborative effort has to be recognised.

5.4. Technology

With regard to technology, several points remain unresolved. Although the requirements of learner-centredness, networking and openness are becoming acknowledged in the design of LMSs, many developments are mere add-ons, and do not challenge the fact that many of the core systems were originally designed for administrative purposes. However, building a PLE on the basis of free Web 2.0 tools only requires that a careful selection of applications be used in terms of safety, stability, and performance. As it is the nature of the web to be under continuous change, with new applications being created and old ones becoming obsolete, new features affecting the usability potential of applications, and changing terms of service effecting the possibilities of use, one has to embrace change and ensure that both students and teachers will be equipped to cope with the change and discover new tools with which to work.

Another point of consideration is that in many organisations the access to external web services can be regarded as a threat as opposed to a resource for extending the learning environment. In such cases, a more limited version of a PLE can be adopted through extending the VLE/LMS already used in the organisation.

6. Conclusion

It is commonly agreed that the potential for learning does not lie in the development of technologies or in the novelty of applications, but rather in the way in which we harness them for learning, i.e., in the ideologies they enable. In this chapter it has been argued that the PLE approach shows great potential for CALL, as it is a step towards active, learner-directed learning that is not detached from its natural social context. When developing their PLEs, language students need to reflect on their learning, find ways to express their progress, and develop new practices. Implementing the PLE framework is not about technology. It is about people, and about change, not about changing the way we understand learning but about the way we distribute responsibility over learning and teaching, respect the individual learners and teachers, and focus on *learning about learning* instead of learning about content. Moreover, in spite of its name, the PLE approach is not about individuals as much as it is about networks, sharing, and creating.

Many of the projects and developments on PLEs have either been promoted by technologists or by individual, enthusiastic teachers. If the concept is to be implemented on a larger scale in higher education, a high level of teacher involvement and motivation are necessary. PLE is a new concept, and is based on a field that is still taking its first steps (integration of Web 2.0 in education). Teachers are the key element, as they are the interface and mediator between learning and curricular requirements. Bringing PLE to educational institutions requires building on teacher experience and on sound pedagogical principles on the one hand, and sufficient support, resourcing and flexibility from the institution, on the other.

Much previous research has shown that a shift in practices of teaching and learning is hard to achieve –changes often remain temporary, superficial or isolated. As an ideology, PLE encompasses a demand for deeper level change in the way we see pedagogy and education: the understanding we have of teaching and learning. Although the approach is not a panacea, it can be seen as one step towards the future of language learning. Placing learners and teachers in focus may increase feelings of agency and ownership and result in permanent change. What can be accomplished is to build on practices, competencies and language repertoires that students with the Lankshear and Knobel's (2007) "new" mindset are familiar with. In the course of the F-SHAPE project we can achieve research-based evidence on the implementation and implications of the PLE approach, thus contributing to the development of technology integration and 21st century pedagogy.

References

Attwell, G. (2007). Personal learning environments – the future of eLearning? *eLearning papers*, *2*(1), 5-5. Retrieved from http://www.elearningeuropa.info/files/media/media11561.pdf

Attwell, G. (2008). Social software, personal learning environments and the future of teaching and learning. Retrieved from http://d.scribd.com/docs/xos1cck6tadkq44z2z4.pdf

Barab, S. A., & Roth, W.-M. (2006). Curriculum-based ecosystems: supporting knowing from an ecological perspective. *Educational Researcher*, *35*(5), 3-13. Retrieved from http://www.aera.net/uploadedFiles/Publications/Journals/Educational_Researcher/3505/3790-01_Barab.pdf

Benson, P. (2001). *Teaching and researching autonomy in language learning*. Harlow: Pearson Education.

Cornell, P. (2002). The impact of changes in teaching and learning on furniture and the learning environment. *New Directions for Teaching & Learning, 92*, 33-42.

Deci, E. L., Vallerand, R. J., Pelletier, L. G., & Ryan, R. M. (1991). Motivation and education: the self-determination perspective. *Educational Psychologist, 26*(3/4), 325-346.

Dickinson, L. (1995). Autonomy and motivation a literature review. *System, 23*(2), 165-174. doi:10.1016/0346-251X(95)00005-5

Downes, S. (2007). Learning networks in practice. *Emerging technologies for learning, 2*, 19-27. Retrieved from http://bit.ly/hZTNBv

Drexler, W. (2010). The networked student model for construction of personal learning environments: balancing teacher control and student autonomy. *Australasian Journal of Educational Technology, 26*(3), 369-385. Retrieved from http://www.ascilite.org.au/ajet/ajet26/drexler.pdf

Felix, U. (2003). An orchestrated vision of language learning online. In U. Felix (Ed.), *Language learning online: towards best practice* (pp. 7-18). Lisse: Swets & Zeitlinger.

Gee, J.P. (2003). *What video games have to teach us about learning and literacy.* New York: Palgrave Macmillan.

Gee, J.P. (2004). *Situated language and learning: a critique of traditional schooling.* London: Routledge.

Guth, S. (2009). Personal learning environments for language learning. In S. Thomas (Ed.), *Handbook of research on Web 2.0 and Second Language Learning.* IGI Global.

Kenning, M.-M. (2007). *ICT and language learning. From print to the mobile phone.* New York: Palgrave MacMillan.

Laakkonen, I., & Juntunen, M. (2009). Tulevaisuuden oppimisympäristöt? Henkilökohtaiset ja avoimet oppimisen tilat. In J. Viteli & A. Östman (Eds.), *Tuovi 7. Interaktiivinen tekniikka koulutuksessa 2009 - konferenssin tutkijatapaamisen artikkelit* (pp. 69-83). Tampere: INFIM. Retrieved from http://tampub.uta.fi/haekokoversio.php?id=298

Lankshear, C., & Knobel, M. (2007). Sampling "the new" in new literacies. In M. Knobel & C. Lankshear (Eds.), *A new literacies sampler* (pp. 1-24). New York: Peter Lang.

Lave, J. (1988). *Cognition in practice: mind, mathematics and culture in everyday life.* Cambridge: Cambridge University Press.

Levy, M., & Stockwell, G. (2006). *CALL dimensions: options and issues in computer-assisted language learning.* Mahwah, New Jersey: Lawrence Erlbaum Associates.

Luukka, M., Pöyhönen, S., Huhta, A., Taalas, P., Tarnanen, M., & Keränen, A. (2008). *Maailma muuttuu – mitä tekee koulu? Äidinkielen ja vieraiden kielten tekstikäytänteet koulussa ja vapaa-ajalla.* Jyväskylä: University of Jyväskylä, CALS.

McLoughlin, C., & Lee, M. (2009). *Personalised learning spaces and self-regulated learning: global examples of effective pedagogy.* Proceedings from ascilite Auckland 2009.

Partnership for 21st century skills. (2009). 21st century learning environments. White paper. Retrieved from http://www.p21.org/documents/le_white_paper-1.pdf

Peña-López, I., & Adell, J. (2010). The dichotomies in personal learning environments and institutions. *Paper presentation. PLE Conference, July 2010, Barcelona.* Retrieved from http://ictlogy.net/20100712-the-dichotomies-in-personal-learning-environments-and-institutions

Reinking, D., & Bradley, B. (2007). *On formative and design experiments: approaches to language and literacy research.* New York: Teachers' College.

Sfard, A. (1998). On two metaphors for learning and the dangers of choosing just one. *Educational Researcher, 27*(2), 4-13. Retrieved from http://www.jstor.org/stable/1176193

Siemens, G. (2004). Connectivism: a learning theory for the digital age. eLearnSpace. Retrieved from http://www.elearnspace.org/Articles/connectivism.htm

Solomon, G., & Schrum, L. (2007). *Web 2.0: new tools, new schools.* Washington: ISTE.

Sykes, J. M., Oskoz, A., & Thorne, S. L. (2008). Web 2.0, synthetic immersive environments, and mobile resources for language education. *CALICO Journal, 25*(3), 528-546. Retrieved from https://calico.org/html/article_715.pdf

Thorne, S. L., & Rheinhardt, J. (2008). "Bridging activities," new media literacies, and advanced foreign language proficiency. *CALICO Journal, 25*(3), 558-572. Retrieved from https://calico.org/html/article_717.pdf

University of Jyväskylä Language Centre. (2010). Teaching philosophy [Website]. Retrieved from https://kielikeskus.jyu.fi/opetus/englanti/teachers-and-teaching-philosophy

Van Harmelen, M. (2008). Design trajectories: four experiments in PLE implementation. *Interactive Learning Environments, 16*(1), 35-46. doi:10.1080/10494820701772686

Warschauer, M. (2000). On-line learning in second language classrooms: an ethnographic study. In M. Warschauer & R. Kern (Eds.), *Network-based language teaching: concepts and practice* (pp. 41-58). New York: Cambridge University Press.

Warschauer, M., & Healey, D. (1998). Computers and language learning: an overview. *Language Teaching, 31*(2), 57-71. doi:10.1017/S0261444800012970

Wenger, E. (1998). *Communities of practice: learning, meaning and identity.* Cambridge: Cambridge University Press.
Wheeler, S. (2010). Anatomy of a PLE [Web log post]. Retrieved from http://steve-wheeler.blogspot.com/2010/07/anatomy-of-ple.html

Websites

EdTechPost wiki: http://edtechpost.wikispaces.com/PLE+Diagrams
Elena's mindmap: http://elenaslivingroom.blogspot.com/2007/12/my-personal-learning-environment-ple.html
F-SHAPE project website: http://fshape.wordpress.com
University of Jyväskylä Language Centre: https://kielikeskus.jyu.fi/en

QuickAssist: Reading and Learning Vocabulary Independently with the Help of CALL and NLP Technologies

Peter Wood[*]

Abstract

Independent learning is a buzz word that is often used in connection with computer technologies applied to the area of foreign language instruction. This chapter takes a critical look at some of the stereotypes that exist with regard to computer-assisted language learning (CALL) as a money saver and an easy way to create an "independent" learning environment. It will also look at what currently available tutorial CALL is able to offer and at how to assess users' independence in this environment. The chapter establishes a working definition of learner independence and shows that tutorial CALL is currently only able to help learners become independent to a limited extent. A paradigm shift in language teaching aimed at promoting learner independence necessitates a shift in the design of dedicated CALL software. As an example of how natural language processing (NLP) technologies can be used to promote independent language learning at an advanced stage, the paper briefly presents QuickAssist, an application which enables learners to work with a German text of their choice using a set of NLP tools, and reports on some findings of a user study.

Keywords: intelligent computer-assited language learning (ICALL), natural language processing (NLP), glossing, independent learning, vocabulary acquisition.

---

[*]9 Campus Drive, Room 521, University of Saskatchewan, Saskatoon, SK, S7N 5A5, Canada.
e-mail: peter.wood@usask.ca

How to cite this chapter: Wood, P. (2011). QuickAssist: reading and learning vocabulary independently with the help of CALL and NLP technologies. In S. Thouësny & L. Bradley (Eds.), *Second language teaching and learning with technology: views of emergent researchers* (pp. 29-43). Dublin: Research-publishing.net.

Chapter 3

1. CALL - the money saver

In this section, I am looking at tutorial CALL applications, their capabilities and shortcomings, and at ways to use natural language processing tools to help advanced language learners.

While many foreign language departments have been seeing severe budget cuts in recent years, they have been struggling to uphold and possibly even improve the quality of their programs. This is at least the result of a survey among the heads of small to medium sized modern language sections in Canada that my department conducted in 2009 (Julien, Makarova, & Wood, in prep.). While costs for both hardware and software might have been prohibitively high a few years back, the infrastructure to administer CALL at universities is now readily available. Can CALL be proposed as a cost-efficient panacea, and can learners manage some or most of the language learning "independently" with the help of technology? Many instructors still have inflated expectations when it comes to CALL (Holland, 1995). I can corroborate this: on various occasions, I was approached and asked whether it would be a good idea to turn some of our offerings into online courses. That way, we ought to be able to increase enrolments and cut down on costs for instructors. Investing into CALL technologies is not wrong, by any means. Sometimes, however, I have a hard time convincing colleagues that investing into CALL cannot go hand in hand with reducing teaching staff or that it will lead to a dramatic decrease in time they will have to spend on preparing lessons or correcting assignments –at least not if the way languages are taught, learnt, and tested does not change dramatically.

Investing in software that is currently available for universities, by and large, involves considerable licensing fees that have to be covered either by the institution itself or by the students. These fees, for the most part, are not one time investments. Either licences expire after a set period, or the software packages have to be upgraded eventually. In addition, there are fees for maintaining and administering a language lab, servers, as well as costs for personnel that take care of online students, correct and grade their work, answer their questions and monitor discussion boards that are part of many modern course packages.

2. Tutorial CALL - the state of the art

In the past, teaching and learning a foreign language implied that instructors and learners had very specific roles. The instructor would decide on the topic of individual classes, would provide input (knowledge) to learners, who in turn were required to reproduce it on request. This is of course oversimplified. Even practitioners of the grammar translation method (Richards & Rodgers, 2001) would eventually expect their students to form utterances independently.

Tutorial CALL programs, on the other hand, cannot do much more than mimic this idealised traditional language teacher. Higgins (1988) uses the term "magister" to refer to CALL applications of this kind and distinguishes them from applications, which he classifies as pedagogues, that afford their users more freedom in making decisions. Levy (1997) uses the terms "tutor" and "tool" to refer to the functionality of programs. Learners can make use of computer applications to complete a specific task, such as looking up an unknown word in an electronic dictionary. Programs of this sort function as tools. The computer as tutor is what most dedicated CALL software, software developed explicitly for language learning, can be classified. It is designed to function like a human instructor. They can provide students with vast amounts of data and exercises to test their knowledge. As long as the set of possible answers to a question remains within manageable bounds, the computer will also be able to provide students with an adequate feedback. It can correct multiple choice and yes/no types of exercises independently. It can even create some of these exercises automatically (Koller, 2007). As long as the learners are at the beginner level, this range of capabilities enables the computer to act almost as a replacement for a human teacher. There are a number of commercial applications that do exactly this.

Using natural language processing tools, computers are also able to deal with more complex tasks, such as analysing short sentences for syntactic (Heift, 1998; Schulze, 2001) and/or semantic correctness (Bailey, 2008) as long as the domain is restricted or the range of possible errors can be anticipated. A few of these so-called ICALL (intelligent computer-assisted language learning)

Chapter 3

applications exist, but only one, Compusensei (Nagata, 1992), is a commercial one. For a detailed discussion of what NLP can accomplish, see Heift and Schulze (2007). However, out of the range of NLP applications available, the language learning software industry has so far only displayed an interest in speech analysis: it is now integrated in many language learning applications where it is successfully used for pronunciation drills. Parsers, corpora and other NLP applications that work robustly have so far not been used in commercial language learning software (Jager, Nerbonne, & Van Essen, 1998; Nerbonne, 2003).

Eventually, however, current computer and software technology reach their limits. While modern parsers are able to work well with complex texts that do not contain any errors, they do not perform reliably when it comes to random learner language (random is used here to indicate a situation where the errors are unpredictable and where the context of the learner input is not predefined). Instructors want their students to be able to construct sentences and texts by themselves. My German students, for example, are required to write short texts after their first six weeks of instruction. At this point, it is necessary for a human corrector to look at the student's text and provide adequate feedback. The amount of "human intervention" that is necessary to correct learner output will increase together with the learner's proficiency level. While tutorial CALL programs can still be used to teach advanced concepts, a human instructor will be necessary to provide feedback on learner language that is random in the above sense. Language learning software that promises to provide a comprehensive course for independent study does so under false pretences, or by providing a learning experience that will sooner rather than later become very artificial because language produced by the learner cannot be adequately analysed.

3. Learner independence

Learner independence, also referred to as learner autonomy, is a widely used buzzword. This has been criticised for a number of reasons. Pennycook (1997) remarks that the notion of independence or autonomy is a western concept. While independence or autonomy have a positive connotation in western society, it might evoke radically different associations in other cultural contexts that place the society above the individual, in which society acts as a sanctuary for the individual. In such a context, a state of autonomy, of being outside society may well be considered undesirable. Schmenk (2006) traces the term autonomy back to ancient Greek philosophy where it was used to describe a political state. This meaning was later adapted by Enlightenment philosophers like Immanuel Kant. From this perspective, as language learners –because of the role they assume in the context of language instruction– are considered to be in need of guidance and support, it would be wrong to call them autonomous.

Many researchers are aware of the inherent problems of both terms and try to use them cautiously. Nevertheless, it is still necessary to define clearly what independence means in a certain context. With respect to the domain of learning, White (2008) locates independence on three different levels:

- Context/Setting: independence can simply mean that learning takes place without a human teacher, but it can also mean that learners have the freedom to make choices, the freedom to select learning opportunities and the freedom to use resources according to their needs.

- Philosophy/Approach: at this level, independence refers to the roles and responsibilities of teachers and learners in the independent learning context. The teacher's role here is to prepare learners to think about their needs. Learners have to develop the ability to look after their own needs.

- Learner Attributes: learners have to develop the attitudes, beliefs, the knowledge and the strategies to take actions that support their learning process.

The stages of autonomy, that Oxford (2008) adapted from Nunan (1997), will be operationalised here to answer the question of the use of CALL to help in the development of learner independence. Concentrating on the role of the learner and the tasks/goals, her model can be summarised as follows:

- At stage one, the learner's role is that of a recipient of information. At this stage a dedicated e-learning system would ideally decide on the goals and provide tasks for the learner and would also give an explanation for the choices it makes.

- At the next stage, the learner acts as a reviewer and selector among system-given options, selecting tasks specific to their individual learning needs and determining the order in which they complete these tasks.

- At stage three, learners adapt tasks provided by the system to their needs.

- Next, learners assume the role of creators and invent tasks to reach the goals they have set.

- Finally, learners become teachers themselves, undertake independent research and help others to acquire a second language.

Taking a look at tutorial CALL applications that are available today, it is clear that they are all able to function adequately as the e-learning system described in stage one. It is important to note that only some of them will actually give learners a comprehensive explanation for the selection of tasks and the order in which they are administered. Ideally, learners should be able to expect more than a summary of the grammar points and other topics covered in the lesson.

Most modern systems will also provide learners with a range of choices as well as the option to create individual learning programs by enabling them to select learning materials and to decide in which order they are presented. I am not aware of any tutorial CALL software that fulfils the functions outlined in stages three and beyond. It could be argued that most systems enable students to create individual vocabulary databases and that complex systems place a large amount of learning elements at learners' disposal, but it is clear that individual needs are hard to predict and that even sophisticated systems would be unable to offer everything. For example, an architect learning Italian in order to read Italian publications on architecture might be able to find a lesson on art history or even texts on some architectural monuments, but nothing that would introduce her to the specific terminology used in her field of interest.

The most important problem that becomes apparent when using Oxford's (2008) model as a benchmark for tutorial CALL software is that there is little that currently available software does in terms of preparing learners to progress to further stages of independence. In order to be able to continue to operate with the limited set of functionality discussed above, the system is forced to keep the learner at stages one or two. Once learners advance past these initial stages, the learning system will either have fulfilled its purpose or become part of a larger pool of resources learners use to proceed in their language acquisition. I would argue that claims made by the producer of tutorial CALL software to provide a comprehensive program that leads learners to a stage of proficiency past an advanced beginner level, are actually misleading. The "Transparent Language German" software is only one example of such software that boasts to teach learners everything to "achieve language proficiency" (details can be found in Wood, 2010b).

Returning to White's (2008) classification of independence, there is another area that developers of tutorial CALL software could take into consideration. While it is clear that CALL applications can not –and will not for some time– uphold the illusion of being an adequate replacement for a human instructor, they can help to develop the kind of skills that White (2008) is pointing to. Including exercises that help develop critical thinking, research tasks, lessons on different learning strategies is certainly possible with currently available technologies. Gradually helping beginning learners to become independent from the system while making them aware of its advanced features (such as dictionaries, Grammar references) would not only help learners, but would also ensure that they would continue to use the application, or at least some of its components in the future as a tool box.

4. Using NLP to promote learner independence

True learner independence, in the sense discussed above, necessarily encompasses a shift in current teaching and learning paradigms. The development of skills for independent learning has to be at the core of every curriculum, but more importantly the traditional roles of instructors and students will have to change dramatically. In a learning situation where learners determine their goals independently and decide on the steps they take to achieve them, there is little room for set syllabi and unified exams. In the remainder of this paper, I am concentrating on NLP software as one example of how CALL can be adapted to promote learner independence at an advanced proficiency stage, and how it can be used in independent learning contexts, with regard to the absence of a human instructor.

As pointed out earlier, NLP applications have been used in tutorial CALL applications, and have been proven to be beneficial at the beginner stage. In this setting, NLP is acting "behind the scenes". Learners are not directly exposed to the parser, nor do they query a corpus or look up words in a dictionary. Exposing learners directly to NLP is not a new idea. Data driven learning has been practised for a number of years. However, the degree of exposure varied in individual approaches. Johns (1991), for example, created learning materials directly for his learners. Learners would then analyse the data in order to explore the semantics of a certain word, common collocations, and syntactic particulars. This approach was considered labour intensive by most instructors (cf. Boulton, 2010), many of whom probably had doubts about the benefits of the method in the first place. Other researchers made the corpus and a query interface available to the students directly. Depending on the underlying technology, using the tools effectively involved a steep learning curve at times.

For QuickAssist, a program that I developed as part of my dissertation, I took an approach similar to the one used in Glosser RuG (Dokter, Nerbonne, Schürcks-Grozeva, & Smit, 1998). In an attempt to follow Colpaert's (2004) software design principles, stipulating that the development has to include a needs analysis, the design, implementation and the evaluation of the software, I researched the availability of CALL software that was suitable for use with advanced learners of German. When it turned out that there was no such software available I started the development that was guided by these principles:

- the program had to be intuitive and easy to use;

- it should be able to provide a wide range of functionality and give users the freedom to chose the learning objects themselves;

- where possible, freely available NLP resources were to be used;

- the program was to be released under the General Public Licence, making it freely available for learners, instructors and developers.

In QuickAssist, users can cut and paste any German text into the application and access a number of NLP tools via a simple and easy to use interface. This was done in order to enable them to work with the application productively without having to learn a query language or have any other sophisticated background in computing. The design and functionality are very similar to a graphical web browser that most learners are sufficiently familiar with. As can be seen from the images below, users are able to click on individual words and are able to look them up in a German-English dictionary using the 'English' button (Figure 1). They can query a corpus for the word and study it in different contexts with the concordancer function by clicking 'Kontext' (Figure 2). This retrieves sentences containing the selected word from the 300,000 sentences German corpus compiled by the Wortschatz project at the University of Leipzig. Moreover, the application provides information on a word's most common neighbours by selecting 'Nachbarn', on its frequencies with the 'Frequenz' function, and on its morphological structure and word paradigms selecting 'Wortbildung' and 'Formen' respectively. It also enables users to look up names of people, places and cultural artefacts in the German version of the Wikipedia (Figure 3). Contrary to Boulton (2010), I do believe that students can be exposed to the underlying technology, provided that they can work with an intuitive enough interface that lets access NLP tools directly.

Chapter 3

Figure 1. Dictionary lookup

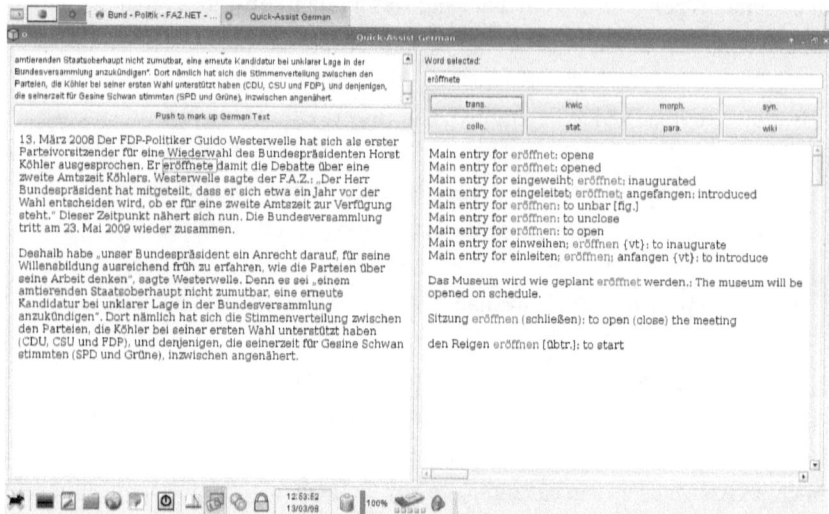

Figure 2. Concordancer output

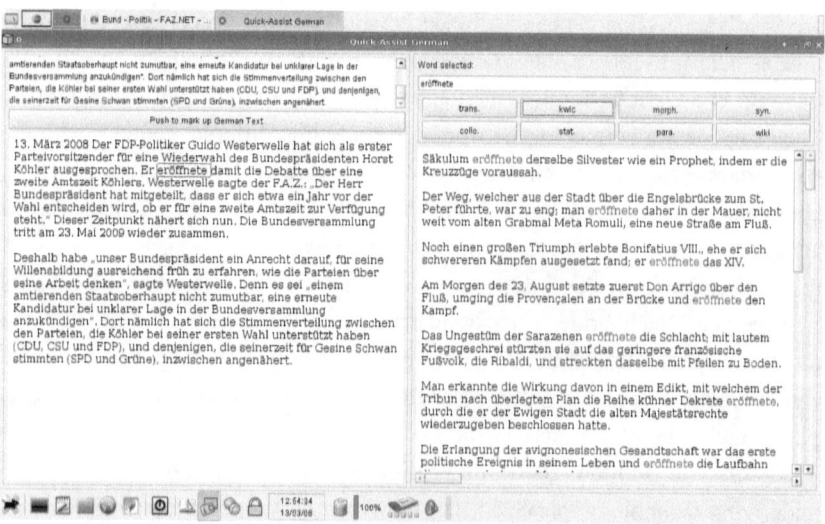

Figure 3.   Query to German Wikipedia

An initial user study found that all four participants were able to use the application without any initial training to work effectively on a task that involved answering comprehension questions on a German text, which contained a number of low frequency vocabulary items, complex compounds, and the names of persons and institutions that the students were not familiar with. Two of the participants also reported after four weeks that they had used the tool successfully for the completion of assignments in their German courses or even for individual research.

One of the more interesting results of this small scale study, I find, is that modern learners are obviously able to learn to work with a piece of software quickly and efficiently. None of my subjects reported that they found the tool too complicated to use. They discovered a number of ways in which the software could be improved and were able to clearly identify the capabilities as well as the limitations of the program. It remains to be shown, but it can be hypothesised that the exposure to electronic media, the familiarity with the Internet and the fact that the computer has become part of everyday life, has had the effect that most of us have developed strategies to filter information, assess the quality of sources, the suitability of resources for a specific task, and others. The age of the users also seems to create a difference in the use of strategies. In the user walkthroughs that were designed in a similar fashion to the ones outlined in Hémard (1999), there were two students in their early twenties, a retired teacher, and a professor emeritus. While both mature learners were trying to read and comprehend the text in a linear fashion, the younger learners used skimming techniques and were also somewhat more selective with the use of the program's functionalities and hence able to answer a greater number of the comprehension questions. A discussion of the user study comprising a detailed description of the learner walkthroughs and the results of a software evaluation by three German instructors is available in Wood (2010a).

After the completion of the initial study, the application was completely rewritten in C++ using the Wt libraries. It is still using the Wortschatz corpus, direct links to the German Wikipedia and canoonet (a lexical and grammatical German dictionary). Instead of using a wordform/baseform list to determine the baseform for dictionary look-ups, the new version uses TreeTagger, which was developed by the IMS Stuttgart. The new version of QuickAssist is web-based and can be used by the general public. The source code of the application is released under the GPL Version 3.0 and will be provided to interested CALL developers upon request.

5. Conclusion

The conclusions that can be drawn from this discussion are that tutorial ICALL software has its place in language teaching. For the time being, it appears that its use will remain confined to the beginning and lower intermediate learners. In order to foster learner independence, CALL software, and other learning software could include content that aims at the development of critical thinking, learning strategies and other skills that make a successful independent learner.

It appears that learners are able to handle a considerable amount of responsibility when it comes to the use of software tools. My subjects displayed an initial tendency to "play around" with features of the program (they would, for example, try to look up function words in Wikipedia). This seems to serve the purpose of getting acquainted with the technology and to probe its limits. After this phase, however, they started to become more and more selective in the use of features and developed strategies to quickly complete individual comprehension tasks.

Instructors are encouraged to give their students the chance to work with NLP tools and learn how to use them for their learning process. All of my subjects expressed excitement about the fact that these tools enabled them to read authentic German texts that were more difficult than what they would normally expect to be reading and that they could do so fairly quickly. While online dictionaries are widely used now by students, few students are aware of what information they can find in a corpus or other NLP tools like morphological analysers.

References

Bailey, S. M. (2008). *Content assessment in computer-aided language learning: meaning error diagnosis for English as a second language.* Unpublished doctoral dissertation. Ohio State University.

Boulton, A. (2010). Data-driven learning: taking the computer out of the equation. *Language Learning, 60*(3), 534-572. doi:10.1111/j.1467-9922.2010.00566.x

Colpaert, J. (2004). *Design of online interactive language courseware: conceptualization, specification and prototyping. Research into the impact of linguistic-didactic functionality on software architecture.* Unpublished doctoral dissertation. University of Antwerp, Antwerp.

Dokter, D., Nerbonne, J., Schürcks-Grozeva, L., & Smit, P. (1998). Glosser-RuG: a user study. In S. Jager, J. Nerbonne, & A. Van Essen (Eds.), *Language teaching and language technology* (pp. 167-176). Lisse, The Netherlands: Swets & Zeitlinger.

Heift, T. (1998). *Designed intelligence: a language teacher model.* Unpublished doctoral dissertation. Simon Fraser University, Burnaby.

Heift, T., & Schulze, M. (2007). *Errors and intelligence in computer-assisted language learning; parsers and pedagogues.* New York: Routledge.

Hémard, D. (1999). A methodology for designing student-centred hypermedia CALL. In R. Debski & M. Levy (Eds.), *Worldcall: global perspectives on computer-assisted language learning* (pp. 215-228). Lisse, The Netherlands: Swets & Zeitlinger.

Higgins, J. (1988). *Language, learners, and computers: human intelligence and artificial unintelligence.* London: Longman.

Holland, V. M. (1995). Introduction: the case of intelligent CALL. In V. M. Holland, J. D. Kaplan, & M. R. Sams (Eds.), *Intelligent language tutors: theory shaping technology* (pp. vii-xvi). Mahwah, NJ: Lawrence Erlbaum.

Jager, S., Nerbonne, J., & Van Essen, A. (Eds.). (1998). *Language teaching and language technology.* Lisse, The Netherlands: Swets & Zeitlinger.

Johns, T. (1991). Should you be persuaded - Two samples of data-driven language materials. *ELR Journal, 4,* 1-16. Retrieved from http://goo.gl/iOMI9

Julien, R., Makarova, V., & Wood, P. (in prep). *How are modern languages departments coping with budget cuts in Canada.*

Koller, T. (2007). *Design, development, implementation and evaluation of a plurilingual ICALL system for Romance languages aimed at advanced learners.* Unpublished doctoral dissertation. Dublin City University, Dublin.

Levy, M. (1997). *Computer assisted language learning: context and conceptualization.* Oxford: Oxford University Press.

Nagata, N. (1992). *A study of the effectiveness of intelligent CALI as an application of natural language processing.* Unpublished doctoral dissertation. Universtiy of Pittsburgh, Pittsburgh.

Nerbonne, J. (2003). Computer-assisted language learning and natural language processing. In R. Mitkov (Ed.), *Handbook of computational linguistics* (pp. 670-698). Oxford: Oxford University Press.

Nunan, D. (1997). Designing and adapting materials that encourage learner autonomy. In P. Benson & P. Voller (Eds.), *Autonomy and independence in language learning* (pp. 192-203). London: Longman.

Oxford, R. L. (2008). Hero with a thousand faces: learner autonomy, learning strategies and learning tactics in independent language learning. In S. Hurd & T. Lewis (Eds.), *Language learning strategies in independent settings* (pp. 41-66). Bristol: Multilingual Matters.

Pennycook, A. (1997). Cultural alternatives and autonomy. In P. Benson & P. Voller (Eds.), *Autonomy and independence in language learning* (pp. 35-53). London: Longman.

Richards, J. C., & Rodgers, T. S. (2001). *Approaches and methods in language teaching*. New York: Cambridge University Press.

Schmenk, B. (2006). CALL, self-access and learner autonomy: a linear process from heteronomy to autonomy. In T. Harden, A. Witte, & D. Köhler (Eds.), *The concept of progression in the teaching and learning of foreign languages* (pp. 75-90). Bern: Peter Lang.

Schulze, M. (2001). *Textana. Grammar and grammar checking in parser-based CALL*. Unpublished doctoral dissertation. University of Manchester, Institute of Science and Technology, Manchester.

White, C. (2008). Language learning strategies in independent language learning: an overview. In S. Hurd & T. Lewis (Eds.), *Language learning strategies in independent settings* (pp. 3-24). Bristol: Multilingual Matters.

Wood, P. (2010a). *QuickAssist. Extensive reading for learners of German using CALL technologies*. Unpublished doctoral dissertation. University of Waterloo, Department of Germanic and Slavic Studies, Waterloo. Retrieved from http://hdl.handle.net/10012/5680

Wood, P. (2010b). Review of Transparent Language system complete edition (German). *Calico Journal*, *28*(1), 229-237. Retrieved from https://calico.org/memberBrowse.php?action=article&id=839

Websites

Canoonet: http://canoo.net
General Public Licence (GPL): http://www.gnu.org/licenses/gpl-3.0.html
QuickAssist: http://linguistics.usask.ca/quickassist/German.wt
TreeTagger: http://www.ims.uni-stuttgart.de/projekte/corplex/TreeTagger
Wikipedia: http://www.wikipedia.org
Wortschatz project: http://wortschatz.uni-leipzig.de

Self-Assessment and Tutor Assessment in Online Language Learning Materials: InGenio FCE Online Course and Tester

Ana Sevilla-Pavón, Antonio Martínez-Sáez, and José Macario de Siqueira*

Abstract

This chapter addresses different modalities of assessment, provides an overview of the assessment processes of the basic skills (reading, writing, listening and speaking) tested by the Cambridge First Certificate in English (FCE) examination, and explores the ways in which the FCE Online Course and Tester –the resources provided through the InGenio CALL authoring shell, content manager and courseware delivery platform– contribute to the effectiveness and efficiency of the assessment of those skills. These materials are flexible enough to be adapted to different degrees of learning autonomy, thus allowing students to assess their own progress while enabling their learning process to be monitored by a tutor or a teacher in those cases where the materials are used by them as a complement for their language lessons. Such is the case of some teachers at the Universidad Politécnica de Valencia (UPV) who are already successfully making use of some of the materials published through InGenio as a way to include additional contents and monitor and assess their students' achievements and progress. One of the most important features concerning these online language learning materials is that they allow students to choose between two main modalities of assessment, one of them enabling them to supervise their own learning process; and the other one leading to the development of their autonomy and sense of responsibility while getting support from a tutor or teacher.

Keywords: modalities of assessment, FCE, online language learning, autonomy.

*Universidad Politécnica de Valencia, Department of Applied Linguistics, Ed. 4P, Camino de Vera S/N, 46022 Valencia, Spain. e-mails: ansepa@doctor.upv.es, anmarsae@doctor.upv.es, jodesi@doctor.upv.es

How to cite this chapter: Sevilla-Pavón, A., Martínez-Sáez, A., & Macario de Siqueira, J. (2011). Self-assessment and tutor assessment in online language learning materials: InGenio FCE Online Course and Tester. In S. Thouësny & L. Bradley (Eds.), *Second language teaching and learning with technology: views of emergent researchers* (pp. 45-69). Dublin: Research-publishing.net.

Chapter 4

1. Introduction

The importance of assessment is derived from both its influence in the way teachers and students address language teaching and learning and the changes it might introduce as far as methodologies, approaches and behaviour of all participants in the language learning process are concerned. Brown and Glasner (2003) consider assessment as one of the key aspects in education and define it as the "dynamic developmental process which develops and changes as the needs arise and as understanding of the process improves" (preface). The washback effect, defined by Messick (1996) as "the extent to which the introduction and use of a test influences language teachers and learners to do things they would not otherwise do that promote or inhibit language learning" (p. 241), is a frequent phenomenon which should also be taken into consideration when dealing with the process of assessment. It is usually found in the language classroom in the form of innovations and new ways of teaching in an attempt to foster students' motivation and the emergence of a greater variety of learning strategies. Teachers usually try to adopt new methodologies and implement new approaches to language teaching as an effort to adapt the contents and materials they develop to meet the students' individual and specific needs, goals, interests and expectations. In this particular case, not only do the students who learn and practice by using the FCE Online Course and who assess their knowledge through the FCE Online Tester try to attain the target language level, but they also aim at passing the official examination. Exam criteria were taken into consideration by the authors of these preparatory materials which were thus adapted to such demands and to the typologies of exercises comprised by the official examination. This fact could be seen as an example of how the washback effect has been present in the process of material design and development. A wide section of exercises included in the course and tester follow the typology, structure and level of the exam. Therefore, students are allowed to practice and assess their knowledge in accordance with the final exam criteria.

This chapter explores some of the key issues concerning the assessment process of skills tested by the Cambridge First Certificate in English Examination[*] and

---

[*]Further information available at Cambridge ESOL webpage: http://www.cambridgeesol.org/exams/general-english/fce.html

the ways in which the InGenio* online preparatory materials contribute to its effectiveness and efficiency in both self-assessment and tutor assessment, with a special focus on the two most recently developed learning materials within the CAMILLE Research Group** at the UPV: FCE Online Course and FCE Online Tester. InGenio is a content manager tool which allows users to develop preparatory materials and activities through a system based on templates. One of the main advantages of the materials created is their adaptability and flexibility. It allows students to have access to two different modalities of assessment and to two different learning options, thus enabling a wider range of students with different characteristics and needs to organise the way in which they intend to face the learning process in the most convenient way, for each of them, so as to obtain better results. Students' self-assessment is the first learning modality offered. It enables students to conduct their own learning process and to assess their own learning achievements in an independent, and autonomous way. Tutor assessment, the other modality provided by these materials, leads to the development of the students' autonomy and sense of responsibility over the learning process, while enabling students to get as much help and support as they need from a human tutor in order to both complete the different tasks and attain the target level of language.

2. The skills tested by the FCE examination

Assessment is a very important component of the learning process. Its importance mainly derives from the fact that it is capable of influencing the way teaching and learning are addressed. Assessment is likely to make teachers and learners, who are the main participants in the learning process, introduce changes in their methodologies, approaches, behaviour and learning strategies. These changes would be based on "the particular kind of knowledge or ability that a test is designed to measure" (Read, 2000, p. 95), that is, the construct, a

---

* InGenio is a free online content delivery and management platform with a number of language courses available. Among them are: Intermediate Online English, Valencià Interactiu – Grau Mitjà, and beginners and elementary courses for learners of Czech and Slovak. The system has been developed by the CAMILLE Research Group led by Dr. Ana Gimeno-Sanz (Department of Applied Linguistics – Universidad Politécnica de Valencia). See http://camilleweb.upv.es/camille for further information.

** CAMILLE stands for Computer Assisted Multimedia Interactive Language Learning Environment

concept which is closely linked to the process of content validity. Fulcher and Davidson (2007) define content validity as "any attempt to show that the content of a test is a representative sample from the domain that is to be tested" (p. 6). Buck (2001) considers that the essential condition for any test to be acceptable is that it measures the appropriate construct, this being the only possible way to ensure validity and usefulness of that assessment. In order to design the right test to measure the four main skills tested by FCE, i.e., reading, writing, listening and speaking, it is important to know the micro-skills and strategies that the candidates need to put into practice in order to ascertain that they have the appropriate level, as well as the way to assess those skills.

When dealing with the assessment of the reading skills, several guidelines about teaching and curriculum planning, mentioned by authors such as Grabe (1991, 2008, p. 81), should be taken into consideration. Reading should be integrated together with other skills within content; the texts should be interesting and related to the candidates' education, hobbies and particular interests; the different reading sub-skills should be measured; silent reading should be fostered, and so should reading comprehension. Furthermore, the person in charge of the assessment should be able to accept different interpretations of the texts, organising skills and strategies systematically and taking into account the characteristics and objectives of each group.

According to Alderson (2000), the reading assessment guidelines also apply to the different levels of understanding to be assessed, which are "literal understanding of a text, an understanding of meanings that are not directly stated in text, or an understanding of the main implications of a text" (p. 7), as well as the distinction between what Gray (1960, in Alderson, 2000, p. 7) called reading "the lines", that is, understanding the literal meaning of a text, reading "between the lines" or inferring meanings, and reading "beyond the lines". This means making critical evaluations and judgements of a text. Because there are so many aspects to take into account when assessing reading, as Alderson (2000) points out, it is very important to find a way to measure reading accurately, considering to what extent the tests reflect and are based on previous research and literature referred not only to the process but also to the product. When trying to find the appropriate way to measure reading comprehension, one of the main things to consider is what the relevant task characteristics are. These can be determined with the help of the following framework (Table 1), designed by Bachman and Palmer (1996).

Table 1. Framework of task characteristics
Adapted from Bachman and Palmer (1996).

Setting	Physical circumstances under which either language use or language testing takes place: • physical characteristics of the setting; • participants involved; • time of the task.
Rubric	Context for the task: Those characteristics that provide the structure for the task and constrain how language users or test takers are expected to respond to these tasks.
Input	Material contained in the task, which test takers need to process in some way, and to which they are expected to respond.
Expected response	Language use that is expected, given the way in which the rubric, or context, for the task is configured, and the particular input that is provided.
Relationship between input and response	• Reactivity: degree of reciprocity, or interaction involved. • Scope: amount and range of input that needs to be processed in order to respond. • Directness: extent to which the response can be made by using information in the input by itself, or whether the language user or test taker must also rely on information in the context or in his or her own real world knowledge..

As far as the use of computers for reading is concerned, it is advantageous for learners because of several features such as the instantaneous access it provides to many kinds of authentic and communicative reading materials through the Web, the capacity to add hypertexts in order to access other texts or useful links as well as additional explanations on vocabulary and grammar, the addition of multimedia files as a complement of the reading materials, and the capacity to control reading speed and other aspects of learning (Levy & Stockwell, 2006). In addition, the Web is a rich source of written materials that can contribute to both the improvement of reading skills to higher levels and the students' cultural competence (Taylor & Gitsaki, 2004). Nevertheless, there is also a series of disadvantages associated with reading on the computer and on the Web. One such disadvantage is the fact that it might be uncomfortable, although this would probably not be an inconvenience if other kind of devices, such as iPads, or more recent developments in screen technology were used instead. Another inconvenience is the fact that it might be harder to find the appropriate texts or excerpts among the huge quantity of materials and information available. In addition, it might be hard to pick the materials with the appropriate level, both linguistically and socially. However, being aware of these drawbacks can help a teacher face them with ease so that a great quantity of useful materials can be used, integrated and adapted to the context of language learning (Dudeney, 2000).

The materials developed to be implemented through the InGenio online platform aim to offer resources to practice the four basic linguistic skills. Concerning reading, InGenio provides the authors with several exercise templates that allow them to create a varied range of activities for autonomous practice and self-assessment. Some of these templates are: reordering, matching, monitoring comprehension, multiple-choice questions (single selection with pull-down menu, single selection menu, and multiple selection), gap-filling exercises, reinforcing new vocabulary, vocabulary building, and word search puzzles. The contents included in the tasks and texts that are part of the exercises are not only devoted to practicing and assessing reading skills but also to helping students think critically and analytically and have a justified or well-founded opinion about some of the world's most important or interesting facts and events. Learners are also provided with more resources such as reference materials, additional explanations and hints, further reading, appropriate feedback according to the student's performance, automatic communication of results through progress reports, and printing-enabled screens.

As for writing, historically it tended to be considered more prestigious and elitist than speaking (Brown & Yule, 1983; Carter & McCarthy, 2006; Gilmore, 2007). Nowadays, it is an essential tool of communication in the global community we are living in. Additionally, there has been a change in the role of writing as it has shifted from "conveying information" to "transforming knowledge to create new knowledge" while helping to predict future professional and academic success. The importance of writing as a predictor might explain the great demand of valid and reliable ways to test writing ability (Weigle, 2009). According to Hamp-Lyons (1991), there are two main ways to assess writing: direct and indirect. The main characteristics of a "direct" test are as follows (Hamp-Lyons, 1991): candidates must write at least one piece of continuous text, they are given a set of instructions or "prompts" but have some freedom in their responses, each test is usually read by more than one trained rater, judgments are tied to a set of sample responses or rating scales, and these judgments are expressed as numbers. In addition, there are other important characteristics such as the limited time frame, generally between thirty minutes and two hours, and the fact that the topic is unknown to test takers in advance (Weigle, 2009, p. 59). The dimensions of tasks for direct writing assessment are specified in Table 2. As for the "indirect" tests of writing or "timed impromptu writing tests", they most often consist of multiple-choice tests of grammar and usage (Hamp-Lyons, 1991).

Table 2. Dimensions of tasks for direct writing assessment
Adapted from Purves, Söter, Takala, and Vähäpassi (1984, pp. 397-398), and Hale (1996), cited in Weigle (2009, p. 63).

Dimension	Examples
Subject matter	Self, family, school, technology, etc.
Stimulus	Text, multiple texts, graph, table
Genre	Essay, letter, informal letter, informal note, advertisement
Rhetorical task	Narration, description, exposition, argument
Pattern of exposition	Process, comparison/contrast, cause/effect, classification, definition
Cognitive demands	Reproduce facts/ideas, organise/reorganise information, apply/analyse/synthesise/evaluate
Specification of: • Audience • Role • Tone, style	• Self, teacher, classmates, general public • Self/detached observer, other/assumed persona • Formal, informal
Length	Less than ½ page, ½ to 1 page, 2-5 pages
Time allowed	Less than 30 minutes, 30-59 minutes, 1-2 hours
Prompt wording	Question vs. statement, implicit vs. explicit, amount of context provided
Choice of prompts	Choice vs. no choice
Transcription mode	Handwritten vs. word-processed
Scoring criteria	Primarily content and organisation; primarily linguistic accuracy; unspecified

Chapter 4

As far as the process of test development is concerned, it occurs in three main stages: design, operationalisation and administration (Bachman & Palmer, 1996). These stages are followed by a very important procedure: scoring, which is used in making decisions and inferences about the performance of the exam takers and therefore must be accurate and derive from appropriate, theoretically-grounded and consistent rating scales and scoring rubrics (Weigle, 2009, p. 108). Writing assessment has overcome dramatic changes due to the impact of technology and increased global communication. In fact, the nature of writing itself has been affected by ICT "in terms of process, norms and standards" (Weigle, 2009, p. 231) and the emergence of scoring of writing by computer is picturing the future of computers as supplements of human raters, especially in the case of large-scale writing assessments such as FCE.

Creativity has a dominant role in the practice of writing, as well as in the practice of speaking. Concerning the InGenio FCE online materials, in the sections devoted to practicing writing and speaking, more freedom is given to students in order to allow them to write and speak about topics that concern them or that they find interesting and attractive. The tasks which are being designed fit the official FCE exam criteria, and try to present these training sections in a more innovative way through more open and reflective approaches. The students also have access to some useful recommendations in order to finally respect the limits fixed by the construct tested by the official exam. Moreover, course designers may need to take into account the type of texts that learners need to write and read in their L2, which could markedly differ from the texts that they write or read in their L1 (Ferguson, 2007). Open input without sound and open-input with sound are among the most useful InGenio templates when it comes to encouraging students "to analyse data and subsequently reason their answers" (Gimeno-Sanz, 2009a, p. 93) and write their own input in the form of rewriting, information transfer, short answers, etc.

As for listening, it is considered as the least understood of all skills (Alderson & Bachman, editors' preface, in Buck, 2001) in spite of being the most important one because of its potential influence in teaching methodologies. It is also difficult to measure at a technical level, and it is time-consuming too, which may explain the frequent reluctance to test it. Nevertheless, it is essential to give listening assessment the importance it deserves, given that the consequent washback could influence teachers and make them aware of the fact that developing listening skills is crucial for students to be able to communicate in the target language. This is especially true in those contexts where the students' L2 is the vehicular language and therefore the main means of interaction. The following listening framework describes its two main components: language competence and strategic competence. Each competence implies different kinds of knowledge, as shown in Table 3 below, adapted from Buck (2001, p. 104).

Table 3. Framework for describing listening ability
Adapted from Buck (2001, p. 104).

Language competence	Knowledge about language that the listener brings to the listening situation. Includes fully automated procedural knowledge and controlled or conscious declarative knowledge: grammatical, discourse, pragmatic, and sociolinguistic knowledge.
Grammatical knowledge	Understanding short utterances on a literal semantic level. Includes phonology, stress, intonation, spoken vocabulary, spoken syntax.
Discourse knowledge	Understanding longer utterances or interactive discourse between two or more speakers. Includes knowledge of the discourse features (cohesion, foregrounding, rhetorical schemata and story grammars) and knowledge of the structure of unplanned discourse.
Pragmatic knowledge	Understanding the function or the elocutionary force of an utterance or longer text, and interpreting the intended meaning in terms of that. Includes understanding whether utterances are intended to convey ideas, manipulate, learn or are for creative expression, as well as understanding indirect speech acts and pragmatic implications.
Sociolinguistic knowledge	Understanding the language of particular sociocultural settings, and interpreting utterances in terms of the context of situation. Includes knowledge of appropriate linguistic forms and conventions characteristic of particular sociolinguistic groups, and the implications of their use, or non-use, such as slang, idiomatic expressions, dialects, cultural references, figures of speech, levels of formality and registers.

Strategic competence	Includes cognitive and metacognitive strategies, or executive processes, that fulfil the cognitive management function in listening. It is the ability to use language competence, and includes all the compensatory strategies used by second language listeners.
Cognitive strategies	Mental activities related to comprehending and storing input in working memory or long-term memory for later retrieval.
Comprehension processes	Associated with processing of linguistic and non-linguistic input.
Storing and memory processes	Associated with storing of linguistic and non-linguistic input in working memory or long-term memory.
Using and retrieval processes	Associated with accessing memory, to be ready for output.
Metacognitive strategies	Conscious or unconscious mental activities that perform an executive function in the management of cognitive strategies.
Assessing the situation	Taking stock of conditions surrounding a language task by assessing one's own knowledge, one's available internal and external resources and constraints of the situation before engaging in the task.
Monitoring	Determining the effectiveness of one's own or another's performance while engaged in a task.
Self-evaluating	Determining effectiveness of one's own or another's performance after engaging in the task.
Self-testing	Testing oneself to determine the effectiveness of one's own language use or the lack thereof.

Out of the three main approaches to assessing listening, that is, discrete-point, integrative and communicative, Buck (2001) considers the communicative approach, characterised by using the language "for the purpose of communication, in a particular situation and for a particular purpose" (p. 83), the most effective one. In this approach, the texts to be listened to are authentic and genuine. There is a well-defined goal and the examinees have to accomplish authentic tasks. The basic idea underlying communicative testing is that these tests emulate the use of language in the real world, which means that the construct to be assessed is richer and more realistic, in such a way that it "allows the examiner to make useful inferences about the examinee's communicative abilities" (Buck, 2001, p. 92). As for the use of technologies in assessing listening, Levy and Stockwell (2006) underline that they should be used in such a way that they provide something extra that was not available through traditional teaching and assessment, in order to enhance learning. The success of multimedia tasks, according to Hoven (1999), depends on the way they are designed as far as individual differences among students, learning styles and preferred learning models are concerned.

The InGenio preparatory materials are not devoted uniquely to practicing through written channels and static texts, but to expand oral and communicative skills by introducing tasks and scenarios aimed at fostering real practice of oral skills. This is done through corpora of audio excerpts (listening) and voice recording systems (speaking) which can be uploaded onto the system for a tutor to assess and subsequently provide appropriate feedback. In the case of completely autonomous practice and assessment, students are provided with models so as to allow them to compare them with their own answers. In particular, concerning the listening skills, the InGenio content manager provides editors with video and audio templates as well as with the means to build up an abundant pool of images and audio and video files. Many of the templates used to practice and assess reading skills could also be used for the listening activities.

Finally, in relation to the assessment of speaking skills, numerous studies point out that this is one of the most complex and controversial aspects within second language teaching (Weir, O'Sullivan, & Horai, 2006). This is due to the difficulties encountered when trying to join the targets of the assessment and the appropriate tasks or instruments that assessment requires (Luoma, 2009). Moreover, speaking is considered the hardest skill to be taught and tested through computers, which might explain the "lack of representativeness" of studies focusing on speaking (Levy & Stockwell, 2006, p. 181). This makes the integration of assessment of communicative speaking into CALL materials a true challenge. Luoma (2009) conceives speaking assessment as a cycle in which the participants involved are the examinees, the interlocutors, the examiners, and the rating/marking criteria. The following illustration (Figure 1), adapted from Luoma (2009, p. 5), outlines the oral assessment activity cycle.

Chapter 4

Figure 1. Oral assessment activity cycle
Adapted from Luoma (2009, p. 5).

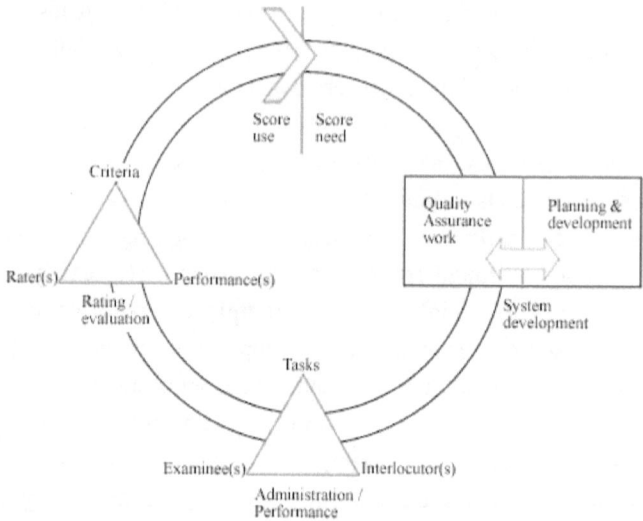

As this graph shows, the cycle starts when the necessity of speaking assessment is perceived; planning and development stages follow, resulting in the definition of the construct. Next, the criteria are determined as well as the way in which the exam is to be administered. Assessment then takes place by means of two interaction processes: firstly, exam administration and candidates' performance in interactions (among the candidates and/or the examiner) in which they show their oral production skills; and secondly, a rating process in which the examiners apply the assessment criteria to the candidates' performance in order to obtain a grade for each of the candidates.

Prior to assessing speaking, the type of speech to be assessed has to be determined: planned or not, formal or informal, etc., as there might be substantial changes in vocabulary choices, grammar constructions or pronunciation depending on the type of discourse (Luoma, 2009). Another factor that could influence the type of speech acts is the social/situational context, which can be determined by using Hymes' (1974) SPEAKING model when planning and describing the construct (Table 4).

Table 4. SPEAKING Model
Adapted from Hymes (1974).

Setting/Scene	"Setting refers to the time and place of a speech act and, in general, to the physical circumstances" (Hymes, 1974, p. 55). Scene is the "psychological setting" or "cultural definition" of a scene, including characteristics such as range of formality and sense of play or seriousness (Hymes, 1974, pp. 55-56).
Participants	Speaker and audience. Linguists will make distinctions within these categories; for example, the audience can be distinguished as addressees and other hearers (Hymes, 1974, pp. 54-56).
Ends	Purposes, goals, and outcomes (Hymes, 1974, pp. 56-57).
Act Sequence	Form and order of the event.
Key	Cues that establish the "tone, manner, or spirit" of the speech act (Hymes, 1974, p. 57).
Instrumentalities	Forms and styles of speech (Hymes, 1974, pp. 58-60).
Norms	Social rules governing the event and the participants' actions and reaction.
Genre	The kind of speech act or event.

Context is the first element Hymes (1974) mentions. It concerns all the aspects and elements that are present at the moment of interaction, i.e., "the linguistic, physic, psychological and social dimensions of the language that is being used" (Luoma, 2009, p. 30). Context also refers to the concrete aspects of the situation in which the interaction takes place, such as the place or the interlocutors' previous experiences of use, what is said and the way it is said in different situations. The implications are that conversation can be led by task designers to a certain extent through the manipulation of the context characteristics by means of the proprieties that are attributed to the tasks and to the activities suggested (Luoma, 2009, p. 30). Nevertheless, conversations cannot be predicted in a very precise manner, as Douglas (1998) points out, because the interlocutors are likely to be influenced by the context features considered by them as the most salient and therefore there might be variation depending on the individuals and on the situations involved in the process.

The integration of speaking tasks in FCE Online Course and Tester is an innovation, since speaking skills are not practised nor tested by most previously-existent self-assessment preparatory FCE materials. These materials tend to give advice about how to prepare for the exam and how to face it, as well as information about its structure and some other details, but they do not allow the candidates to practice and to assess their speaking abilities. Nevertheless, this feature had already been predicted by Gimeno-Sanz (2009b), who foresaw the design of speaking tasks through voice recording in the InGenio online content delivery and management platform which would then add up to the already implemented features:

> Although voice recording has not been programmed into the system, it is nevertheless possible to design exercises where the learner is requested to record his or her own utterances by accessing the Windows Media Player, which can be called up and minimised when not in use. Evaluation of oral production will be subject to learner comparison with a pre-recorded model or by tutor intervention. Future developments include incorporating voice recognition software into the InGenio system (Gimeno-Sanz, 2009b, p. 94).

Apart from being an innovative aspect, the inclusion of speaking tasks in these preparatory materials would also be an advantage of the online format of the FCE Course and Tester. The lack of flexibility of the printed versions makes the assessment of the speaking ability an unfeasible task whereas the characteristics of the electronic format that benefits from the recent advances in technology facilitate this kind of assessment. In fact, there are many other advantages about the use of technologies such as computers for the assessment of speaking. One of these advantages is the reliability of the assessment, which can take the form of semi-assisted interviews recording the answers of the examinees to a set of questions, the performance of the candidate thus being safely saved and stored, ready to be subsequently assessed by a qualified rater. Another positive aspect is the authenticity of the tasks based on audiovisual repertoires. In addition, the use of ICT can provide a high degree of interactivity, and very often it has a positive impact and washback effect in the classroom. Furthermore the practicality, for both the examiner and the examinee, of the use of a system based on computational linguistics together with the possibility to assess speaking more objectively are two additional advantages of the use of technology. In fact, the use of e-tools such as voice recording systems allows for the collection of data while facilitating the evaluation of these data and the possibility to access them in case a revision of the results is needed.

3. Self-assessment and tutor assessment in FCE Online Course and Tester

The modalities of assessment offered by the materials of the InGenio authoring tool and learning management system (Figure 2) developed by the CAMILLE Research Group at the Universidad Politécnica de Valencia, such as FCE Online Course and Tester, are self-assessment and tutor assessment.

Figure 2. The InGenio authoring tool homepage

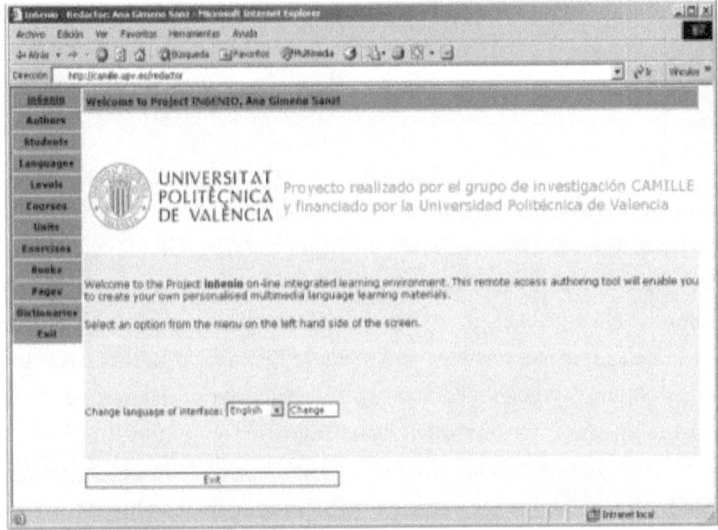

The courses and materials published through the content manager platform InGenio allow users to follow the self-assessment modality. It includes a greater variety of materials and activities so as to cater for the needs of learners with different learning styles and preferences, thus enabling them to use the materials in the most convenient way. These materials include a greater number of reference materials (Figure 3), additional explanations, extra readings and extra self-assessment activities in order to help those students who are mainly learning with less or no support from a human tutor. These features have the advantage of enabling students to conduct their own learning process and to evaluate their own learning achievements in an independent, autonomous and individual way.

Figure 3. InGenio Editor's interface for reference materials

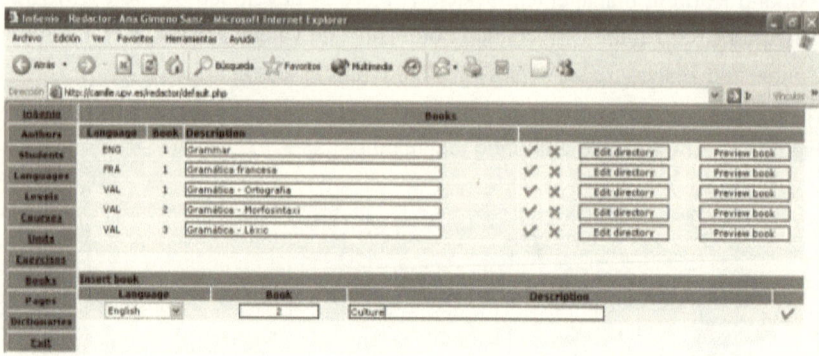

InGenio also provides two modalities of activities: automatically corrected and tutorised activities. On the one hand, the users can find automatically corrected activities, since once the student has completed an exercise or task, the system offers immediate feedback by using the information provided by the authors of the exercises (correct answers and specific feedback). In this case, students receive automatically generated messages in response to the number of correct or incorrect answers. On the other hand, tutorised activities are those which require human intervention by providing personalised feedback programmed or provided by the author of the exercise. This is the case in some of the exercises dealing with oral and written production, where responses are generally more elaborate or cannot be limited in order to give students automatic feedback. The following examples (taken from Gimeno-Sanz, 2009b) show the template where content designers can introduce their feedback (Figure 4), the automatic feedback by items in the way students see it (Figure 5), and the general feedback measured by rate of efficiency (Figure 6).

Figure 4. Author feedback form in InGenio

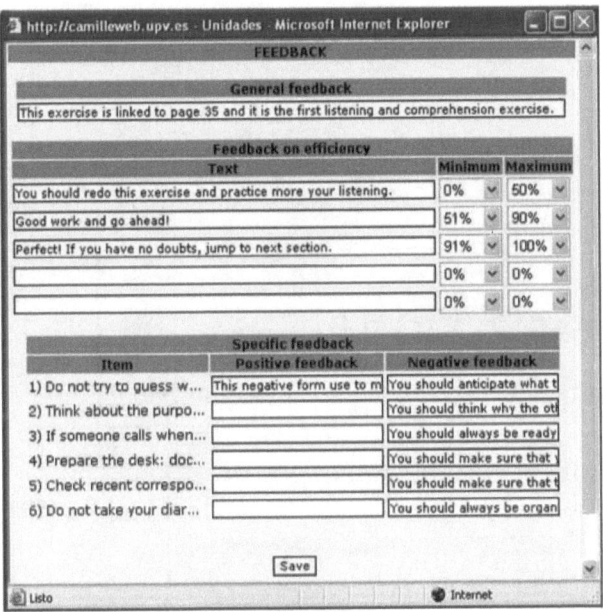

Figure 5. Feedback by item

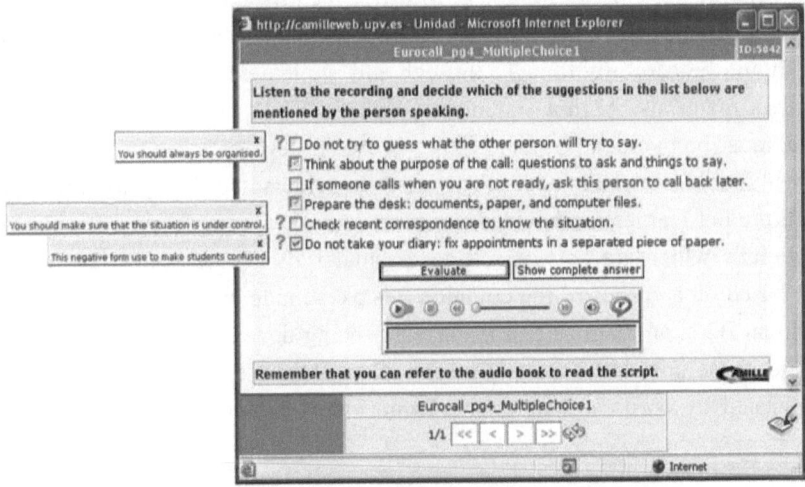

Chapter 4

Figure 6. Feedback measured by rate of efficiency

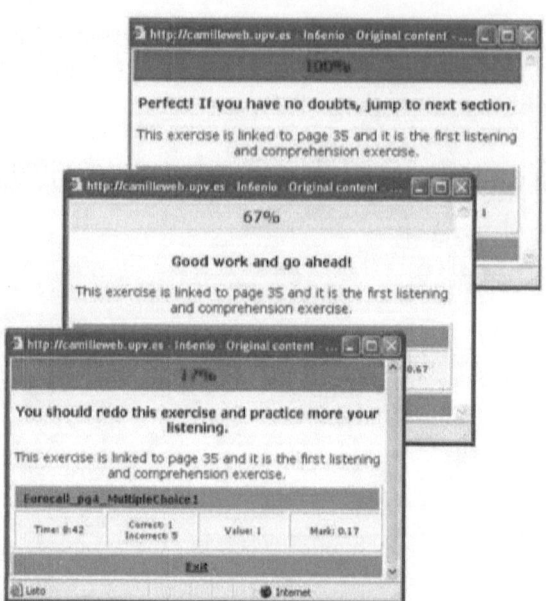

Feedback, obviously, is a key component of these materials as "it should always be clear what kind of mistake has been made", and it is a useful means to "provide not only awareness as to where the mistake lies, but also how to improve the learner's performance" (Gimeno-Sanz, 2009a, p. 88). Moreover, it should be carefully thought through and implemented when writing self-access materials. Abrupt statements such as "No", "Incorrect, try again", etc. must be avoided (Gimeno-Sanz, 2009a, p. 88). In order to provide the most suitable kind of feedback, content providers should try to anticipate and predict learners' behaviour and reactions when completing exercises or activities which are part of self-access materials. These predictions could be based on a corpus of the common mistakes made by Spanish speakers in official B2 examinations that is currently being developed. The information about these mistakes has mainly been taken from the literature based on or informed by corpora such as the Cambridge Learner Corpus (CLC)[*], but

---

[*] Further information available at http://www.cambridge.org/es/elt/?site_locale=es_ES.

further improvements will include analysing the Universidad Politécnica de Valencia students' results in the exam simulations and enriching the InGenio corpus with information about the mistakes the students made.

As for the materials designed for the tutor assessment modality, they provide more support to be used in the classroom context and include resources such as materials specifically designed to provide support for the tutor, a teachers' guide, and also detailed performance reports (Figure 7) about the students and other tracking devices (Gimeno-Sanz, 2008, p. 54). The positive aspect of this modality is the fact that it helps students to become autonomous learners (see Sevilla-Pavón, Martínez-Sáez, & Gimeno-Sanz, in press), by fostering their sense of responsibility in the learning process while providing students with help, guidance and support.

Figure 7.   InGenio student's assessment report

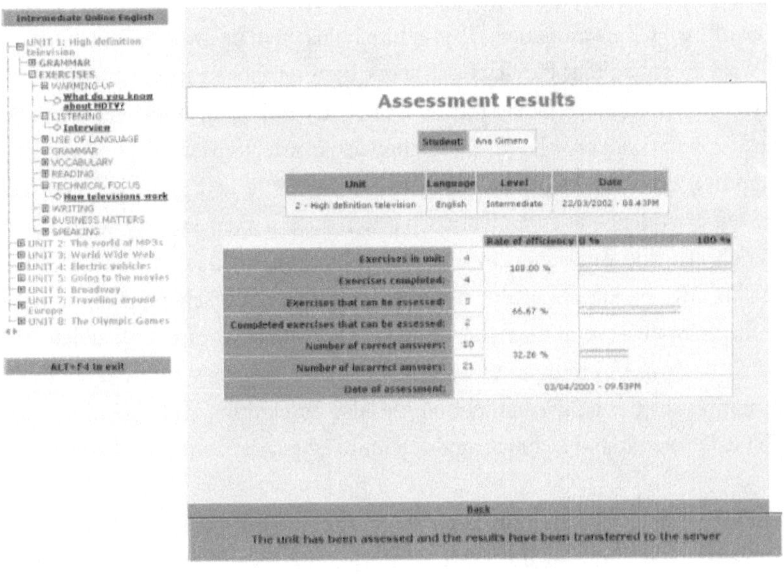

InGenio FCE Online Course and Tester also give students access to test simulations, similar to the actual FCE examination in terms of level, structure,

Chapter 4

exercise typology and administration mode*. The current development work of the CAMILLE Research Group is now focused on relating and adapting the content of these materials to the scientific and technical context of the Universidad Politécnica de Valencia. This is being done with a view to enriching the students' specific knowledge (e.g., their technical and scientific vocabulary) so as to help them become better professionals in the future. At the same time, these materials aim to enable the students to prepare for an examination that would certify their B2 level of English in accordance with the Common European Framework of Reference for Languages (CEFRL), a new requirement to earn their degree according to the guidelines fixed by the UPV as part of the implementation of the Bologna Process.

The self-assessment exercises and simulations included in the FCE Online Course and Tester benefit from numerous advantages of ICT, such as reliability, interactivity, authenticity, practicality, objectivity, and quick collection/evaluation of data. In this way, students are given the opportunity to face a similar situation to that of the FCE examination. This in turn helps them be aware of their strengths and weaknesses so that they can still work hard on those particular aspects they need to improve before facing the actual test. By doing so, students are likely to get better results not only linguistically but also in affective terms, since being able to improve and even to predict their outcomes before taking the test can foster their self-confidence and motivation while reducing their anxiety levels. These materials also allow designers to generate online assessment elements that provide valuable information about the students, available for teachers at any point so that they can observe and assess adequately the progress of every student. This is particularly useful in those cases in which these materials are used not only in preparation for the FCE examination but also as learning and assessment tools specifically oriented to technical and scientific languages learning.

The FCE Online Course and Tester develop their full potential when used in combination, the first of these preparatory resources being an online course

---

*These simulations are computer-based and therefore their administration mode is the same as that of the computer-based FCE, the computerised version of the FCE examination which was launched in January 2010 (further information available at http://www.cambridgeesol.org/exams/exams-info/computer-based-testing.html).

with different kinds of exercises –similar to the ones included in the FCE papers–to be completed first; and an assessment program including self-assessment exercises and simulations of the actual online examination, to be completed once the online course is finished and the students feel ready to face an examination situation. Prior to the design of simulations, a great number of exercises had to be compiled in a corpus of B2 exercises accessible through an online database. These exercises are either independent or based on given texts, the latter being more abundant than the former since texts are also predominant in the actual FCE examination papers. The simulations can be generated upon the users' request, the great number of texts and exercises included in the database allowing for numerous and randomised combinations.

In the development of these preparatory materials, the two main previous aspects underscored by Buck (2001) have been taken into account. First of all, the ultimate objective, which would be to succeed in the FCE examination and thus to ascertain the B2 level of English of our students, follows the application of the guidelines of the Bologna Process and of the Action Plan on Language Learning and Linguistic Diversity*. Then, the profile of the potential examinees is considered, which in our case would be that of students of technical and scientific degrees at UPV aged between 18 and 25, who need to prove their B2 level of English –one of the means fixed by the UPV to do so is a success in the FCE official exam. As for the successful put into practice, Messick's (1996) advice to avoid construct-underrepresentation and construct-irrelevant variance is also being followed. On the one hand, construct-underrepresentation occurs when "the test is too narrow and fails to include important dimensions or facets of the construct" (Messick, 1989, p. 34). On the other hand, construct-irrelevant variance (which is also called surplus construct irrelevancy) takes place when "the test contains excess reliable variance that is irrelevant to the interpreted construct" (Messick, 1989, p. 34), i.e., when the test assesses abilities which are not included in the theoretical description of the construct. Avoiding these inconveniences is a sine qua non requirement in assessment because the correct

---

*Further information can be found at http://europa.eu/legislation_summaries/education_training_youth/lifelong_learning/c11068_en.htm.

or incorrect interpretation of the scores, which in turn influences the validity of the decisions we make based on those scores, depends on the theoretical and operational soundness of our construct.

4. Conclusion

The InGenio FCE Online Course and Tester are good examples of the way in which the use of ICT in language learning can contribute to the effectiveness and efficiency of the assessment process of basic skills such as reading, writing, listening and even speaking in two main modalities: student self-assessment and tutor assessment. The students are allowed to choose between these two different modalities of assessment on account of the flexibility of these materials. Their choice depends on their needs, preferences, learning styles and personal characteristics. This is possible thanks to the fact that the students can choose whether to use these materials as part of a blended-learning course (i.e., attending classes and also practicing online), by completing the course and tester contents autonomously while being monitored by a tutor, or following the course in a completely autonomous way (both by paying attention to the automatic feedback reports that show their results and by comparing their answers with the models provided in those cases where automatic correction is not possible).

The self-assessment modality enables students to conduct their own learning process and to assess their own learning achievements in an independent, autonomous and individual way. The tutor assessment fosters the development of the students' autonomy and sense of responsibility while enabling them to get as much help and support from a human tutor as they need. Both modalities have the common goal of making students think critically about themselves and to enable them to make decisions and judgements about their own progress, in spite of the fact that this is done in different ways depending on the modality chosen.

The criteria and the objectives of these materials, as well as the contents and the way these are organised, have been determined by the guidelines of the Action Plan on Language Learning and Linguistic Diversity of the European Union as well as by the characteristics of the FCE. In this way, the FCE Online Course and Tester are intended to make students develop their communicative abilities in English. This is addressing the necessity that European universities set up a clear and coherent linguistic policy that takes into account linguistic and cultural diversity, as established by the European Commission, while pursuing the goal of helping students acquire a B2 level of English. This level enables them to pass the FCE exam, which is a prerequisite for them to be able to graduate from UPV.

The CAMILLE Research Group will continue working in order to improve its FCE preparatory course and tester in terms of quality, user-friendliness, efficiency, and usefulness. Trying to foster the students' autonomy and to prepare them better for a global society in which the ability to communicate and to interact fluently and spontaneously with speakers of other languages, especially in English, is becoming more and more important.

Acknowledgements

Acknowledgements are due to the Valencian Regional Government (Generalitat Valenciana) for funding Ana Sevilla-Pavón's and Antonio Martínez-Sáez's research grants (FPI).

References

Alderson, J. C. (2000). *Assessing reading*. Cambridge: Cambridge University Press.
Bachman, L. F., & Palmer, A. S. (1996). *Language testing in practice*. Oxford: Oxford University Press.
Brown, G., & Yule, G. (1983). *Discourse analysis*. Cambridge: Cambridge University Press.
Brown, S., & Glasner, A. (Eds.). (2003). *Assessment matters in higher education: choosing and using diverse approaches*. Buckingham and Philadelphia: The Society of Research into Higher Education and Open University Press.
Buck, G. (2001). *Assessing listening*. Cambridge: Cambridge University Press.
Carter, R., & McCarthy, M. (2006). *Cambridge grammar of Englis*h. Cambridge: Cambridge University Press.

Douglas, D. (1998). Testing methods in context-based second language research. In L. F. Bachman & A. D. Cohen (Eds.), *Interfaces between second language acquisition and language testing research* (pp. 141-155). Cambridge: Cambridge University Press.

Dudeney, G. (2000). *The Internet and the language classroom*. Cambridge: Cambridge University Press.

Ferguson, G. (2007). Teaching writing in a second language: an overview of principles and practice. In R. Plo Asastrué (Ed.), I. Andrés Monte (Coord.), Ministerio de Educación y Ciencia, Secretaría General de Educación, Instituto Superior de Formación del Profesorado, Secretaría General Técnica, Subdirección General de Información y Publicaciones, *El desarrollo de competencias en lenguas extranjeras: textos y otras estrategias* (pp. 31-63). Madrid: Ediciones Gráficas Arial.

Fulcher, G., & Davidson, F. (2007). *Language testing and assessment: an advanced resource book*. London: Routledge.

Gilmore, A. (2007). Authentic materials and authenticity in foreign language learning. *Language Testing*, 40(2), 97-118. doi:10.1017/S0261444807004144

Gimeno-Sanz, A. (2008). *Aprendizaje de lenguas asistido por ordenador: herramientas de autor para el desarrollo de cursos a través de la web*. Valencia: Servicio de Publicaciones de la Universidad Politécnica de Valencia.

Gimeno-Sanz, A. (2009a). How can CLIL benefit from the integration of information and communication technnnologies. In M. L. Carrió Pastor (Ed.), *Content and language integrated learning: cultural diversity* (pp. 77-102). Bern: Peter Lang.

Gimeno-Sanz, A. (2009b). Online courseware design and delivery: the InGenio authoring system. In I. González-Pueyo, M. C. Foz Gil, M. Jaime Siso, & M. J. Luzón Marco (Eds.), *Teaching academic and professional English online* (pp. 83-106). Bern: Peter Lang.

Grabe, W. (1991). Current developments in second language reading research. *Tesol Quarterly*, 25(3), 375-406. Retrieved from http://www.jstor.org/pss/3586977

Grabe, W. (2008). *Reading in a second language: moving from theory to practice*. Cambridge: Cambridge University Press.

Gray, W. S. (1960). The major aspect of reading. In H. Robinson (Ed.), *Sequential development of reading abilities* (Vol. 90) (pp. 8-24). Chicago: Chicago University Press.

Hale, C. (1996). *Wired style: Principles of English usage in the digital age*. San Francisco, California: HardWired.

Hamp-Lyons, L. (Ed.). (1991). *Assessing second language writing in academic contexts*. Norwood, New Jersey: Ablex.

Hoven, D. (1999). A model for listening and viewing comprehension in multimedia environments. *Language Learning & Technology*, 3(1), 88-103. Retrieved from http://llt.msu.edu/vol3num1/hoven/index.html

Hymes, D. H. (1974). *Foundations in sociolinguistics: an ethnographic approach.* Philadelphia: University of Pennsylvania Press.

Levy, M., & Stockwell, G. (2006). *CALL dimensions: options and issues in computer-assisted language learning.* Mahwah, New Jersey: Lawrence Erlbaum Associates.

Luoma, S. (2009). *Assessing speaking* (5th ed.). Cambridge: Cambridge University Press.

Messick, S. (1989). Validity. In R. Linn (Ed.), *Educational measurement* (3rd ed., pp. 13-104). Washington DC: American Council on Education.

Messick, S. (1996). Validity and washback in language testing. *Language Testing*, 13(3), 241-256. doi:10.1177/026553229601300302

Purves, A. C., Söter, A., Takala, S., & Vähäpassi, A. (1984). Towards a domain-referenced system for classifying composition assignments. *Research in the Teaching of English*, 18(4), 385-416. Retrieved from http://www.jstor.org/pss/40170996

Read, J. (2000). *Assessing vocabulary.* Cambridge: Cambridge University Press.

Sevilla-Pavón, A., Martínez-Sáez, A., & Gimeno-Sanz, A. (in press). *Assessment of competences in designing online preparatory materials for the Cambridge First Certificate in English Examination.* Paper presented at the EuroCALL Conference 2010, Université de Bordeaux.

Taylor, R., & Gitsaki, C. (2004). Teaching WELL and loving IT. In S. Fotos & C. M. Browne (Eds.), *New perspectives on CALL for the second/foreign language classroom* (pp. 129-145). Seattle: Lawrence Erlbaum Associates.

Weigle, S. C. (2009). *Assessing writing* (6th ed.). Cambridge: Cambridge University Press.

Weir, C., O'Sullivan, B., & Horai, T. (2006). Exploring difficulty in speaking tasks: an intra-task perspective. In P. McGovern & S. Walsh (Eds.), *The British Council: IELTS Research Reports 6* (pp. 119-160). Canberra: British Council & IDP Australia.

Website

CAMILLE Research Group: http://camilleweb.upv.es/camille

Mobile-Assisted Language Learning: Designing for Your Students

Agnieszka Palalas[*]

Abstract

Mobile-assisted language learning (MALL) can augment second language teaching and learning by taking it into the real world. Authentic communicative situations in conjunction with the cultural artefacts and metalinguistic clues offered by the context can promote active learning; however, as respondents of the study presented in this chapter observed, this dynamic process of situated learning has to be supported by access to peers and facilitators, information and linguistic resources, as well as tools for capturing and distributing linguistic information. Moreover, out-of-class language learning has to be guided by a relevant pedagogical task which encompasses language-in-action activities and motivates students to work and communicate with others. When interacting with others in a socio-cultural milieu of the real world, students can rely on mobile technology to provide the necessary cultural artefacts and tools. This chapter reports on a design-based research (DBR) study seeking to enhance English as second language (ESL) students' aural skills with help of mobile devices. Owing to the comprehensive feedback from an interdisciplinary group of students, the design of our MALL solution has evolved from a set of podcasts to a suite of learning tools which enable access to a networked community of practice and other resources required for the completion of language tasks.

Keywords: mobile-assisted language learning (MALL), real-life language tasks, learner-generated content, MALL instructional design, design-based research (DBR).

---

[*]George Brown College, Toronto, Canada; Doctoral Candidate, Athabasca University, Canada. e-mail: agaizabella@rogers.com

How to cite this chapter: Palalas, A. (2011). Mobile-assisted language learning: designing for your students. In S. Thouësny & L. Bradley (Eds.), *Second language teaching and learning with technology: views of emergent researchers* (pp. 71-94). Dublin: Research-publishing.net.

Chapter 5

1. Introduction

This chapter reports on how the conceptualisation of mobile-assisted language learning design was refined through the enhanced understanding of the needs of students and their specific context. It aims to demonstrate how students' feedback gathered through multiple stages of collaborative inquiry, coupled with the expertise of practitioners and the knowledge derived from research, theory and best practices, engendered a new conceptual approach to the design of mobile second language instruction. Initiated by L2* students' demands for innovative English for special purposes (ESP) instruction, which would allow them to learn English out-of-class in their own time, this investigation into effective MALL solutions has progressed from an exploratory study (Palalas, 2009) to a longitudinal design-based research project. The first two phases of the ongoing DBR study and the resultant findings are the focus of this chapter. The DBR investigation drew on what had been learned in the earlier exploratory research project, a brief synopsis of which is presented below.

The exploratory study commenced at George Brown College (GBC) in Toronto, Canada, in 2007. It sought to augment classroom learning by designing MALL solutions which would promote out-of-class listening practice, thus offering added language learning without increasing classroom time. The resulting mobile learning tasks were then tested as part of a hybrid ESP course. This English for Accounting course aimed to optimise L2 students' academic success at the college and consequently to help them secure jobs commensurate with their qualifications. Its curriculum blended in-class, online and mobile learning to address both the language and socio-cultural competencies required by the Canadian workplace.

Building on the inherent affordances of the iPod Touch, which was the main technology under study**, audio and video podcasts were created in-house for on-the-go access. Other open access ESL podcasts and vodcasts were also available to

---

* L1: speakers of English as their first language; L2: speakers of English as their second language.

** iPod Touch devices were loaned to students for the period of the exploratory study; one student chose to use her own mobile phone instead.

students for flexible retrieval. These included selected ESLpod, Business English Pod, and TED videos as well as Whaddaya Say audio recordings. Additionally, students were encouraged to use their handheld devices to communicate by blogging and via email, as well as to record their written reflections using the Notes feature. Nonetheless, to curtail the difficulties resulting from typing using small keyboards and the cost of connectivity (Kukulska-Hulme & Shield, 2008), the mobile devices were used primarily for the provision of pre-loaded listening and video content. This MALL approach was tested in a fifteen-week pilot which concluded in August 2009.

During the pilot-course, feedback pertaining to the effectiveness of the MALL activities and student satisfaction was collected from twelve L2 students and four practitioners. Using qualitative and quantitative measures, this exploratory study also examined students' learning and took a closer look at what types of activities students preferred to engage in and why. While participants expressed high levels of satisfaction with the MALL component of the course, it was found that the mobile devices were used primarily as media players. Minimal levels of interaction were observed and the connectivity features of the mobile devices were hardly utilised. Learning was thus limited to non-reciprocal listening and rote memorisation of vocabulary. It became evident that the instruction had to be modified in order to promote effective second language learning, encompassing communication and benefiting from the inherent capabilities of mobile devices. In addition, a number of mobile learning advantages and caveats were identified which provided a better understanding of students' experience with mobile technologies. Consistent with mobile learning literature (Kukulska-Hulme, 2005; Kukulska-Hulme & Pettit, 2009; Kukulska-Hulme & Shield, 2008; Naismith, Lonsdale, Vavoula, & Sharples, 2004; Pachler, 2009; Sharples, 2009), students cited flexibility, portability, access to resources and convenience as the key benefits of mobile learning, whereas cost and limited connectivity were identified as its primary shortcomings. Informed by these findings and the latest mobile learning research, the question of effective MALL design was revisited in a new DBR study which commenced in September 2009. The next section introduces the current study.

2. Investigating effective MALL design: design-based research

As mentioned in the introduction, the current DBR study draws on the findings of a two-year investigation of MALL solutions addressing the development of aural skills in adult college students. The main purpose of the study is to distil a set of design principles for effective mobile-assisted listening learning objects (LO). The main question guiding this investigation is:

> What are the characteristics of an effective pedagogically sound LO for students' mobile devices through which adult ESP students in a community college enhance their listening skills while expanding their learning outside of the classroom?

The primary focus of the question rests on what constitutes an effective pedagogically sound MALL resource. The investigation into the vital elements of a successful design involves multiple iterative cycles of the LO design, development, and evaluation. Therefore, supplementary research questions congruent with the various phases of the study have emerged and will continue surfacing in the process to guide the ongoing inquiry. This chapter concentrates on the informed exploration and enactment phases, which are the first two stages of the four-phase study. Throughout the multiple cycles of those two phases, a number of questions were asked of the research participants as they were creating and testing the subsequent versions of MALL listening learning objects. The two key questions pertaining to the effectiveness of mobile learning activities and the affordances of mobile technologies were:

> 1. Based on the MALL resources you tested and other m-learning ESP materials, what are the characteristics of effective listening activities/resources for mobile devices?

> 2. How do you usually use your mobile device for learning, work, and leisure? Which of these uses should be adopted in the design of MALL listening activities/resources?

To distil the vital characteristics and understand their relationships necessitates interdisciplinary feedback from L2 students, designers, programmers, English as second language practitioners and m-learning researchers. Moreover, such feedback has to reflect the specific needs of the George Brown College L2 students and their educational, linguistic and cultural context. That context and more importantly student voices have shaped the design of the preliminary MALL LOs as well as the theoretical framework adopted by the study. The remainder of this chapter discusses the evolving conceptual framework of the DBR study, the findings of the two completed stages and how they have informed future research at GBC.

2.1. Theoretical framework

To ensure pedagogically sound design of mobile listening activities, sociocultural theory (SCT) was initially adopted as the framework for the study. Vygotsky-inspired sociocultural theories share the concept of higher-order cognitive functions being culturally mediated and communicative processes as "inherently cognitive processes [...] indivisible from humanistic issues of self-efficacy, agency, and the capacity to lead a satisfying if not fulfilling life" (Thorne, 2005, p. 403). Accordingly, social interaction and the internal cognitive process of thinking are strongly interconnected in "a dialectic unity in which publicly derived speech completes privately initiated thought" (Lantolf, 2000, p. 6). The activity of mind cannot be realised without interaction with others through culturally organised activity. Hence, social relationships and culturally constructed forms of mediation play a central role in human cognition (Lantolf, 2000, 2004). For learning to occur, recurring interaction with the cultural-historical context and other people is sine qua non. All interaction and communication with others and the world is thus mediated by culturally constructed artefacts including language and technology (Lantolf, 2000, 2004; Pachler, 2009). Users see those cultural artefacts as meditational means for "interpersonal (social interaction) and intrapersonal (thinking) purposes" (Lantolf, 2000, p. 6) and tools that serve a specific purpose (Thorne, 2005). Furthermore, as learners develop, they gain increasing control over those tools (Lantolf, 2000) and as a result develop their communicative skills.

As indicated above, SCT integrated the constructivist concepts of mediation, goal-oriented activity, the zone of proximal development (ZPD) (Vygotsky, 1978), and interaction with others in a socio-cultural milieu. In the MALL context, this translates to designing instruction which promotes communication with others in a relevant setting, through goal-oriented activities. It calls for an inclusion of collaborative communicative activities mediated by the mobile technology across time and space to accommodate cognitive and social processes. While learning language in action, learners need access to others as well as to information, feedback, and help systems which can be provided through the appropriate software (Hoven, 1999). For the learner to achieve independent performance, interactivity should be combined with the scaffolding support of facilitators and peers (Vygotsky, 1978) or appropriate forms of computerised context-sensitive help.

Mobile technologies do, indeed, facilitate the support of a networked community of practice and learning situated in the real-life setting. Using handheld devices learners can engage in interaction not only with others, but also with their environment (Sharples, Taylor, & Vavoula, 2007). The context of learning is thus a significant construct which embraces the environment in which learners operate, with all its inherent components and actors.

The two context-related perspectives on mobile learning adopted in the study are: context-independent learning when the learner is using travelling or dead time to learn using mobile devices, and context-aware (contextual) mobile learning when the learning activity relates to the location (physical, geographical or logical) of the actors and the context in which they are moving (David, Yin, & Chalon, 2009). It is the latter perspective that had been identified in the exploratory study at GBC as a critical element of engaging communicative MALL activities. Consequently, the current theoretical framework also integrates the notion of situated learning with its emphasis on the authentic context and social interaction (Brown, Collins, & Duguid, 1989; Lave & Wenger, 1991) as well as "apprenticeship" learning based on "activity in and with the world" (Lave & Wenger, 1991, p. 33). Seen through this conceptual lens, MALL can be defined as language learning enabled by the mobility of the learner and location, portability of handheld devices (Kukulska-Hulme, 2005; Mwanza-Simwami, 2009; Naismith et al., 2004), human interaction across multiple situations mediated by mobile technology within a networked community of practice (Sharples et al., 2007), embedded in contexts which are relevant and pedagogically sound (Laurillard, 2007) and informed by the real-life context in which the learning takes place.

2.2. Method

It is the intent of this DBR study to produce two key outputs which Plomp (2009) refers to as educational interventions and design principles (intervention theory). The combination of two parallel goals, namely, the design of MALL learning solutions and the development of a corresponding instructional design (ID) framework, makes design-based research a suitable approach for the purpose of this real-world practice study (Brown, 1992; Plomp, 2009). Interventionist and practical in nature, DBR is "a systematic but flexible methodology aimed to improve educational practices through iterative analysis, design, development, and implementation, based on collaboration among researchers and practitioners in real-world settings, and leading to contextually-sensitive design principles and theories" (Wang & Hannafin, 2005, p. 7).

To ensure "rigorous, research-based cycles within a technology-based instructional design effort" (Bannan, 2009, p. 53), the integrative learning design framework (ILDF) (Bannan, 2009) has been adopted. The ILDF model encompasses four phases of (1) informed exploration, (2) enactment (3) evaluation: local impact, and (4) evaluation: broader impact. These phases and their cycles are, in fact, iterative and they tend to overlap. The first two phases have been completed and they are summarised below.

2.2.1. The informed exploration phase

To better understand the ESP student needs, informed exploration focused on comprehensive investigation of the target audience and practitioners' perceptions. Data collected in the exploratory study were revisited and enriched with additional comments from both returning and new research participants, all of a diverse cultural and demographic backgrounds. These included twenty-one adult L2 learners, eleven of whom were from the original Accounting pilot-course, six from the School of Design, and four were Programming students from the School of Technology. Practitioner perspective was represented by two Design faculty, two Programming faculty, and three Communications/ESL professors. Qualitative feedback was collected from all participants via three semi-structured focus groups with the three individual groups of students and five faculty meetings supplemented with email communication. In addition, an online survey was conducted with a random sample of 182 L2 George Brown students regarding the type of mobile devices they use, how and when respondents use them, as well as data plans they subscribe to. The data gathered from this interdisciplinary group was then coded, interceded, and analysed for the most frequent themes using the NVivo software. The results highlighted the systemic social, cultural, and organisational influences and constraints on the MALL intervention design. These findings coupled with comprehensive review of relevant literature on second language learning, mobile learning and instructional design, resulted in a theoretical construct of the MALL listening LO, which has served in the subsequent stages as an ideal providing "a vision and a guide as well as a significant component of the measuring stick by which the ideal, as instantiated in actions within a real context, is measured" (Anderson, 2007, slide 48). The prototype of this ideal was produced in the next phase which is discussed below.

2.2.2. The enactment phase

In this highly visible production phase (Anderson, 2007), prototype MALL listening learning objects were designed and developed by the researcher in cooperation with the School of Design and School of Technology students and practitioners. First, twelve post-graduate Design students, including six L2 speakers, completed the design of MALL learning objects as part of their course curriculum. They had access to an ESL instructional designer through ten weekly in-class meetings. Design students' feedback was collected through those meetings, two focus groups, and email correspondence. Their creations were then handed over to a group of two L1 and two L2 programmers who, through multiple cycles of redesign, development and prototype testing, further enhanced the perspective on the MALL design. Having faced multiple stumbling blocks in terms of the conceptual framework as well as technology, the interdisciplinary team of students and practitioners collaborated on the design through weekly face-to-face meetings, online Elluminate* sessions, as well as email and wiki communication. Design, Programming and ESP students created a strong network through which they have also exchanged their expertise and feedback with the researcher and the faculty. They engaged in the systematic adaptive work of sharing the learning through formal and informal collaborative practices including planning, researching, problem solving as well as individual and collective ID tasks.

While the students documented the design and development process through their assignments and design logs, their feedback was recorded by way of researcher notes and audio recordings from the face-to-face and virtual Elluminate meetings. The data collected from all students and practitioners was once again coded and analysed using NVivo. Its main themes constituted the basis for the refined conceptual model which is presented in the findings and discussion sections.

2.2.3. Findings

The informed exploration and enactment phases of the study produced contextually-grounded knowledge based on the interdisciplinary feedback collected from language learners, student designers and student programmers as well as practitioners. It is primarily the student perspective, however, and the investigation of their "mobile habits" that triggered the re-conceptualisation of the design approach. These findings are presented below using selected verbatim quotes from research participants. They have been arranged to tell the story with students' words and to encapsulate the main themes of the feedback obtained from the L2 learners.

---

* Elluminate Live! is a web conferencing program; it offers an array of communication and presentation tools. It was used in the study for the purpose of synchronous online meetings with practitioners.

Chapter 5

As mentioned before, student participants were asked two key questions; the first one aimed to identify the main characteristics of effective listening activities/resources for mobile devices. The following responses are representative of all L2 students' opinions pertaining to the first question:

> *All that helps you practice how to understand other students and other people not only at school.*
>
> *Most important characteristic is that we can listen when we are not busy and we can practice pronunciation and vocabulary.*
>
> *I like the videos from work that show the culture office behaviours. I think that this is important to learn about what's important at work and also new things to immigrants... and to listen to accounting vocabulary.*
>
> *I really like the podcasts that I can listen to when I'm on the TTC [Toronto Transit Commission] but sometimes I catch myself that I stop to listen and to concentrate. I also stop when I'm not sure what it means. So it's better if I could ask about the meaning when I listen instead of to wait when I meet my friends... When we meet with the teacher she can help us or other students can help me... maybe we could [get help] over the phone.*
>
> *When we work with our mobile phones we are isolated, like I am isolated when I am in the Accounting courses because my English is not so good; but when we meet once a week and do team assignments, we feel part of the group... I don't know if that can be done through the phone, but belonging is very important.*
>
> *Sometimes the mobile learning does not keep me interested because it's like listening to the radio, you can stop if you want to or if you are tired. When we are in the ESL class the teacher forces us to get up and do things. Something like that is needed on the phone.*

> *The best assignment was when we had to prepare radio interview. First I was very nervous but then we ensured that it was interesting to us and to the class. The recording directions were not clear but we figured it out...the most important characteristics are clear directions, real problems connected to our program, and examples from other students...you are proud when you create your own project, many students are creative, and I enjoyed to listen to their programs.*

> *Some of the tasks should be more demanding... more like real case studies not ESL exercises.*

> *... works for me but I'm not sure about everybody; we all should talk for ourselves.*

Students further elaborated on the salient functionalities of handheld devices in their comments to the second question: how do you usually use your mobile device for learning, work, and leisure? Which of these uses should be adopted in the design of MALL listening activities/resources?

> *I use my phone usually for to text and call my friends. I also check my email and Facebook... I don't have the Internet but it would be good to help with my homework.*

> *Like everybody, I communicate with my friends and classmates, also [colleagues] at work, both for leisure and work; we communicate for fun and to get things done.*

> *Listening to music is for pleasure, but I listen also to radio, some podcasts [the teacher suggested] and other that my classmates found.*

> *People can learn from TED, YouTube and special websites for different topics.*

Chapter 5

> ... other students said to me to use YouTube
> and iTunes but I don't know yet.
>
> You find information from Wikipedia, or answers.
> com, or use audio Google app.
>
> I have dictionary and apps that you can practice words...
> flash cards that with audio would be better.
>
> For help with English, I use my dictionary or
> there are translators for iPhone.
>
> Audio dictionary? I didn't know... then you can check a
> word when I don't know what people say to me.
>
> Usually, I make photos with my phone to send to my friends,
> but you can use pictures when don't know the word and you
> want to explain something, or for you to ask someone later.
>
> When we did interviews for our radio, different students used
> different recorders. It depends on what you can afford. The teacher
> put us in groups so we had all tools we need for the assignment.
>
> You can use what you have on your phone, you can listen
> or type, you can learn or have fun... it's your choice.
>
> I cannot do the same like other students because
> they have more expensive phones.
>
> To help you learn you can ask teacher for lesson podcasts.
>
> For media, I normally send my favourite pictures and songs, and I listen
> to songs;... I take photographs and send to show what I like... but maybe
> we can listen to other people favourite songs and talk about them.

Students identified a number of interconnected components of a potential MALL solution and their properties. Before I propose how to incorporate all of them into a new design framework, the abovementioned results are summarised and their pedagogical implications are discussed.

3. Discussion: implications for the MALL design

Learners' needs have to be integrated in the design of any student-centered instruction. Our L2 students emphasised that it is the key goal of language learning to be able to communicate in any life situation as part of a community. In fact, it is the very purpose of learning to be "prepared to deal with novel contexts that are going to be encountered beyond the classroom" (Larsen-Freeman, 2002, p. 43), and mobile technology affords learning out-of-class and thus engenders situated practice and flexible learning across space, time, and contexts (Sharples, 2009).

Consistent with earlier findings (Palalas, 2009), GBC students valued out-of-class ESP practice and the opportunity to learn in their own time. In their language practice learners wanted to focus on listening comprehension, advanced vocabulary, field-specific terminology, pronunciation, and socio-cultural competencies. A majority of respondents also emphasised a need for activities which would engage and motivate them despite the physical absence of such extrinsic factors as the facilitator or peers. The pilot course students had indicated that the hybrid course sustained their high levels of motivation primarily on account of the weekly face-to-face meetings and the feeling of belonging to the community of practice which they had not experienced in other college courses. Due to what the learners themselves considered as their inadequate language skills, their learning was hindered by affective barriers and the feeling of being emotionally and socially distant from their peers. Subsequently, some respondents elaborated on the notion of community of practice and a need for technology-enabled opportunities in order to socialise. Socialisation with peers indeed promotes language acquisition (Kramsch, 2002). Apart from the emotional and social aspects of interaction, the significance of learning support available via the network was also accentuated. Hence, to maintain high levels of engagement and to provide both on-demand and delayed help, mobile students have to be able to seamlessly connect to their peers and facilitators. A number of web-based and phone-based digital resources can provide language help; however, the facility to interact with the community of practice is deemed particularly vital to m-learning. Lacking the physical proximity, mobile learners could, in fact, benefit from collaborative activities integrating communication via mobile devices in conjunction with in-person meetings at the participants' convenience. Consequently, collaborative tasks organised around joint goals form the focus of our MALL design.

In terms of other means of just-in-time learning help, dictionaries, glossaries and digital translators are used by L2 students to support communication and repair miscommunication. Additionally, learners resort to visual artefacts, such as photos taken with their phone cameras or images which can be accessed through their mobile devices. Students select these resources based on their needs and the technology available to them. As mature students and experienced language learners, many of our respondents indicated readiness to select from the tools, applications, and resources available on their mobile device. They recommended searching audio and video distribution portals such as YouTube, TED and iTunesU for existing podcasts and mini-ESL lessons. Students also identified audio flashcards and audio podcasts related to their personal interests as useful for language practice. While our learners autonomously explored a variety of MALL resources, they expressed a need for guidance through the vast amount of information, and wished for learning activities and materials to be organised around pedagogical tasks. Accordingly, it is essential to provide learning and technology help options which encompass access to peers and experts, language task-specific help, and a selection of web-based or locally residing language resources for mobile devices. Scaffolding derived from communication with others as well as mobile access to a choice of resources are critical; however, the facilitator should relinquish some of the control and empower the learners to accept more responsibility for learning (King, 1993).

All in all, the ability to access appropriate authentic materials and reference sources, to be guided by well-designed tasks relevant to students' interests, and to actively engage in synchronous and asynchronous communication with "connected" others have been identified as indispensable properties of the MALL design. Leveraged by mobile technology, the flexibility of interaction and expression within a web of learning can be further enhanced using various modalities and tools of choice. As indicated by our respondents, students record their own notes in text and audio, they take photos, they enjoy recording and uploading interviews, and they recommend creating and publishing mini-presentations using their mobile devices. Equipped with audio, video, and text capabilities, mobile devices afford communication through multiple means of representation. This allows for listening competencies to be taught in a more authentic environment integrating all four language skills (Rost, 2002).

Another concept interwoven throughout the learner feedback was that of student-generated materials. Respondents took pride in their creations and were willing to share their artefacts with others. As noted by McGarr (2009), when challenged to create their own materials, students have to engage their critical thinking and comprehend the content thoroughly. McGarr (2009) posits that "student generated content can also facilitate peer learning and contribute to a supportive and constructive [learning] environment" (p. 317). Therefore, drawing on constructionist theories, our MALL activities encourage learners to create tangible meaningful artefacts and thus enhance the learning experience (Ackermann, 2002). Students' engagement in meaning-making while designing relevant projects and sharing them within the community will facilitate their learning (Papert & Harel, 1991).

As mentioned above in the theoretical framework discussion, in order for that learning to occur, communicative activities should be embedded in real-life settings. Context, along with technologies and other cultural artefacts mediate meaning-making. Students reported, for example, informally utilising context to convey meaning when they snapped photographs of items they wanted to communicate about with interlocutors. Apart from capturing images and symbols, language learners can benefit from a wealth of visual and audio clues surrounding them in an authentic communicative situations. Language in-action is emergent and dynamic (Lafford, 2009; Van Lier, 2000). "Language use is contingent on the communicative needs of the participants in particular speech situations—in particular, times and places (Lafford, 2009, p. 675). Language practice should, indeed, incorporate opportunities for impromptu revision and adjustment of speech when language "emerg[es] from a person's situatedness or participation in a physical and social world" (Kramsch, 2002, p. 11). "The environment provides a 'semiotic budget' [...] within which the active learner engages in meaning-making activities together with others who may be more, equally, or less competent in linguistic terms" (Van Lier, 2000, p. 252). Overall, context affords meaningful interaction through an array of supports and cultural artefacts mediating communication. The GBC second language learners are surrounded by authentic language in-action at the College, at their workplace, and in the streets of Toronto. It is, thus, viable and beneficial to these learners to participate in MALL activities involving communication in these real-life contexts.

To sum up the main characteristics of our MALL instructional design, we seek to promote collaborative active learning situated in the real-world environment. MALL activities are built to allow interaction, communication, access to resources and people within the networked community of practice. The LOs are designed with respect to the technologies students have access to and to their preferences. Therefore, our MALL design promotes a collaborative approach which allows learners to combine various facilities and channels of communication that their diverse mobile devices afford.

Examples of MALL tasks based on the findings of our study include, among others, student-generated audio-visual descriptions of Toronto landmarks, an audio repository of English idioms, an audio dictionary, phone blogging, a Toronto scavenger hunt and radio interviews conducted by students. The pedagogical tasks entail listening comprehension practice, following audio instructions, in-situ communication, audio data collection, collaborative inquiry, multimedia artefacts creation and distribution, as well as peer review of student-generated content. Students work with audio and video recordings simulating real-life communication in an authentic workplace as well as language examples and themes obtained from their college program courses. Moreover, students are required to communicate with their peers and other people either through rehearsed audio recordings or in impromptu speech situations, such as when faced by a scavenger hunt challenge or a phone inquiry. The majority of tasks involve listening comprehension practice, followed by recording of audio files which capture the usage of English in the real world. These steps are completed either individually or collaboratively, depending on the task. Subsequently, the student-generated artefacts are exchanged and peer-evaluated. To provide further opportunities for interaction, students are also encouraged to complete their tasks, and in particular the scavenger hunt and the Toronto landmarks challenges, either in a group or in pairs. Varied degrees of teacher scaffolding and mediation are required and can be provided in person, via email or by telephone. The type and timing of the expert support and coordination will be further investigated in the subsequent stages of the study; so will the balance between the flexibility of individual work vis-à-vis the benefits of collaborative activities.

The above-mentioned mobile learning activities are integrated into a complete MALL LO solution which provides a conceptual model for subsequent designs and their refinement. This MALL learning suite incorporates the following tools and resources, all of which can be downloaded onto the mobile device or be retrieved directly from the web-based mobile site:

- task-specific directions and resources: audio podcasts and related text-based materials;

- a selection of device-specific applications or web-based tools for creation of multi-media artefacts, e.g., audio recorders, ipadio software;

- information pertaining to the use of built-in CMC tools (audio podcasts and scripts);

Chapter 5

- information regarding the pedagogical approach and proven language learning strategies, partially student-generated (audio podcasts and scripts);

- help options including communication with the facilitator and peers, FAQ site and a Wordpress class blog;

- proven linguistic references and language resources, including free software and applications deemed by respondents as affordable;

- uploading and publishing tools for student-generated artefacts;

- viewing options for collaboratively created databases and their constituent items;

- repository of students' questions and impromptu reflections;

- summative evaluation of all the constituent parts of the suite (text-based survey).

All the above components are interconnected to form a network of actors, tools, information sources, affordances and student-generated artefacts which enable out-of-class learning embedded in the real-life environment. Students can access information and co-construct knowledge by entering the MALL network through the devices of their choosing at a convenient time. While guided through the pedagogical tasks, the learner has a choice of what tools and resources to select.

Using an ecological metaphor, which has been proposed for the future phases of the study (Hoven & Palalas, in press), it is likely that some elements of our MALL system will not be used by some students, but they have to be available as potential affordances or pointers to affordances. The essential components of the MALL eco-system have been combined into one whole solution, more specifically the MALL suite, which functions through the interconnections of its constituents. The properties of any of the elements of the whole solution can be investigated and understood only in terms of their interactions with the learner. Thus, our students are the critical link in the web. It is through the observation of their activity and the dynamic process of learning espoused by the MALL solution that the study will seek to determine the optimal instructional design for acquiring ESP aural skills.

4. Conclusion and future research

In this chapter, I have demonstrated how student feedback stimulated collaborative investigation into MALL instruction and the evolution of its design. From an m-learning language solution which relied primarily on audio and video podcasts, our MALL design evolved to offer flexible language learning which has a potential of being interactive, engaging, authentic, contextualised, connected and supported by appropriate feedback and scaffolding.

Owing to the interdisciplinary character of the DBR study and the opportunity to iteratively validate our design with college "language learners as language users in natural environments" (Kramsch, 2002, p. xi), the project has been able to generate a student-centered learning solution. In the resultant model of mobile-assisted language learning, the learner is viewed as a negotiator of contextual meaning and the ways to arrive at that meaning. He/she can select from affordances offered by the context, including mobile technologies and other cultural tools required to mediate the meaning.

As members of the community of practice, students collaboratively construct an ecological environment within which they interact, socialise, help each other and thus learn. Synonymously to the view of language as an open system (Larsen-Freeman, 2002), our MALL suite is seen as a system which can evolve in an "organic" process of learning. Learners generate artefacts and events which in turn inform and thus expand the MALL suite. At the same time, the system has to be flexible enough to be adaptable and transferable from context to context and from learner to learner.

What elements of the system are vital and what are their relationships? The design of those essential components and how they connect and inform each other will be investigated in the ongoing research. Other central questions necessitate further exploration and predominantly those pertaining to (1) how dynamic communication and the use of affordances in the real-life context can be optimised through the MALL design, (2) what degrees of collaboration amongst learners are preferred, and (3) what language expert support is required before, during and after MALL tasks. These questions are a focus for the next stage of research. In September 2010, another iteration of the design-development cycle commenced following the formative evaluation of the MALL prototype conducted during the evaluation within a local context phase. At time of writing, only partial data have been collected. Concurrent with the MALL solution re-design and construction, subsequent versions of design principles will be soon sketched and fed back into the system. Based on the feedback concerning the design, development and evaluation of those educational interventions, a set of interconnected design guidelines will be extracted. These heuristic principles will form a framework which will capture the knowledge about whether, when, how and why the intervention and its unique elements work in the specific context.

The resultant design principles will be formulated to guide ESP practitioners and they will not be "intended as recipes for success, but to help others select and apply the most appropriate substantive and procedural knowledge for specific design and development tasks in their own settings" (McKenney, Nieveen, & Van den Akker, 2006, p. 119).

References

Ackermann, E. (2002). *Piaget's constructivism, Papert's constructionism: what's the difference? Future of Learning Group Publication.* Retrieved from http://goo.gl/XSeGX

Anderson, T. (2007). Design-based research: a new research paradigm for Open and Distance Learning [Slideshare slides]. Retrieved from http://www.slideshare.net/terrya/design-based-research-new-research-paradigm

Bannan, B. (2009). The integrative learning design framework: an illustrated example from the domain of instructional technology. In T. Plomp & N. Nieveen (Eds.), *An introduction to educational design research* (pp. 53-73). SLO: Netherlands Institute for Curriculum Development.

Brown, A. L. (1992). Design experiments: theoretical and methodological challenges in creating complex interventions in classroom settings. *Journal of the Learning Sciences*, *2*(2), 141-178. doi:10.1207/s15327809jls0202_2

Brown, J. S., Collins, A., & Duguid, P. (1989). Situated cognition and the culture of learning. *Educational Researcher*, *18*(1), 32-42. Retrieved from http://www.jstor.org/stable/1176008

David, B., Yin, C., & Chalon, R. (2009). *Contextual mobile learning: principles and nutritional human being case study*. Proceedings from IADIS International Conference Mobile Learning 2009, Barcelona, Spain.

Hoven, D. (1999). A model for listening and viewing comprehension in multimedia environments. *Language Learning and Technology*, *3*(1), 88-103. Retrieved from http://llt.msu.edu/vol3num1/hoven/index.html

Hoven, D., & Palalas, A. (in press). *(Re)-conceptualizing design approaches for mobile language learning*. CALICO Special Issue: CALL in Canada.

King, A. (1993). From Sage on the stage to guide on the side. *College Teaching*, *41*(1), 30-35. Retrieved from http://www.jstor.org/stable/27558571

Kramsch, C. (2002). Introduction: how can we tell the dancer from the dance? In C. Kramsch (Ed.), *Language acquisition and language socialization: ecological perspectives* (pp. 1-30). London: Continuum.

Kukulska-Hulme, A. (2005). Introduction. In A. Kukulska-Hulme & J. Traxler (Eds.), *Mobile learning: a handbook for educators and trainers* (pp. 1-6). London: Routledge.

Kukulska-Hulme, A., & Pettit, J. (2009). Practitioners as innovators: emergent practice in personal mobile teaching, learning, work and leisure. In M. Ally (Ed.), *Mobile learning transforming the delivery of education and training* (pp. 135-156). Athabasca University: AU Press.

Kukulska-Hulme, A., & Shield, L. (2008). An overview of mobile assisted language learning: from content delivery to supported collaboration and interaction. *ReCALL*, *20*(3), 271-289. doi:10.1017/S0958344008000335

Lafford, B. A. (2009). Toward an ecological CALL: update to Garrett (1991). *The Modern Language Journal*, *93*(s), 673-696. doi:10.1111/j.1540-4781.2009.00966.x

Lantolf, J. P. (2000). Introducing sociocultural theory. In J. P. Lantolf (Ed.), *Sociocultural theory and second language learning* (pp. 1-26). Oxford: Oxford University Press.

Lantolf, J. P. (2004). Sociocultural theory and second and foreign language learning: an overview of sociocultural theory. In K. Van Esch & O. S. John (Eds.), *New insights into foreign language learning and teaching* (pp. 13-34). Frankfurt am Main, Germany: Peter Lang Verlag.

Larsen-Freeman, D. (2002). Language acquisition and language use from a chaos/complexity theory perspective. In C. Kramsch (Ed.), *Language acquisition and language socialization: ecological perspectives* (pp. 33-46). London: Continuum.

Laurillard, D. (2007). Pedagogical forms of mobile learning: framing research questions. In N. Pachler (Ed.), *Mobile learning – towards a research agenda* (pp. 153-175). University of London: WLE Centre, Institute of Education.

Lave, J., & Wenger, E. (1991). *Situated learning: legitimate peripheral participation*. New York: Cambridge University Press.

McGarr, O. (2009). A review of podcasting in higher education: its influence on the traditional lecture. *Australasian Journal of Educational Technology, 25*(3), 309-321. Retrieved from http://www.ascilite.org.au/ajet/ajet25/mcgarr.pdf

McKenney, S., Nieveen, N., & Van den Akker, J. (2006). Design research from a curriculum perspective. In J. Van den Akker, K. Gravemeijer, S. McKenney, & N. Nieveen (Eds.), *Educational design research: the design, development and evaluation of programs, processes and products* (pp. 67-90). New York: Routledge.

Mwanza-Simwami, D. (2009). Using activity-oriented design methods (AODM) to investigate mobile learning. In G. Vavoula, N. Pachler, & A. Kukulska-Hulme (Eds.), *Researching mobile learning: frameworks, tools and research designs* (pp. 97-122). Bern, Switzerland: Peter Lang AG International Academic Publishers.

Naismith, L., Lonsdale, P., Vavoula, G., & Sharples, M. (2004). *Report 11: Literature review in mobile technologies and learning*. Nesta FutureLab Series. Retrieved from http://goo.gl/VQwaK

Pachler, N. (2009). Research methods in mobile and informal learning: some issues. In G. Vavoula, N. Pachler, & A. Kukulska-Hulme (Eds.), *Researching mobile learning: frameworks, tools and research designs* (pp. 1-16). Bern, Switzerland: Peter Lang AG International Academic Publishers.

Palalas, A. (2009). Using mobile devices to extend English language learning outside the classroom. In D. Metcalf, A. Hamilton, & C. Graffeo (Eds.), *mlearn 2009: 8th World Conference on Mobile and Contextual Learning*. Proceedings (pp. 179-183). Florida: University of Central Florida.

Papert, S., & Harel, I. (1991). Situating constructionism. In S. Papert & I. Harel (Eds.), *Constructionism*. Ablex Publishing Corporation.

Plomp, T. (2009). Educational design research: an introduction. In T. Plomp & N. Nieveen (Eds.), *An introduction to educational design research* (pp. 9-36). SLO: Netherlands Institute for Curriculum Development.

Rost, M. (2002). *Teaching and researching: listening*. Harlow, England: Longman.

Sharples, M. (2009). Methods for evaluating mobile learning. In G. Vavoula, N. Pachler, & A. Kukulska-Hulme (Eds.), *Researching mobile learning: frameworks, tools and research designs* (pp. 17-39). Bern, Switzerland: Peter Lang AG International Academic Publishers.

Sharples, M., Taylor, J., & Vavoula, G. (2007). Theory of learning for the mobile age. In R. Andrews & C. Haythornthwaite (Eds.), *The SAGE handbook of e-learning research* (pp. 221-247). London: Sage.

Thorne, S. L. (2005). Epistemology, politics, and ethics in sociocultural theory. *The Modern Language Journal*, *89*(3), 393-409. doi:10.1111/j.1540-4781.2005.00313.x

Van Lier, L. (2000). From input to affordance: social-interactive learning from an ecological perspective. In J. P. Lantolf (Ed.), *Sociocultural theory and second language learning* (pp. 245-259). Oxford: Oxford University Press.

Vygotsky, L. S. (1978). *Mind in society: the development of higher psychological processes*. Cambridge, MA: Harvard University Press.

Wang, F., & Hannafin, M. J. (2005). Design-based research and technology-enhanced learning environments. *Educational Technology Research & Development*, *53*(4), 5-23. doi:10.1007/BF02504682

Sources cited

Business English Pod (n.d.). [English language learning website]. Retrieved from http://www.businessenglishpod.com

ESLpod (n.d.). English as a Second Language Podcast [English language learning website]. Retrieved from http://www.eslpod.com/website/index_new.html

Chapter 5

iTunesU (n.d.). [Web-based distribution system for educational content]. Retrieved from http://www.apple.com/education/itunes-u

TED (Technology, Entertainment, Design) (n.d.). [Web-based distribution system for presentations and talks]. Retrieved from http://www.ted.com

Weinstein, N. (2001). *Whaddaya say?: Guided practice in relaxed spoken English* (2nd ed). Pearson Education USA.

Wordpress [Web-based open source blog publishing application]. Retrieved from http://wordpress.org

A Design for Intercultural Exchange – An Analysis of Engineering Students' Interaction with English Majors in a Poetry Blog

Linda Bradley[*],
Berner Lindström, Hans Rystedt, and Magnus Gustafsson[**]

Abstract

Web based writing platforms allowing for exchanges across the world are increasingly being used in education. These recent forms of textual practice are highly related to conditions offered by the technology, allowing users, who previously were primarily consumers, to become producers of text. This chapter investigates student interaction over a blog in an intercultural student exchange between native speakers and non-native speakers of English in higher education analysing and interpreting poetry. The groups of students involved in this study belong not only to different academic disciplines, but also differ in terms of nationality and language background. In the blog posts, the students' cultural voices are heard, offering a meeting between very contrasting groups. Scrutinising the student postings, the threaded discussions show ways that students thematise content and meaning in the poems. The results show that there are a number of features at play in an intercultural environment where language and translation issues are prominent parts of the student discussions, offering extended perspectives to the students' initial views. Collaborative efforts in such a diverse environment are important when negotiating meaning and extending students' understanding of poetry.

Keywords: blog, intercultural interaction, collaboration, negotiating meaning.

[*]Chalmers University of Technology, Sweden. e-mail: linda.bradley@chalmers.se

[**]Valuable input has been given by her supervisors Professor Berner Lindström and Ph.D. and Assistant Professor Hans Rystedt as well as her colleague Ph.D. Senior Lecturer and Director Magnus Gustafsson. e-mails: berner.lindstrom@gu.se, hans.rystedt@ped.gu.se, magusta@chalmers.se, respectively.

How to cite this chapter: Bradley, L., Lindström, B., Rystedt, H., & Gustafsson, M. (2011). A design for intercultural exchange – an analysis of engineering students' interaction with English majors in a poetry blog. In S. Thouësny & L. Bradley (Eds.), *Second language teaching and learning with technology: views of emergent researchers* (pp. 95-122). Dublin: Research-publishing.net.

Chapter 6

1. Introduction

It is becoming increasingly common that web based environments are used as meeting spaces within language learning in higher education (cf. Conole, 2008; Lomicka & Lord, 2009). Frequently the lingua franca is English, which implies that non-native speakers of English will need to express their ideas in English and native speakers will encounter persons with other language backgrounds. For this reason, among many, environments that enhance web based group activities, such as blogs are considered beneficial for extending students' communicative repertoire, since they will have a possibility to engage with others in inspiring ways in order to learn about other cultures (Dippold, 2009; Lee, 2010). Such expectations are also expressed by Gee (2004) who claims that "people learn best when their learning is part of a highly motivated engagement with social practices which they value" (p.77).

The purpose of this study is to explore the interaction that evolves when such a web based environment is introduced to literature courses where students use a blog[*] as their platform for interaction in a web based poetry exchange between an American and a Swedish university. The exchange, which has been part of the course assignment for six years, involves two diverse groups belonging to different disciplines, mainly within the fields of engineering and English. The aims of the exchange are not only to increase the students' understanding of poetry and how readers in different contexts understand poems, but also to prepare students for future careers in a society where competences in language and communication are important features.

A sociocultural perspective on culture promotes questions of how people relate to and interact with one another. Through web based interaction, new venues for groups are created, which in turn have raised questions of how individuals become members of such groups, and how they contribute to the group's identity and culture (Levy, 2007). Exchange interaction through social networking is suggested to encourage the group's reflective collaborative

---

[*]Project homepage, http://crossculturalcollaboration2010spring.blogspot.com.

writing (Lee, 2010). 'Culture' is to be understood as patterns of human knowledge and shared attitudes in practices such as an organisation or a group. The development of culture is in this sense caused by "situated social interaction together with practical activity in the material world" (Thorne, 2003, p. 39; Vygotsky, 1978, 1986). In this chapter, cultural aspects are thus coupled with the fact that the two groups of students come from different countries and have different educational backgrounds, which, it is assumed, will affect the content and outcomes of their intercultural web based interaction.

2. Background

Educational projects in which digital tools are used play a critical role in intercultural* communication (cf. Thorne, 2003; Ware & Kramsch, 2005). In the literature there are a number of studies targeting exchanges in language learning through digital media focusing on intercultural interaction, also referred to as "telecollaboration" studies (cf. Belz, 2003; O'Dowd, 2010). For the development within language learning, these media have generated openings to enhance multilingual and multicultural aspects of language learning in global exchanges (cf. Kramsch & Whiteside, 2008; Thorne, 2003). The exchanges have "raised questions about the traditionally monolingual and monocultural nature of language education" (Kramsch & Whiteside, 2008, p. 646), in exposing learners to various varieties of language whose outcomes are hard to predict in advance. When learning English, for instance, there is cultural diversity between those who speak the language as standard English, non-standard English or English as a foreign language, to mention but a few (Dewey, 2007). The challenge in meetings between NSs (native speakers) and NNSs (non-native speakers) is emphasised in existing exchanges. Collaboration here frequently takes unpredictable turns, which can lead to new experiences that learners claim are not achievable through their study of literature alone, but through interaction with peer learners. By engaging in

---

*The terms 'intercultural' and 'cross-cultural' are synonymously used in the literature, when referring to exchanges between language learners of different nationalities. In this study, though, 'intercultural' will be used, indicating that the exchange stretches over different cultural fields.

Chapter 6

an exchange the concept of communicative competence is thus extended by adding an intercultural dimension (O'Dowd, 2010).

Most intercultural language learning exchanges reported by means of digital media are performed through e-mail, chat or discussion forum. There are only a few studies with a language learning focus, suggesting ways of using blogs to enhance cultural learning and connection with other disciplines (Lomicka & Lord, 2009). In a study by Ducate and Lomicka (2005), two blog projects of students of French and German are described, where the groups were set the task of co-constructing ideas about French, German, and American cultures. The students were encouraged to form their own new perspectives about other cultures with the intention of promoting critical thinking. Regarding culture, "students gained access to current events accompanied by a German perspective that they would not have received in the foreign language classroom" (Ducate & Lomicka, 2005, p. 417). By exploring cultural topics outside their textbook in reading their classmates' perspectives on topics in a blog, the users got "the insider's perspective on various cultural topics, thus leading to better understanding of other cultures and what shapes them" (Ducate & Lomicka, 2005, p. 413). It is suggested that the students formed new understandings by taking an active part in being productive on the blog. In addition, there is some research suggesting the potential of using literature in intercultural digital exchanges in language learning (Warschauer, 1999). In a study by Müller-Hartmann (2000) of joint reading of literary texts in an e-mail exchange, assignments including the analysis of literature are claimed to be "highly suitable for activities or tasks in intercultural learning" (p. 131).

A key aspect highlighted in previous studies is the fact that users' previous experience with digital tools has a bearing on their communication. Thorne (2003) describes three case studies of NSs meeting NNSs where computer mediated communication (CMC) tools create conditions for language learning and building linguistic as well as cultural relationships. The nature of "production, consumption, and co-construction of meaning and intention when intercultural communication is mediated by such tools" is investigated (Thorne, 2003, p. 41). The outcomes of this study show that tools such as e-mail, chat, and instant messaging are profoundly affected by the cultures in which they are used. This is termed "cultures-of-use", i.e., "the manner in which these tools mediate everyday communicative practice" (Thorne, 2003, p. 38).

Studies of intercultural digital exchanges commonly describe miscommunication between participants caused by several issues. Frequently, there is a combination of conditions involved, related both to the digital tool and to the differences in nationality and language background. Investigating the impact of telecollaboration, Belz (2003) presents a detailed case study of an e-mail based exchange between two German students and one American. The analysis points at the necessity of being provided with the right input for interaction in order to avoid breakdown in communication. The students in this study lacked adequate knowledge of culture-specific patterns of interaction and the impact of their interactional styles eventually damaged the relationship beyond repair.

Another example of miscommunication, dealing with learners of German in the US and learners of English in Germany, is reported by Ware and Kramsch (2005). The students were involved in a telecollaboration of asynchronous writing on a discussion board. The project was designed to examine how participants on both sides engaged with language learning online and how they evaluated their experiences in the exchange. The article discusses a misunderstanding between a German and an American student leading to a breakdown in communication. Reasons given for the breakdown in communication included a number of issues, such as asynchronous technology, classroom assignment, language skills, teacher engagement as well as students not being adequately prepared for the exchange. According to O'Dowd (2003), there is a risk that intercultural exchanges that fail to function properly will reinforce stereotypes. However, through analysing and reflecting upon the interaction it is agreed that intercultural exchanges have the potential to reach further than mere "superficial pen-pal projects where information is exchanged without reflection" (O'Dowd, 2003, p. 121).

The general view in the field of intercultural communication embraces the fact that there are a number of issues that need to be considered. Merely having the required prerequisites of a common language and digital medium is not always enough. Since there are other aspects at play in specific communicative traditions, outcomes cannot always be managed by the participants. Consequently, there are a number of conditions to take into account that might lead to communication breakdowns and therefore it is "over-simplistic to blame one single factor to explain an exchange's lack of success" (O'Dowd, 2010, p. 7). In addition, if the interaction takes an unpredicted turn, which is a natural consequence when members of different cultures interpret each other's intentions, this must be viewed as something which in itself can contribute to the learning process. This is also alluded to by Thorne (2003) and Ware and Kramsch (2005), who claim that differences in expectation and misunderstanding lead to learning opportunities for the students engaged in cross-linguistic exchanges.

Having the implications of multifaceted cultural encounters in mind, this study focuses on students' interaction on a blog with the purpose of analysing poetry. The digital tool together with the pedagogical design and the content for discussion have been elaborated on during several years of exchange.

3. Pedagogical design

The intercultural poetry exchange was designed as part of two single-term university literature courses, Fiction for Engineers in Sweden and World Literature in the US. The exchange took place in spring 2010, for a period of less than two weeks in the middle of term. The students were set to analyse the Swedish poet Tomas Tranströmer, as part of their respective literature courses which involved reading works by different authors.

All in all there were 15 students from Sweden and 21 from the US. The students from the Swedish university were technology students, primarily master's students from various engineering disciplines, such as computer science, mechanical engineering, biotechnology, chemical engineering and interaction design. From the US, the students were mainly freshmen, majoring in English, but also one student with a history major and one with a double major in English and vocal performance. The students were divided into seven peer groups on the blog, with both Swedish and American students in each blog group.

There was little instruction in the classroom prior to the exchange, since the pedagogical strategy employed involved students elaborating on their postings without being too heavily guided by teachers. Therefore, the teachers were not part of the interaction on the exchange, but left the students to discuss the poems on their own, within their groups. All information pertaining to the exchange was posted on the blog start page, including thorough guidelines regarding objectives and instructions for three "letters" that were to be posted as part of the assignment. The time frame was intense with less than two weeks between the first and last letter. The content selected for discussions consisted of three poems by Tomas Tranströmer*, both the original poem and translations of the poem by different translators: *I det fria* together with two English translations: *In the Clear* and *Out in the Open*, *Andrum: Juli* together with four English translations: *Breathing Room: July; Breathing Space July; Breathing Space July*; one without title, and *Spår* together with two English translations: *Track* and *Tracks*.

Before Letter 1, the students were requested to read the three poems by Tomas Tranströmer that were posted on the blog and then respond to one, two, or all three. They were to choose words or short central phrases, motivating their significance and suggesting a theme of discussion. In the instructions prior to Letter 2, guidelines were given as to how to proceed when giving response to the peer group. For Letter 3, apart from giving response to the peer students' reflections, the instructions were to find or to create a multimodal expression in the form of an alternative way of capturing the theme or mood of one of the poems.

Concerning the background to the poetry exchange, the first exchange took place in 2004. During the first two years, the web based environment consisted of a discussion forum hosted at the Swedish university. However, for practical and administrative reasons of not being able to host the forum on the university

---

*Poems are linked from the project homepage http://crossculturalcollaboration2010spring.blogspot.com

Chapter 6

server, the exchange was moved to a blog in 2006, which was more transparent and flexible. The blog has been the environment for the exchange since then.

In addition to the change of technology, the teachers have also modified the pedagogical design by altering the contents over the years. Each year of the exchange one specific well anthologised poet has been chosen for the exchange, either an American or a Swedish poet, such as T.S. Eliot, Emily Dickinson and Tomas Tranströmer. The Swedish poet has been translated into English by a few different authors. One reason for choosing the particular Swedish poet was that at the time of the exchange, there was limited analysis available online about the poems, making the students' posted interaction more original, not reporting on existing established analyses.

4. Research questions

Using an asynchronous social software platform such as a blog for interaction within an educational environment implies using a meeting space that caters for a chronological, structured exchange of ideas over vast physical distances. This study analyses the interaction taking place in an intercultural student exchange blog. The particular exchange took place during a limited time frame bringing together two groups of students from different backgrounds. They were engaged in interaction through their postings on the blog where they discussed their understanding of the poetry being analysed.

Of central concern was to investigate student blog interaction in an educational environment and how it was possible for two such diverse groups with different backgrounds, regarding academic discipline and nationality to make sense of each other's viewpoints. Concerning the content of the blog postings, topics for discussion were put forward by the students themselves. The development of the content into discussion threads was founded on the students' discussions of the poems, emanating from the various topics based on the translations provided and their understanding of the poems. Therefore, the analysis is based on the following questions:

When blogging in an educational environment with the objective of analysing poetry:

1. What does the educational framing mean to the students' approach to the blogging activity?
2. How is the students' cultural belonging displayed in their blog posts?
3. How are threads developed when the students thematise content and meaning of the poems?
4. What discussions of language and translation issues are enacted by the students?

5. Method

Due to its chronological construction, a blog environment lends itself to parallel and targeted scrutiny of postings. This persistent representation of communicative interaction is what Thorne (2003) calls "CMC residua", i.e., on-screen or printed out log files that can be "scrutinized and reflected upon by researchers and participants and can help to locate specific developmental episodes" (Thorne, 2003, p. 57). Written records of all student interaction are saved, from the very first to last posting of the exchange, preserving the content in the order in which it was saved on the blog.

The analysis of the student postings in this study was data driven, based on a close examination of the interaction taking place in the postings of the seven blog groups studying Tomas Tranströmer in spring 2010. The reason for focusing on the most recent exchange was catching the most current debates from the student exchanges. The design has been refined over the years and this is the first time a Swedish poet has been used since the exchange moved from a forum to a blog environment.

The procedure of analysing the blog postings was started after the termination of the exchange. Following an initial examination of the blog postings in their entirety, each blog group was then scrutinised individually, investigating the postings of each individual contributor in chronological order. The text in the blogs was then systematically coded and sorted into categories related to prominent, recurrent features in the postings. These features were tagged with a number and a letter. Each participating student was assigned a colour code in order to facilitate tracing of the participants' entries. The seven blog groups were then investigated in detail, tracing commonly distinguishable items found in the postings. These postings were related to cultural areas, such as disciplinary and national belonging and the interaction process taking place. Consequently, each item was traceable, making it possible to follow the trail of a specific item and how it was intertwined with other items. The analysis is thus based on the joint formation of posted content developed by the participants.

In accordance with ethical guidelines, the students gave their consent to participating in the research project. The names of the participants in the examples given have been altered in order to preserve their anonymity.

6. Results

A web based writing environment used in education allows participants to engage in joint production of content on a specific space. This can be compared with a classroom setting where it is possible to hide by not contributing to the discussions or by not being able to make oneself heard. The results deal with the interaction taking place and how it is developed in the students' joint writing.

Donato (2004) suggests that it is possible for learners to 'mutually construct' assistance in the same way as experts scaffold novices, forming what he calls "a collective expert" (cited in Lantolf & Thorne, 2006, p. 283). In the texts posted by the students, it is possible to trace how the interaction develops within the groups; from their initial choice of threads that are to be analysed in the poems, to their discussion, offering interpretations and eventually referring to the outcomes as facts that promote new insights to those involved.

Certain recurring features are visible when scrutinising the content of the postings in the blog groups. These are related to blogging as an assignment within a pedagogical design, how students' backgrounds are made visible, the topics the students elicit and how language and translation is discussed. After having made these more general observations explicit, the analysis of four specific problems are thus presented, *Blogging in an educational environment; Displaying diversity in background; Forming threads thematising content and meaning of poems;* and *Discussions of language and translation issues in an intercultural environment.*

6.1. Blogging in an educational environment

Blogging within an educational setting implies targeting certain assignments or specific interactive exchange aspects (Lee, 2010). There is a clear connection between assignment descriptions and how the web based interaction is initiated by students in a blog designated for analysing poetry. Therefore, it is possible to see that the students are concerned about following the instructions posted on the blog start page in their interaction, taking elements from the guidelines into account. In the instructions to Letter 2, for instance, the students are requested to "refer specifically to at least two members of the group by name, attempting to cite at least two groupmates". All of the student groups fulfil the task of including at least two members of the group in their responses in their second letters.

Another aspect is the set form that blogging within an educational environment invites its users into. In the student postings, there are few deviations from the instructions given. The participants introduce themselves, suggest a few central words or phrases to bring up from the poems, stay within the stipulated number of words, all according to how they perceive the given guidelines. The following quote is from Letter 2 showing how one of the students from Group 2 refers to one of the poems chosen by the other peers:

> *It seems like most of you took a liking to the "Track(s)" poem, so I'll start off by sharing my reflection on your comments.*
> (Swedish student, Group 2, Letter 1)

The student fulfils the guidelines, following the model presented in the instructions of giving his views of previous postings. Furthermore, this quote reflects the style of content displayed in the student interaction. The student applies a polite and reflective tone, pointing out a specific theme of interest that struck him when reading the poems in relation to what is being posted previously in the blog.

Sticking to the set blog structure is something that the students generally do when contributing with content in their postings. Therefore, for example in group 7, even though two students get a comment from another blog group member having an opposing view on a matter, neither of the students replies nor defends themselves, since they have both already posted their third and final letter of the exchange and feel they have completed their assignment. In a non-educational setting, however, posing a question in a blog discussion would more likely imply answering.

The fact that blogging is integrated in the institutional educational setting is thus indicated in several ways. The groups are formed according to the instructions given, which is something that points out the basic organisation of the exchange as educationally situated. The students generally adhere to the educational norms implying that given an assignment the instructions should be followed. This means that even though the blog affords interactional exchange to be driven by the content or ideas presented, the students do not fully engage in a content driven discussion, since participating in a way that is formally demanded has higher priority.

6.2. Displaying diversity in background

Throughout the postings, the students' cultural belonging and how they position themselves is displayed. The diversity in the student body, the students from the Swedish university being a few years older engineering students than their US peers, creates an interesting mix in the exchange. Some of the students from the Swedish university are exchange students from Germany and France, having limited understanding of Swedish, but the others had the advantage of knowing the original language of the poems being discussed. The American students are younger, native speakers of English, majoring in English. Most of these students introduce themselves as being familiar with poetry and competent in its interpretation.

Disciplinary characteristics are specifically visible in certain places. One such occasion is in the introductions when the students point out their disciplinary belonging in relation to previous experience of literature studies. The following quote is an example from one of the students of technology:

> *The course 'Fiction for Engineers' is my first genuine literature*
> *course at an advanced level and I love how different it is from*
> *the normal day differential equations and mechanics.*
> (Swedish student, Group 2, Letter 1)

The student states that he has a lack of experience of literature courses at an advanced level and gives a brief introduction to his everyday activities of "differential equations and mechanics". The literature students also emphasise their disciplinary background, when specifying their previous experience of literature:

> *I'm a freshman English major at Clemson University.... I absolutely*
> *LOVE poetry and prose, so I'm really excited about this project.*
> (American student, Group 2, Letter 1)

To some extent, the disciplinary belonging is revealed through the formulation of posts. An example of this is found in the next quote where one of the significant themes in the exchange, the existence of 'train' in the poem Track is brought up. One of the engineering students elaborated on seeing the poem as an equation, removing the word 'train' to see how this affected the poem:

> *The train is significant. The first thing I did in order to*
> *convince myself that the train is important for the poem was*
> *to remove it from the equation. Without the train the night is*
> *still a night, the field is still a field but a different field..."*
> (Swedish student, Interaction Design and Computing, Group 7, Letter 1)

Chapter 6

The student has a sequential presentation, systematising his analysis, using mathematics as a tool, introducing elements from engineering discourse. The function of language is of primary concern in this quote, where removing a parameter has an effect on the whole sentence. The next quote is written by one of the literature students. It displays a different viewpoint, approaching the poem from a linguistic perspective:

> *There is no title and his wording is also more concise and gives a structural flow to the poem with a steadier rhythm. The translation by May Swenson suggests a more literal interpretation because of the use of active verbs such as "swayed" and "outflung" as opposed to "swaying" and "released."*
>
> (American student, English major, Group 7, Letter 1)

In this example, the student is more descriptive, highlighting the rhythm and the specific verb forms in the poem. Central components of the poem are targeted through using word and structure functions as analytical tools.

The disparity in the background of each individual contributor created a dynamic relationship, adding to the understanding of cultural diversity discussed by Dewey (2007). A wide range of elements are brought up around the poems, something that is used as a resource. This is frequently mentioned by the students, for instance in the reconfirmation by one of the Swedish students in his second letter claiming that "*I like to reiterate that I'm a computer science guy, and therefore analyse the poem different*" (Swedish student, Group 5, Letter 2). The student refers to his disciplinary background stating that it entails a specific way of reading poetry. He claims that due to the difference in background, his analysis is different. Given the fact that this is a setting where some of the students have presented themselves as being more experienced in analysing poetry, he gives an account for his lack of experience.

However, as the process of being engaged in the interaction unfolds, the role of being a literature student or an engineering student gradually becomes of subordinate importance. Instead, most of the points highlighted from the poems in the exchange are related to general issues that concern humankind, irrespective of disciplinary belonging.

6.3. Forming threads thematising content and meaning of poems

Concerning how students engage in developing their analysis of the poems by thematising contents they lift from the poems, they shape the content of the blog together through elaborating on topics suggested by fellow writers. As the interaction expands, suggestions and responses form the groups' ways of negotiating meaning of the poems. It is possible to see how threads develop within the exchange groups, into a joint interpretative project.

Regarding the content being formed, there are an average of 14 discussion threads initiated by the members in Letter 1 of each blog group. From these, a little less than half of the threads are picked up and mentioned by at least one other student in the blog group. 20 % of the threads are followed up between three and eight times, which indicates there is very active blogging taking place. Such extensive interaction may promote the formation of new understanding, in line with Ducate and Lomicka (2005), who suggest that it is by being active in producing content on the blog that students form extended understandings.

One such example of development of a theme is from Group 7, where the significance of "train" from the poem *Spår* is brought up and discussed in eight postings by five students in this peer group. Following the processing of this word in the chronological postings, there is joint development of the perspectives this word brings to the understanding of the poem. In Letter 1, one of the Swedish students introduces the concept:

> ... *The train is significant. The first thing I did in order to convince myself that the train is important for the poem was to remove it from the equation. Without the train the night is still a night, the field is still a field but a different field, the town lights are still flickering on the horizon and unruly thoughts still wash over my mind. But*

> *the train changes the view, changes the location. This is not a field, it is a field with a resting train, a train that has covered hundreds of miles but is now suspended in place, its bulk pushing down on the track. The train casts haunting shadows across the field in the moonlight, each of the shadows accumulating into a greater whole. The train adds depth and atmosphere to the scene (if you let it)...*
>
> (Swedish student 1, Letter 1)

In Letter 2, three American students include reflections on the significance of the train in their postings, adding on to the previous postings. This is the first posting by one of them, referring to the original posting displayed in the previous quote:

> *I agree with Johan's thought on the train from the poem Tracks. The train does add a deeper quality to the poem that would be easily overlooked. I read the poem with the train in my thoughts and then again, this time removing the train as Johan suggested. It is quite clear that without the train the poem loses something, I cannot put my finger on it now, but hopefully through further discussion we can find the train's true purpose. I really liked Johan's description of what the train adds. "Haunting shadows" and "accumulating shadows" really gives an eerie but calming feeling to the literary piece...*
>
> (American student 1, Letter 2)

Following the postings regarding the significance of "train" by the group, this concept is brought up an additional four times in Letter 3 by another Swedish student, by two of the aforementioned American students, and by the Swedish creator of this theme, who summarises the discussion in his last letter.

Another example of a common theme, brought up in six of the seven blog groups, concerns whether or not the gender of the translator has any implications regarding the interpretation of the poem. By following two contrasting groups, Group 1 and Group 5, it is evident that the postings take different turns in different groups. In both groups this theme causes postings, however displaying different outcomes.

In Group 1, a group member initially claims that the difference in gender of the two translators affects the tone in the translation:

> *"The female translation seems to have a softer, emotional tone, whereas the male translator's version seems to give more of a straight, descriptive tone"*
> (American student, Letter 1)

This is disputed by another student who connects to previous contributions by claiming that other issues apart from the gender of the translator need to be considered, for instance the poet's background and previous work:

> *"...it's very important to consider a poets earlier works to put the translation into context rather than draw conclusions from the gender"*
> (Swedish student, Letter 2)

There are eight postings negotiating this topic until the group comes to the conclusion that stereotypical generalisations are not applicable in modern society, where so much more than "gender" is at play.

In Group 5, however, when the gender of the author is raised as a topic of discussion, it differs from the structure of the previous group. In this group, the contributors act more as individuals, adding their views but not connecting their reasoning into a joint discussion. The next two quotes illustrate this, interpreting the significance of the gender of Tranströmer, the author himself, for understanding of the content in two different poems *Spår* and *I det fria*, respectively. The first student explains gender from a perspective of what the times were like in the fifties, when the poem was written:

> *"...since the poem was written in the fifties that there may have been an issue of female repression."*
> (American student, referring to *Spår*, Letter 3)

The next student does not connect with or refer to the previous student's remark that the poem was written in a specific period in history having significance for the understanding of the poem. Instead, this student points to the author's Christian background as being significant in relation to gender:

> "...the man is digging/poking in the field, the choice of male gender might be an indication of Tranströmer originating from a Christian context with the man being central."
>
> (Swedish student, referring to I det fria, Letter 3)

There is neither reference between nor after these two postings dealing with the similar topic, within the group. Instead, the two posts display two individually posted reflections about the author, which are not developed further within the group.

Even though there is considerable variation in themes discussed within the seven exchange groups, there are a few themes which are brought up in all groups, such as man's connection to nature, selection of paths of life, and issues concerning death.

6.4. Discussions of language and translation issues in an intercultural environment

Another aspect visible in the blogs, apart from the disciplinary belonging, is that tied to local cultural settings and language issues. Among the different viewpoints displayed, the most conspicuous ones are those related to explicit statements about language translation. The fourth research question concerns how discussions on language are enacted by the students when they analyse the poems. Half of the students in the exchange, who do not understand Swedish, are dependent on the translated versions of the poems offered by the translators in order to understand the poems. The Swedish students, on the other hand, have access to the poems in the original language, Swedish, together with the English translations. This caused some engagement by the students. Below is an example explicitly expressed by one of the Swedish students:

> "I'm the only one so knee deep in Swedish that I can analyze the poem in respect to Tranströmers original, what power I hold. ;)"
>
> (Swedish, Group 1, Letter 2)

Adding the emoticon at the end of the sentence softens this otherwise strong statement. Using appropriate jargon from web-based language, downplays the strong statement in the message, displaying efforts at maintaining a good relationship. Removing this symbol could potentially entail misunderstanding of the meaning and intention. It is claimed by Thorne (2003) that users' previous experience of communicating with digital tools affects the way in which they use them. Using emoticons in this blog exchange mirrors conventions of other social network environments that are applied by the students in the present context.

The advantage of understanding the mother tongue of the poet is also reflected in the American students' writing:

> *"I was particularly interested in the discrepancies between the original Swedish poems and the translations that we have to read. I have no knowledge of the Swedish language, so I only have the translations to go by. Niclas and Jonas, I envy your obvious advantage there. :)"*
> (American student, Group 2, Letter 2)

The benefit of understanding the original language, Swedish, is a theme frequently expressed by the American students. Since the three poems were provided with at least two translations each, one of the issues brought up in the blogs was the discrepancy in understanding, through the different translations. Having access to the poet's own language is something that is expressed as desirable. Emoticons are frequently used as a stylistic element in blogging, implying a softer tone to formulations.

The next selection of quotes show ways that students try to find answers in their analyses through language translation. In the first quote, an American student points out the importance of being supplied with relevant translation for understanding the content from the poet's point of view. In the preceding postings the two Swedish students in the blog group have made a comparison between the Swedish original and the American translations, which justifies this American student's initial understanding:

Chapter 6

> *"I liked Swenson's version of the poem better to begin with,
> and I was happy to know that her translation was more
> closely related to the original Swedish than Bly's."*
> (American student, Group 2, Letter 2)

The student puts forward the notion that a native Swedish speaker possesses specific credibility, which implies that native speakers can have a closer understanding of the true meaning of the poems. The American student expresses gratitude to learn that one of the Swedish students has verified the way he understands the poem.

The next quote shows how an American student is trying to determine a correct translation of the content of one of the poems by requesting the assistance of native Swedish speakers. The student contrasts the interpretations offered by two Swedish students:

> *"Philip wrote that Robert Bly's Track was more accurate
> while Andreas said the opposite, believing that May
> Swenson's translation is the more correct version"*
> (American student, Group 1, Letter 3)

The student in this quote expresses an opinion indicating that there is a more or less accurate meaning embedded in the original language, which is reflected in language formulations and exact translations.

Concerning translation, the students are frequently struggling with concepts at word level. There are a number of instances where this issue is brought up in the postings. One such example is in Group 2, where one of the American students brings up the word "synranden" from the poem *Spår*, in Letter 1, asking if this is equivalent to the English word "horizon", due to its corresponding placement in the text. Two of the Swedish students give similar explanations in reply to this request, independent of one another in Letter 2. They claim that the two words are synonyms, that there is a Swedish word "horisont" which is more directly compatible with "horizon" and that "synranden" implies "as far as one can see with the naked eye", which is more metaphorical. In Letter 3, the student posing the question expresses her appreciation for getting this insight, also reflecting on the fact that native speakers are blessed with an enhanced view of knowing a more appropriate meaning of single words.

An example of how joint construction of understanding of words takes different paths is displayed in discussions of the word "ultra-rapid". The Swedish word "ultrarapid" is being used in the Swedish version of *Andrum: Juli* and referred to as "ultra-rapid" in one of the English translations, whereas the synonym "slow motion" is used in the other three English translations. The discussion on this topic, consisting of eight threads in Group 7, tries to shed light on the distinction between these words, even using a video-clip from YouTube. The group does not come to a joint understanding of this concept. In fact, it is clear from the following quote that one of the American students misinterprets the input from his peers:

> "I would have never of thought that the word would mean the opposite in Swedish as it does in English. During my reading of the poem this confused me, but with the Swedish students help it was much clearer."
> (American student, Group 7, Letter 3)

This statement indicates the student never understands the fact that the two words have similar meaning in Swedish and in English. Since none of the participants in the peer group are persuasive enough in their efforts to clarify meaning, the outcomes of the joint efforts of understanding are not helpful enough here. Instead, as evidenced by the quote, it is not clear that he has understood this concept.

Athough there is clearly some miscommunication in this exchange, there are no significant instances of breakdown in communication as described by for example Belz (2003) and Ware and Kramsch (2005). There are certain features that are problematic for the students. In some of the postings, students try sharing a culture-specific experience, which is a complex endeavor. It entails not only communicating a specific context but also the use of foreign words to express

Chapter 6

that context. One such example is explaining the traditional Swedish April Fools' Day nonsense rhyme being recited on April 1 in Sweden, in connection with performing a practical joke; *April, april din dumma sill, jag kan lura dig vart jag vill*. The student is aware of the fact that there is no corresponding idiom in English and that the concept needs to be experienced in order to understand it. Nevertheless, he tries to explain it together with giving a direct translation of the idiom from Swedish to English:

> *"...considering the date, in Sweden we have a tradition and a childhood verse which goes something like: April, April you silly herring I can fool you with anything"*
> (Swedish student, Group 2, Letter 3)

This quote illustrates that communicating something that is inherent in another culture and linguistic context, making it comprehensible, is an advanced and demanding task. Foreseeing how this will be received by the American reader is indeed difficult.

In fact, there are a few local cultural traces in the blogs which go beyond a mere word level. One such example is referring to "the feeling of a summer day in the Swedish archipelago" (Swedish student, Group 2, Letter 1). Though the words can be understood, the feature is something that might be hard to envision by someone who has never visited the Swedish coast on a beautiful summer day.

7. Discussion and conclusion

Blogs are increasingly being used for educational purposes (Murray & Hourigan, 2008). This implies that students are asked to interact in environments where they are not always particularly experienced or used to interacting (Mortensen, 2008). Although these emerging web based tools generally require low level technical skills, they call for elaborated writing skills. The blog as a writing environment requires a certain style of posting, which is generally informal and personal.

From an interactive perspective, a blog environment caters for commentary and descriptions of events in the form of an online diary, which can be seen in the results of this study.

Blogs provide an arena that encourages self-expression and creativity (Huffaker, 2004) Also, blogging provides students with a "high level of autonomy while simultaneously providing opportunity for greater interaction with peers" (Williams & Jacobs, 2004, para. 35). This type of asynchronous writing environment caters for reflection by its contributors, since it only allows one posting at a time. In the assignment for this project, the main threads being posted were named "letters", which adheres to the original idea of blogging of being informal and presented chronologically. Accordingly, the discursive quality of posts in blogs can be both of a private nature, where the person writes for personal reasons, as well as of a more social nature where there is an expectation of an audience being out there (Lantolf & Thorne, 2006). In this study it is evident that even when blogging is used within an institutional context, the affordances of the blog technology as suggested above are picked up and made use of by the participants.

Using social software such as a blog in a targeted way in language education allows for student engagement in a joint project. There were certain expectations from the students of what they were supposed to communicate in the blog geared at analysing poetry, which can be seen in relation to how the assignments were fulfilled. The design around the exchange involved very little restriction of the students' interaction and there was also very limited preparation prior to the exchange. The students were only informed that they were going to participate in an exchange as part of their respective courses. The writing guidelines, however, posted on the exchange web site gave detailed instructions of the frames and prerequisites of what was expected of the student posts. As far as the contents were concerned, the topics brought up in the exchange were entirely created by the students themselves, which also implied very active participation. However, as was shown in the analyses, blogging in an educational setting is constrained, primarily by the fact that the activity is driven by the given task or assignment and how this is supposed to be organised and performed. We might even talk about blogging in an educational setting as "educational blogging" to point out

Chapter 6

the fact that blogging in an educational institutional context becomes something partly different from blogging in an everyday context. However, the analysis also implies that there is ample room for the students to take initiatives, set the agenda for discussions and carry out these discussions.

The analysis of the postings clearly demonstrates how the students position themselves and collaborate in a joint writing project. Disciplinary background and local cultural belonging is presented or revealed in a number of places throughout the blogs, offering a meeting between two very contrasting groups. In this exchange, although there were some instances of miscommunication, there were no instances at all of breakdown in communication as reported in other studies (cf. Ware & Kramsch, 2005). On the contrary, the difference between the students stood out as the driving force for the discussions, creating a dynamic environment.

The asynchronous nature of a blog suits reflective writing, such as poetry discussions, well, since the time frames are more expanded than real-time chat, for instance. Blogs allow for negotiating meaning of various concepts in the poems in a number of discussion threads created by the students. In addition, blog environments present the chronological postings of participants, making it possible for the writers to trace the contents of the posted threads easily. In fact, the 'delay' created by the environment in combination with the conversational collaboration has the potential to enhance the learning impact of the intervention in the respective courses. Furthermore, the overlap between the content and the medium emphasises how forums and blogs are "unfinished business" (Mortensen, 2008, p. 452). This openness caters for flexible ways of sharing individual reflection as a collaborative enterprise and as mutual opportunity for learning. Consequently, the analysis suggests that despite the fact that cultural, individual as well as collective causes influence the ways students perceive Internet communication tools, and thus their learning, informed design and use of virtual environments can facilitate learning not easily achieved in traditional environments.

Concerning language differences, the issue of translations and negotiating meaning was identified in the interaction. The interpretation of the poems for half of the students in the exchange was totally reliant on the variants of translations offered and not the poet's own, original phrases in Swedish. The interaction took place in English, the native language of the half who did not understand the poet's original words. In the discussions which focused on language and translation issues negotiated by the students, a number of specific words and expressions were raised where translations and comparison of their meaning in the two languages were elaborated on. In the postings, there were instances where the students both agreed and disagreed on the meaning of concepts.

Within the course frames there is a temporal and spatial boundary, which is characteristic of digital tools when used in an educational environment. The efforts students need to make when taking part in a cultural exchange with asynchronous technology cater for a high level of performance. From first individually posting reflections to making iterations, the tool offers promising possibilities to extend the students' interaction. Not only does it enable students to become more active on their own but also to be engaged in joint projects of interpretation and construction of meaning. It is suggested that the delay inherent to asynchronous environments provides a means to "reinject both space and time into communication" (Brown & Duguid, 1996, para. 67) which is beneficial for those involved, allowing for extended reflection (Wegerif, 2007). In the case of communicating more reflective content, e.g., interpreting poems, the delay between message and response adds time to evaluate the analysis of poems.

In the last letter of the exchange, some of the students reflect on the significance of the various peer backgrounds. A Swedish student makes the following comment:

> "I wonder how important our different backgrounds played a role in our respective opinions, was it just our culture, our educative background or, most probably, our personal life?"
>
> (Swedish student, Group 6, Letter 3)

The quote suggests downplaying the significance of cultural backgrounds in favour of emphasising how individual experience of human life might be more important for achieving shared meanings. With that suggestion, this final quote accentuates that in a blog exchange, it is as much the joint collaborative efforts as the specific backgrounds of the participants that are important for negotiating meaning. So, for these students, trying to make sense of others is a complex matter connected equally to single conditions as well as to an array of intertwining cultural aspects.

References

Belz, J. A. (2003). Linguistic perspectives on the development of intercultural competence in telecollaboration. *Language Learning & Technology, 7*(2), 68-99. Retrieved from http://llt.msu.edu/vol7num2/pdf/belz.pdf

Brown, J., & Duguid, P. (1996). The social life of documents. *First Monday, 1*(1-6 May). Retrieved from http://firstmonday.org/htbin/cgiwrap/bin/ojs/index.php/fm/article/view/466/387

Conole, G. (2008). Listening to the learner voice: the ever changing landscape of technology use for language students. *ReCALL, 20*(2), 124-140. doi:10.1017/S0958344008000220

Dewey, M. (2007). English as a lingua franca and globalization: an interconnected perspective. *International Journal of Applied Linguistics, 17*(3), 332-354. doi:10.1111/j.1473-4192.2007.00177.x

Dippold, D. (2009). Peer feedback through blogs: student and teacher perceptions in an advanced German class. *ReCALL, 21*(1), 18-36. doi:10.1017/S095834400900010X

Donato, R. (2004). Aspects of collaboration in pedagogical discourse. *Annual Review of Applied Linguistics, 24*, 284-302. doi:10.1017/S026719050400011X

Ducate, L. C., & Lomicka, L. L. (2005). Exploring the blogosphere: use of web logs in the foreign language classroom. *Foreign language annals, 38*(3), 410-421. doi:10.1111/j.1944-9720.2005.tb02227.x

Gee, J. P. (2004). *Situated language and learning: a critique of traditional schooling*. New York: Routledge.

Huffaker, D. (2004). The educated blogger: using weblogs to promote literacy in the classroom. *First Monday, 9*(6-7 June). Retrieved from http://firstmonday.org/htbin/cgiwrap/bin/ojs/index.php/fm/article/view/1156/1076

Kramsch, C., & Whiteside, A. (2008). Language ecology in multilingual settings. Towards a theory of symbolic competence. *Applied Linguistics, 29*(4), 645-671. doi:10.1093/applin/amn022

Lantolf, J. P., & Thorne, S. L. (2006). *Sociocultural theory and the genesis of second language development.* Oxford: Oxford University Press.

Lee, L. (2010). Fostering reflective writing and interactive exchange through blogging in an advanced language course. *ReCALL, 22*(2), 212-227. doi:10.1017/S095834401000008X

Levy, M. (2007). Culture, culture learning and new technologies: towards a pedagogical framework. *Language Learning & Technology, 11*(2), 104-127. Retrieved from http://llt.msu.edu/vol11num2/pdf/levy.pdf

Lomicka, L., & Lord, G. (Eds.). (2009). *The next generation: social networking and online collaboration in foreign language learning.* San Marcos, Texas: CALICO Monograph Series, Vol 8.

Mortensen, T. E. (2008). Of a divided mind-weblog literacy. In J. Coiro, M. Knobel, C. Lankshear, & D. Leu (Eds.), *Handbook of research on new literacies* (pp. 449-466). Routledge.

Müller-Hartmann, A. (2000). The role of tasks in promoting intercututural learning in electronic learning networks. *Language Learning & Technology, 4*(2), 129-147. Retrieved from http://llt.msu.edu/vol4num2/muller/default.html

Murray, L., & Hourigan, T. (2008). Blogs for specific purposes: expressivist or socio-cognitivist approach? *ReCALL, 20*(1), 82-97. doi:10.1017/S0958344008000719

O'Dowd, R. (2003). Understanding the "other-side": intercultural learning in a Spanish-English e-mail exchange. *Language Learning & Technology, 7*(2), 118-144. Retrieved from http://llt.msu.edu/vol7num2/odowd/default.html

O'Dowd, R. (2010). Online foreign language interaction: moving from the periphery to the core of foreign language education? *Language Teaching,* 1-13. doi:10.1017/S0261444810000194

Thorne, S. L. (2003). Artifacts and cultures-of-use in intercultural communication. *Language Learning & Technology, 7*(2), 38-67. Retrieved from http://llt.msu.edu/vol7num2/thorne/default.html

Vygotsky, L. S. (1978). *Mind in society: the development of higher psychological processes.* Cambridge, MA: Harvard University Press.

Vygotsky, L. S. (1986). *Thought and language.* Cambridge: The MIT Press.

Ware, P. D., & Kramsch, C. (2005). Toward an intercultural stance: teaching German and English through telecollaboration. *The Modern Language Journal, 89*(2), 190-205. doi:10.1111/j.1540-4781.2005.00274.x

Warschauer, M. (1999). *Electronic literacies: language, culture and power in online education.* Mahwah, NJ: Lawrence Erlbaum Associates.

Wegerif, R. (2007). *Dialogic education and technology: expanding the space of learning.* New York: Springer Science.

Williams, J. B., & Jacobs, J. (2004). Exploring the use of blogs as learning spaces in the higher education sector. *Australasian Journal of Educational Technology, 20*(2), 232-247. Retrieved from http://www.ascilite.org.au/ajet/ajet20/williams.html

Developing Sociolinguistic Competence through Intercultural Online Exchange

Mathy Ritchie*

Abstract

The main goal of this study was to investigate whether computer-mediated communication (CMC) intercultural exchange offers the conditions necessary for the development of the sociolinguistic competence of second language learners. Non-native speakers (NNS) of French in British Columbia interacted through CMC with native speakers (NS) of French in Quebec over the course of one university semester. Drawing on the sociocultural perspective, this study used a qualitative approach to analyse the collected data. The data included the transcripts of text-based chat discussions and of a discussion forum. The framework used to guide the sociolinguistic inquiry consisted of The Common European Framework of Reference for Languages (Council of Europe, 2001). The findings of this study suggest that intercultural CMC exchange offers positive conditions for the development of the sociolinguistic competence. NNS were exposed to stylistic variation and made minor changes in their use of sociolinguistic elements, showing that they developed sensitivity to the vernacular style used by NS. The results also allow for a general description of the sociolinguistic elements involved in this type of exchange.

Keywords: language learning, computer-mediated communication, sociolinguistic competence, online intercultural exchange, French as a second language.

*Simon Fraser University in Burnaby, British Columbia, Canada. e-mail: mritchie@uvic.ca

How to cite this chapter: Ritchie, M. (2011). Developing sociolinguistic competence through intercultural online exchange. In S. Thouësny & L. Bradley (Eds.), *Second language teaching and learning with technology: views of emergent researchers* (pp. 123-141). Dublin: Research-publishing.net.

Chapter 7

1. Introduction

Intercultural exchanges (between native and non-native speakers) by means of computer-mediated communication have created research and pedagogical interest because they provide opportunities for learners to participate in intercultural dialogue while simultaneously developing the necessary strategies to perform successfully in the activity (Thorne, 2005). Through CMC, language learners have the opportunity to communicate in meaningful ways and to be exposed to contextualised authentic language, two factors described as essential for the development of the communicative competence of learners.

This chapter presents an investigation of a CMC exchange between native speakers (NS) and non-native speakers (NNS) of French as a possible way to improve language learners' sociolinguistic competence. Like many language learners, the NNS in British Columbia involved in this study have not had many opportunities for interactions with native speakers and their culture outside the classroom. The goal of this study was to find out whether a CMC exchange with NS in Quebec would be beneficial for the development of their sociolinguistic competence.

1.1. CMC in the second/foreign language classroom

Many second and foreign language educators have embraced the use of CMC in the classroom for the simple reason that it allows language learners to engage in authentic communication with native speakers who can provide them with "expert" feedback. Besides this principal characteristic, CMC also offers the opportunity for extensive language practice, for intercultural learning, for the development of the autonomy of learners, and for reflection on form and content (Hanna & de Nooy, 2009). As Chapelle (2010) points out, plenty of studies have demonstrated in the last fourteen years that CMC offers conditions that foster language skills development, but more studies are needed to describe how learners interact and learn in this environment.

Synchronous CMC (communication in real-time such as text-chat) has generated a lot of support because it mimics oral conversation without involving the potential pressure of a face-to-face discussion. Thus, chat has been described as a conversation in slow-motion (Payne & Whitney, 2002). Furthermore, it allows learners to use a discourse that is similar to an oral conversation while also providing them with more time to concentrate and to reflect on the form and content of their intervention (Warschauer, 1996). In these interactions, language learners do not have to worry about pronunciation and judgment from classmates. Studies have shown that students participate more frequently and more equally in online discussions when compared to regular face-to-face in class discussion (Beauvois, 1997; Warschauer, 1996). Moreover, online discussions allow for a more learner-centered environment where students are willing to take more risks and use less of their first language to communicate than in face-to-face interactions (Abrams, 2006).

1.2. Sociolinguistic competence

Many SLA researchers have been interested in looking at the sociolinguistic competence because they have acknowledged language learners' difficulties in acquiring and using the full range of speech styles or in developing "stylistic variation" (Dewaele, 2004). Sociolinguistic competence refers to the learner's "knowledge of the sociocultural rules of language and discourse" (Brown, 2000, p. 247). In his definition, Brown includes learners' sensitivity to dialect or variety, choice of register, naturalness, and knowledge of cultural references and figures of speech. Tarone and Swain (1995) define this competence as the ability of the members of a speech community to adapt their speech to the context in which they find themselves. For example, a more formal variety will be used in an interview whereas an informal register, a "vernacular" style will be used amongst friends. Lyster (1994) defines the concept of sociolinguistic competence as the "capacity to recognise and produce socially appropriate speech in context" (p. 263).

Research on sociolinguistic competence in SLA has mainly focused on the linguistic variants used by native speakers and second language (L2) learners and on the conditions required to acquire these variants. One interesting finding is that L2 learners will generally overuse formal variants and underuse informal variants in similar communicative situations (Nadasdi, Mougeon, & Rehner, 2005; Tarone & Swain, 1995). According to Dewaele (2004), the overuse of formal variants by NNS is one fairly consistent result of research studies on stylistic variation linked to the lack of access to the community of practice of NS and the exposition to one communicative context that is the classroom.

Results regarding the conditions required for its development have shown "the important effect of informal contact with the target language, both through native-speaker contact in general and, more particularly, in the target-language community" (Howard, 2006, p. 381). Other research studies have shown that learners who have spent time in the target language community increased their use of informal sociolinguistic markers. Such studies on French language have focused on the omission of "ne" in negative sentences (Dewaele & Reagan, 2002; Rehner & Mougeon, 1999; Sax, 2003), the use of the pronoun "on" versus "nous" (Sax, 2003), and the learning of social routines and colloquial vocabulary (MacFarlane, 2001).

Although sociolinguistic competence is recognised as an important aspect of L2 learners' competency, it remains a concept difficult to grasp, to define and to teach. Indeed, this competence involves the learning of the sociocultural principles that determine the norms of appropriate behavior and language use of a specific community, which is difficult to teach in a classroom (Hinkel, 2001). Besides suggesting prolonged and regular contact with NS, suggestions and strategies on how to foster the development of that competence are lacking in language instructors' curriculum. The use of an intercultural CMC exchange may be an alternative solution for addressing the issue of sociolinguistic competence development in the second/foreign language classroom. Indeed, research studies have shown that in this environment, language learners pay attention to the form of language used by NS such as different registers and they are inclined to imitate these language uses (Davis & Thiede, 2000; Hanna & de Nooy, 2003, 2009; Savignon & Roithmeier, 2004; Uzum, 2010).

Very few studies so far have looked at the potential of an intercultural CMC exchange for the development of competences related to the use of language in context such as the sociolinguistic competence. Belz and Kinginger (2002) investigated the learning of the acquisition of pronouns of address (specifically, the use of tu/vous and du/Sie). Results showed that by interacting through e-mail in the L2, learners were forced to choose the appropriate pronoun. The researchers argue that L2 learners were provided with a wide range of discourse options and with timely assistance from native-speaking peers.

2. The study

During the spring semester of 2007, two groups of students met online for nine weeks to discuss cultural topics on the course management system Moodle. On this web platform, students were able to send and receive e-mail, enter an assigned chat-room and participate in a discussion forum that included all the participants. Each student was required to participate in a minimum of six chat sessions and three discussion forums. Students were put randomly in groups of three to five students that were generally made up of two students from Quebec (native French speakers, NS) and two students from British Columbia (non-native speakers, NNS) for the online chat. In total, fourteen groups were assigned to specific chat-rooms. The discussion forum included all of the students from both groups.

2.1. Participants

The participants in British Columbia (n=24) were enrolled in an intermediate French as L2 class that focused on the development of oral and written skills and on culture. More than half of the students had been to a French speaking area or community before (65%). Half of the students answered that they were never or rarely using French outside the classroom. The other half answered that they were speaking French occasionally with friends and family or with customers at work. The group was composed of students with various cultural backgrounds; 60% of them declared having English as a first language and 45% declared speaking English only normally at home. The other languages spoken at home were: Mandarin, Cantonese, Gujarati, Korean, Arabic, and Spanish.

Chapter 7

Participants in Quebec (n=29) were enrolled in a course on French literature and culture that was designed for French speakers. The college was situated in a major Canadian city in the province of Quebec and characterised by its multicultural diversity. The official language in Quebec is French and Quebec is the only Canadian province whose population is mainly francophone, constituting 79.6% of the population (Office of Commissioner of Official Languages, 2007). However, results from the post-study questionnaire revealed that a little less than half of students considered themselves Francophones. The other half of the students answered that they had been living in Quebec for a period between three years and seventeen years and also came from different cultural backgrounds. Despite the heterogeneity of this group, they are called native speakers of French in this study because the course they were taken required a native-like level of French and because their instructor considered them to be native speakers.

2.2. Methodology and analysis

Drawing on the sociocultural perspective, this study used a qualitative approach to analyse the collected data. The aspect of sociocultural theory mostly represented in second language acquisition (SLA) research is that "the human mind is always and everywhere mediated primarily by linguistically based communication" (Lantolf, 2002, p. 104). As a mediated process, SLA is seen as developing when learners engage in social interactions, often with more capable social members. Within this approach, learners are seen as active agents because they learn by the act of socialising with others. Sociocultural theory recognised that use and learning are inseparable and that consciousness emerges from practice (Magnan, 2008). This social view of language acquisition considers the complexity and richness of SLA and includes other realms of inquiry and practice such as culture and discourse.

The corpus analysed included forty-three discussion threads. Each thread was examined with the use of a grid describing the use of participants' sociolinguistics elements. The grid was designed with the help of the common European framework reference for languages (CEFRL) which has a thorough section on sociolinguistic competence. The qualitative analysis of the transcripts was divided in three main parts. The first part focused on describing which elements of the sociolinguistic competence were displayed in the discourse of the participants in the online chat and in the discussion forum. The second part focused on identifying differences in the use of the sociolinguistic elements by NS and NNS. It was assumed that the NS would use the appropriate sociolinguistic elements in each specific context and that different ways of using these elements by NNS would point out a lack of development of their sociolinguistic competence. This way of measuring the competence was proposed by Rehner (2002). She suggested that variation in advanced learners be measured by comparing how they alternate between forms that are used by NS. One way to do so is by observing whether they use the expressions used by NS in the same communicative situations. Finally, the third section focused on looking for changes over time in the use of specific sociolinguistic elements in the discourse of NNS with the objective of finding sociolinguistic development.

The common European framework reference for languages was used as a guide rather than as an evaluation tool in this investigation and was not presented to the participants. This framework provided the most detailed description of the elements included in the sociolinguistic competence when compared to other frameworks such as the standards for foreign language learning in the 21st Century (American Council on the Teaching of Foreign Languages, 1999) or with the core French provincial language curriculum in British Columbia (British Columbia Ministry of Education, 2001). The CEFRL organised learners' competences in two broad categories: general competence and communicative competence. The communicative competence is described as containing three components: linguistic competence, sociolinguistic competence and pragmatic competence. The categories included in the sociolinguistic competence are: markers of social relations, politeness conventions, expressions of folk-wisdom, register differences, and dialect and accent. The last category, dialect and accent, was not used in the analyse of the discourse of the participants because it is generally concerned with the oral form of language.

Chapter 7

3. Results

3.1. Sociolinguistic elements

The results of the first analysis showed that most of the sociolinguistic elements were displayed in the exchanges as shown in Figure 1.

Figure 1. Display of sociolinguistic competence elements with CMC tools

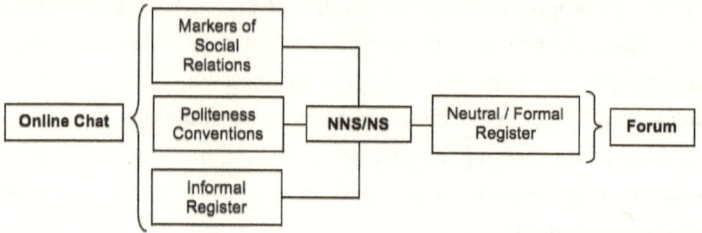

In the online chat sessions, participants used markers of social relation such as greetings on arrival and departure, and expletives such as "Oui, c'est tellement génial!" *(Yes, it is so great!)*. They also expressed politeness either by showing interest in one's well-being, which was done mostly in the greetings on arrival and departure, by expressing admiration towards someone's experience, and by expressing affection and gratitude towards one another. The chat sessions were characterised by the use of an informal register. The usual capital letter and the period to mark the beginning and the end of a sentence were not always displayed, sentences were incomplete, and there was an extensive use of exclamation marks and points of ellipsis (...). The content of the message appeared to be more important than the form as a lot of typing errors, spelling and grammar mistakes were left by the participants. A few expressions that would normally be found in an oral conversation like "cool", or "ouais" for "oui" or "euh" to show hesitation, were also observed in some chat discussions.

The category "expressions of folk wisdom" does not appear in Figure 1 because very few of these expressions were found in the discourse of the participants. For example, one NS wrote "chacun ses goûts" *(to each his own taste)* and another one wrote "à toi l'honneur" *(you do the honors)*. These fixed formulae found in proverbs and familiar quotations are more likely to appear in graffiti, t-shirts slogans, TV catch phrases and posters than in daily conversation (Council of Europe, 2001, p.120). Therefore, it is not surprising that the online chat did not foster their use.

The discussion forum which displayed a more formal register seemed to offer a better context for expressions of folk wisdom. Still, these expressions occurred infrequently. Besides giving the opportunity to NNS to write in a more formal manner, the discussion forum did not display elements of the other categories. Yet, if participants had had to comment on each others' paragraph, more of these elements would probably have been displayed. For example, when responding or commenting on the paragraph of one student in particular, we can assume that the participant would have used greetings and would have paid attention to politeness conventions. However, because the discussion forum fosters the use of a more formal register, participants would have used these elements in a more formal manner. Consequently, the use of the discussion forum and the chat in this way, would have allowed L2 learners to see how NS use the sociolinguistic elements in the different online contexts and would have exposed them to greater stylistic variation.

3.2. Differences in use between NS and NNS

The analysis of the discourse of NS and NNS showed similarities and differences in the use of sociolinguistic elements. Similarities were found in their use of address form; both groups called each other by their first names and used the pronoun "tu" when talking to someone in particular. Similarities in use were also found in the way they took turns in the exchange and in their way of using positive politeness.

Differences were found in the choice of words for greetings, in the choice of words for expletives, and in the expressions of negative politeness. Table 1 and Table 2 recapitalise some of the differences found between NS and NNS in regards to the use of sociolinguistic elements.

Table 1. Differences in use between NS and NNS

Expressions	NNS	NS
Bonjour/Au revoir	76	15
Salut/Allo/Bye-bye	37	72
Je pense que	38	20

Table 2. Examples of choice of expletives

NS	NNS
• Ouais finalement!! *(Yes finally!!)*	• Au oui!?!?!? C'est fantastique. *(Ah yes !?!?!? It's fantastic.)*
• Ooooo nice!! *(Oh, nice!)*	• Je vois!! c'est bien! *(I see!! That's good!)*
• Oui, c'est tellement génial!! *(Yes, it so great!!)*	• Ah oui, c'est intéressant!! *(Ah yes, that's interesting!!)*
• Aaaa cest cool sa!! *(Aaaa that's cool!!)*	• Vraiment, tu es super! *(Really, you are super!)*
• Trop génial: super chanceuse! *(Too great: super lucky!)*	• C'est intéressant!! *(That's interesting!!)*

Table 1 shows that the favored word for greetings on arrival was the word "bonjour" for NNS where the words "salut" and "allo", two more informal words for greetings, were the preferred choice for NS. The greetings on leaving the most used for NS was the English word "bye" or "bye-bye" which is quite informal in French, and for NNS, it was "au revoir" which is a more neutral expression. Similar findings were found for the choice of expletives. The expressions used by NNS were less colloquial than the ones used by the NS as shown in Table 2. For example, NNS used expressions such as "C'est intéressant!!" *(That's interesting!!)* and NS used a mix of English and French, as in "C'est cool ça", used "ouais" instead of "oui", and used specific combinations of words such as "tellement génial" *(so great)* and "super chanceuse" *(super lucky)*. NS' expletives belong to an informal register and they seem to represent a "vernacular variety" of speech used by some of the francophone youth of this college. Finally, NNS showed a lack of strategies for expressing negative politeness such as "hedges" in their discourse to avoid making absolute statements. Indeed, NNS used the expression "je pense que"

(I think that) almost twice the times as NS did as shown in Table 1. NS used as many hedges as their counterparts but they chose other strategies. For example, they used other introductory phrases such as "Je crois que" *(I believe that)*, tag questions such as "n'est-ce pas?" *(isn't that so?)* and approximators of degree such as "généralement" *(generally)*.

3.3. Development of sociolinguistic competence

A closer look at the elements used by NNS showed a few examples of changes over time. Changes were found in greetings on arrival and departure, in choice of expletives, and in the use of strategies to express hedges. The following extract shows a possible influence of the NS on the choice of words for greetings for the NNS (S* and C*).

(1) Chat-room 3, Chat 3

- S*: Bonjour Joel *(Hi Joel)*
- J: allo!! *(Allo!)*
- S*: allo Caroline *(Allo Caroline)*
- C*: Bonjour Sabina... bonjour Joel *(Hi Sabina... hi Joel)*
- J: allo Caroline!! *(Allo Caroline!!)*
- E: salut, le monde!!! *(Hi everyone!!!)*
- C*: Salut Erica *(Hi Erica)*
- S*: ... salut Erica *(Hi Erica)*
- E: salut Caroline! Salut Sabina, salut Jo!!! je suis super contente de vous voir! *(Hi Caroline! Hi Sabina, hi Jo!!! I am super happy to see you!)*

In this extract, the NS (J and E) wrote "allo" and "salut". Both NNS (S* and C*) wrote "bonjour" but also "allo" and "salut" in response to the words use by the NS. In further exchanges, they also kept on using "bonjour" most of the time, S* using "allo" once in chat 5 and C* using "salut" in chat 6. It seems that in this group, the NS had an influence on the greetings the NNS chose to use. Similar results were found in the choice of words for greetings on departure in the same group.

Chapter 7

(2) Chat-room 3, Chat 4

- **J:** bref je suis désolé mais je vais devoir vous laissez!
  (So I am sorry but I have to go!)
- **J:** Bye Bye tout le monde! *(Bye Bye everyone!)*
- **J:** xxxxxx *(Kisses)*
- **S*:** Je comprends. Je dois partir aussi
  (I understand. I have to go too.)
- **S*:** Au revoir *(See you soon.)*
- **C*:** Au revoir Joel! …bonne soirée
  (Good-bye Joel! …Have a nice evening)
- **J:** toi aussi ☺ *(You too)*
- **E:** Bonne jsoirée. désolée, je me prenais une pomme
  (Have a nice evening. Sorry, I was getting an apple)
- **C*:** LOL.. mais byee byee à vous! *(LOL..but bye bye to you!)*
- **S*:** bye *(Bye)*
- **E:** bye bye! *(Bye bye!)*
- **C*:** okay, au revoir tout le monde!! *(O.K., see you later everyone!)*

In this extract, the NNS (S* and C*) naturally chose "au revoir" at first; then in response to the NS who selected "bye bye", they wrote it as well. Again, it seems that they are very receptive to the expressions used by the NS.

A few expletives were modeled by the NNS. For example, the word "cool" was used in the third session by a NNS in response to a NS that was using this expression regularly. In general, the expletives used by the NS were not modeled by the NNS. The English words such as "cool", "wow", and "nice" were not used by the NNS perhaps because they were making an effort to use French words only. Other expletives including words from the oral informal register such as "ouais" instead of "oui" for "yes" or expressions which may sound funny to English speakers such as "j'adore" which means "I love it" or "génial" used for "great" and "super" were also not selected by NNS. NNS might have chosen consciously not to use these forms because they "belong" to the community of practice that represents this specific group of NS. Dewaele (2004) talks about "in group" membership to describe how members of a group use specific speech patterns to show that they "fit in". L2 learners using these words could be seen as out of place and could bring unwanted effects from the interlocutors. This means that a strong trust relationship must take place before NNS have the desire, and most importantly feel welcome, to identify with a group of NS. However, the exchange allowed NNS to notice how these elements were used by NS of their age and might have contributed to their knowledge on stylistic variation.

In the case of the use of hedges, some NNS have used a different strategy besides "je pense que". In the extract below, the participants are discussing multiculturalism in Canada and one of the NNS (C*) used other strategies in response to the NS.

(3) Chat-room 3, Chat 4

- **E:** j'avoue la diversité, le mélange des deux en toi fait quelque chose de nouveau *(I agree diversity, the mix of both in you make something new)*

- **C*:** Canada est un pays de multiculturalisme.. si **en général** preuve de tolérance et d'ouverture d'esprit les uns envers les cultures-- **comme Erica a dit**
  (Canada is a country of multiculturalism.. if in general proof of tolerance and openness of the ones towards other cultures—like Erica said)

- **E:** mais, je trouve que les gens ici cont formidables et je n'ai jamais perdu de vue qui je suis. Sabina, toi, tu es un méchant cocktail d plusiquers nationalités, n'est-ce pas?
  (But, I find that people here are awesome and I never lost sight of who I am. Sabina, you, you are a powerful mix of several nationalities, are you?)

- **S*:** Ils sont autres difficultes aussi (comme la discrimination etc.) mais **je pense que** les avantages de multiculturisme sont plus importants
  (They have other difficulties too (like discrimination etc.) but I think that the advantages of multiculturalism are more important)

- **C*: Donc, vous aimez le multiculturisme de Canada?**
  (So, you like the multiculturalism in Canada?)

In this extract, "Je pense que" is used only once by S*. C* added to her idea the phrase "en general" meaning "in general" and also "comme Erica a dit" meaning "like Erica said" in her first intervention in this extract. Both of these phrases are used as strategies to avoid making absolute statements or to distance herself from the statements. In her last intervention, she asks a question which also shows that she developed another strategy. It is possible that she has developed these strategies by modeling the discourse of the NS which could show the development of her sociolinguistic competence.

The changes observed in the discourse of the NNS seemed to have occurred in reaction to the language behaviour of the NS. These results are similar to the ones by Lee (2004) who found that L2 learners interacting with NS recognised different registers, discourse patterns and style and imitated these new language forms by integrating some of them in their own discourse.

4. Discussion

This CMC exchange provided an environment which was conducive to the development of NNS' sociolinguistic competence. By chatting online with NS of the target language, NNS saw how NS used the sociolinguistic elements in their discourse through their choice of words for greetings, in the way they express positive and negative politeness and in their choices of expletives. The discussion forum was used to display a more formal register, to which NNS were able to adapt.

The results of this research study did not reveal enough changes to show evidence of sociolinguistic competence development for the NNS. However, the changes observed indicated that some of the NNS were sensitive to the way NS used the sociolinguistic elements. As pointed out by Rehner (2002), researchers looking at measuring sociolinguistic development of L2 are faced with speakers with a repertoire in a state of flux. This state of flux is influenced by several independent variables such as social characteristics, situational variables, the influence of the first language(s), the degree of exposure to the L2, and the type of input received through instructors and pedagogical material. Therefore, the few changes observed in the discourse of the NNS are difficult to interpret.

In addition, some participants might have been less ready than others to acquire knowledge about sociolinguistic rules. Dewaele (2004) suggests that sociolinguistic knowledge has to become "proceduralised" before users can make automatic decisions about appropriateness (p. 315). It means that the L2 learners in this research study might have needed more time before starting to use new linguistic forms. Added to this, is the suggestion that the NNS might not have been ready to use the vernacular style represented by this group of NS. It might mean that a strong trust relationship must be built before NNS have the desire, and most importantly feel welcome to identify with a group of NS.

Seen in the perspective of sociocultural theory, the exchange provided the conditions necessary for second language acquisition as L2 learners engaged in meaningful social interactions with more capable social members. As Lee (2004) observed, learners participating in online discussions are active agents as they are pushed by their motivation to socialise with others to produce coherent discourse that goes beyond linguistic and grammatical accuracy.

5. Conclusion and further reflections

Computer-mediated communication exchange with NS seems to be a valuable substitute to face-to-face interactions to develop the sociolinguistic competence for those who do not have the opportunity to immerse themselves in the target language environment. In this study, the use of a discussion forum and of an online chat to communicate with NS allowed L2 learners to experiment with two language registers, one of them being difficult to access in their learning environment. With these exchanges, they noticed the way NS used various sociolinguistic elements. Some NNS seemed to have modeled these language behaviors as some changes were observed in their discourse.

Further research is needed to establish which factors could maximise the development of this competence. For example, research could determine the type of explicit instruction to be provided during the exchange to maximise students' development. Research studies could also look at how L2 learners perceived the use of other registers other than the neutral and the formal register. For example, is there a certain confidence level that L2 learners need to achieve before they decide to integrate more idiomatic forms in their discourse? Or, is there a certain degree of relationship that has to be reached before learners want to identify with the speakers of the target community or before NS accept NNS as part of their in-group? It would also be interesting to see how online interactions with NS compare to face-to-face interactions with NS in regard to the development of sociolinguistic competence. For example, does it have the same beneficial effect on learners? Does it need to last longer to have the same beneficial effect? In addition, it would be most interesting to see if learners who show an improvement in their sociolinguistic competence in an online text-chat could transfer their competence to an oral conversation.

This study proposed that contact with NS by way of new communication technologies is one way of solving the question of how to teach sociolinguistic competence in the L2 classroom. In more general terms, this study aimed to emphasise the importance of contact with the target language and culture in the development of language learners' skills. This study will add to a growing body of research on CALL and more specifically on research involving computer-mediated communication exchange between native speakers and non-native speakers.

References

Abrams, Z. I. (2006). From theory to practice: intracultural CMC in the L2 classroom. In L. Ducate & N. Arnold (Eds.), *Calling on CALL: from theory and research to new directions in foreign language teaching* (pp. 181-210). Texas: CALICO Monograph Series.

American Council on the Teaching of Foreign Languages (1999). *Standards for foreign language learning in the 21st century*. Yonkers, NY: ACTFL.

Beauvois, M. H. (1997). Computer-mediated communication: technology for improving speaking and writing. In M. Bush (Ed.), *Technology enhanced language learning* (pp. 165-184). Lincolnwood, Illinois: National Textbook Company.

Belz, J. A., & Kinginger, C. (2002). The cross-linguistic development of address form use in telecollaborative language learning: two case studies. *The Canadian Modern Language Review, 59*(2), 189-214. doi:10.3138/cmlr.59.2.189

British Columbia Ministry of Education. (2001). *Integrated resource package, core French 5 to 12*. Victoria: BC MOE Curriculum Branch.

Brown, H. D. (2000). *Principles of language learning and teaching*. New York: Addison Wesley Longman.

Chapelle, C. A. (2010). Research for practice: a look at issues in technology for second language learning. *Language Learning & Technology, 14*(3), 27-30. Retrieved from http://llt.msu.edu/issues/october2010/commentary.pdf

Council of Europe. (2001). *The common European framework of reference for languages*. Cambridge: Cambridge University Press.

Davis, B., & Thiede, R. (2000). Writing into change: style shifting in asynchronous electronic discourse. In M. Warschauer & R. Kern (Eds.), *Network-based language teaching: concepts and practice* (pp. 87-120). Cambridge: Cambrige University Press.

Dewaele, J.-M. (2004). The acquisition of sociolinguistic competence in French as a foreign language: an overview. *Journal of French Language Studies, 14*(3), 301-319. doi:10.1017/S0959269504001814

Dewaele, J.-M., & Reagan, V. (2002). Maîtriser la norme sociolinguistique en interlangue française: le cas de l'omission variable de 'ne'. *Journal of French Language Studies, 12*(2), 123-148. doi:10.1017/S0959269502000212

Hanna, B. E., & de Nooy, J. (2003). A funny thing happened on the way to the forum: electronic discussion and foreign language learning. *Language Learning & Technology, 7*(1), 71-85. Retrieved from http://llt.msu.edu/vol7num1/pdf/hanna.pdf

Hanna, B. E., & de Nooy, J. (2009). *Learning language and culture via public internet discussion forums*. New York: Palgrave Macmillan.

Hinkel, E. (2001). Building awareness and practical skills for cross-cultural communication in ESL/EFL. In M. Celce-Murcia (Ed.), *Teaching English as a second or foreign language* (pp. 443-458). Boston, MA: Heinle & Heinle.

Howard, M. (2006). Variation in advanced French interlanguage: A comparison of three (socio)linguistic variables. *The Canadian Modern Language Review*, *62*(3), 379-400. doi:10.3138/cmlr.62.3.379

Lantolf, J. P. (2002). Sociocultural theory and second language acquisition. In R. B. Kaplan (Ed.), *The Oxford hanbook of applied linguistics.* Oxford: University Press.

Lee, L. (2004). Learners' perspectives on networked collaborative interaction with native speakers of Spanish in the US. *Language Learning & Technology*, *8*(1), 83-100. Retrieved from http://llt.msu.edu/vol8num1/pdf/lee.pdf

Lyster, R. (1994). The effect of functional-analytic teaching on aspects of French immersion students' sociolinguistic competence. *Applied Linguistics*, *15*(3), 263-287. doi:10.1093/applin/15.3.263

MacFarlane, A. (2001). Are brief contact experiences and classroom language learning complementary? *The Canadian Modern Language Review*, *58*(1), 64-83. doi:10.3138/cmlr.58.1.64

Magnan, S. S. (2008). The unfulfilled promise of teaching for communicative competence: insights from sociocultural theory. In J. P. Lantolf & M. E. Poehner (Eds.), *Sociocultural theory and the teaching of second languages* (pp. 351-381). London: Equinox Publishing.

Nadasdi, T., Mougeon, R., & Rehner, K. (2005). Learning to speak everyday (Canadian) French. *The Canadian Modern Language Review*, *61*(4), 543-563. doi:10.3138/cmlr.61.4.543

Office of Commissioner of Official Languages. (2007). *The official languages of Canada's population.* Retrieved from http://www.ocol-clo.gc.ca/html/stats_e.php

Payne, J. S., & Whitney, P. J. (2002). Developing L2 proficiency through synchronous CMC: output, working memory, and interlanguage development. *CALICO Journal*, *20*(1), 7-32. Retrieved from https://calico.org/html/article_327.pdf

Rehner, K. (2002). *The development of aspects of linguistic and discourse competence by advanced second language learners of French.* Unpublished PhD thesis. OISE/University of Toronto, Toronto.

Rehner, K., & Mougeon, R. (1999). Variation in the spoken French of immersion students: to "ne" or not to "ne", that is the sociolinguistic question. *The Canadian Modern Language Review*, *56*(1), 124-154. doi:10.3138/cmlr.56.1.124

Savignon, S. J., & Roithmeier, W. (2004). Computer-mediated communication: texts and strategies. *CALICO Journal*, *21*(2), 265-290. Retrieved from https://calico.org/html/article_207.pdf

Sax, K. (2003). *Acquisition of stylistic variation in American learners of French*. Unpublished PhD thesis. Indiana University.

Tarone, E., & Swain, M. (1995). A sociolinguistic perspective on L2 use in immersion classrooms. *The Modern Language Journal, 79*(2), 166-178. Retrieved from http://www.jstor.org/stable/329617

Thorne, S. L. (2005). Pedagogical and praxiological lessons from Internet-mediated intercultural foreign language education research. In J. A. Belz & S. L. Thorne (Eds.), *Internet-mediated intercultural foreign language education* (pp. 2-30). AAUSC, Boston: Thomson Heinle.

Uzum, B. (2010). An investigation of alignment in CMC from a sociocognitive perspective. *CALICO Journal, 28*(1), 135-155. Retrieved from http://goo.gl/Dewz5

Warschauer, M. (1996). Comparing face-to-face and electronic discussion in the second language classroom. *CALICO Journal, 13*(2-3), 7-26. Retrieved from https://www.calico.org/html/article_604.pdf

Second Language Learning by Exchanging Cultural Contexts through the Mobile Group Blog

Yinjuan Shao*

Abstract

Although much attention has been devoted to learning a second language in the authentic language environment, learners still have limited opportunities to stay there for a longer time. The internet has opened up a gateway for learners to a virtual foreign world while mobile technology is bringing more features from the real world. In this study we explored the use of a mobile group, recording and sharing learners' real experiences in the target culture, and helping learners who are far away from the target language surroundings to enhance the understandings of 'real' language use in 'real' culture. Two studies were conducted separately with two different groups physically in the learners' own country and the target language country. The contexts of the real culture have been delivered and discussed within these two groups. Results show a spontaneous shift from using native language to second language in the target culture and students' learning motivation and language efficacy have been improved.

Keywords: mobile group blog, context transition, context socialising, second language learning.

---

*Nanyang Technological University, Singapore. e-mail: yinjuan@gmail.com

How to cite this chapter: Shao, Y. (2011). Second language learning by exchanging cultural contexts through the mobile group blog. In S. Thouësny & L. Bradley (Eds.), *Second language teaching and learning with technology: views of emergent researchers* (pp. 143-168). Dublin: Research-publishing.net.

Chapter 8

1. Introduction

From social-constructivist perspectives, language learning is regarded as the result of interactions between learners, teachers, and other sources of the target language in socio-educational contexts (Williams & Burden, 1997). The term context might have various implications in different specialties. In technology enhanced learning (TEL), it not only covers the physical space, social situations, learning resources, learning culture and technology-mediated learning environment but also embraces the learners' experience and history (Chalmers, 2004; Mercer, 1992; Smagorinsky & Fly, 1993). Issues of context have been particularly highlighted in encouraging learners' learning in the real world. Hymes (1972) pointed out that the key to understanding language in context is to start not with language but with context. Particularly for second language learners, one of the most significant current discussions is that the ideal situation of second language learning is in the real world. Learning in the real world indicates more autonomy and mobility of learners, which could fit in with the affordances of mobile technology. Mobile-assisted language learning (MALL) currently is found as a worthwhile solution to support second language acquisition and learning flexibility (Attewell & Savill-Smith, 2003; Kukulska-Hulme & Traxler, 2005).

1.1. Context and language learning

Atkinson (2002) contended that learning is a part of everyday life and argued that language is intertwined with and inseparable from experiences, cultural knowledge, emotions, and self-identity. Learning a language is the process of appropriating the cultural resources or voices of local communities in broad social contexts. It is impossible for language learners to be quarantined from the "real world" and considered as a set of asocial, amoral skills to be mastered; they are always shaped, produced, and consumed in relation to broader social and cultural conditions (Burr, 1995; Collentine & Freed, 2004; Wertsch, 1991). Herron's (1994) findings indicated that comprehension in a foreign language is facilitated by richness of context. The social context, especially time and space, are often incorporated into learning design and attract a growing number of educators and learners to be involved in both the real and the virtual world (Hirst, 2004; Kelton, 2007). The conversations or dialogical exchanges should be conceived spatially or temporally, not only as meaningful texts or actions, but also in relation to the reproduction and production of different spaces and times (Leander, 2001). Kramsch (1993) also exhorted the reflection of the historical situatedness and local context of language in the learner's interlanguage when they encounter authentic interactions in the target culture. Tracing the context of using second language in the real language surroundings also invests learners' trajectories in new learning resources for remote learners.

1.2. Mobile technology and context

Mobile technology is one of the recent effective technologies to support learning in the real world. Mobile technology affords more accessibility to learning resources whenever and wherever learners are (Sharples, 2007). This indicated two significant advantages for learning in different contexts: flexibility of time and flexibility of locations. In reflecting these advantages educators have noted some outstanding features that mobile technology can offer for second language learning.

1.2.1. Flexible access to learning spaces

Günther, Winkler, Ilgner and Herczeg (2008) argued that there is no longer a fixed and well-defined space for learning, but multiple and intertwined learning scenarios and culture. Mobile technology then could support learning at the right time at the right place (Ogata & Yano, 2003), offering great opportunities of learning in the real world and linking with the virtual world. Access and exposure to engaging, authentic, and comprehensible contexts in the target language is essential for successful language learning (Zhao, 2003). Learner's autonomy and authentic problem solving are central to second language education (Meyer & Bo-Kristensen, 2009). Mobile technology offers learners free access to acquire linguistic phenomena not only in the present context but across contexts, retrieving and delivering information in everyday life. As Kukulska-Hulme (2006) noted:

Chapter 8

> Mobile learning promises to deliver closer integration of language learning with everyday communication needs and cultural experiences. Mobile devices may be used for learning at home, in a classroom, in a social space, on field trips, in museums and art galleries, in work contexts or as part of everyday learning (Kukulska-Hulme, 2006, p. 122).

1.2.2. Promoting synchronous interaction remotely

Since language learning is a social activity (Norbrook & Scott, 2003; Warschauer, 1999), it is impossible to perform successful language learning without interaction. Interactions exist between the learner and the technology, between the learner and the learning environment and between the learner and other learners. Several studies found that mobile technology could improve the interaction of teacher-to-learner and learner-to-learner (e.g., Collins, 2008; Dias, 2002; Kukulska-Hulme & Shield, 2008; Thornton & Houser, 2005). The mutual information channel via mobile technology, information delivering and information gathering succeeds in these supports. Thomas (2005, cited in Cobcroft, Towers, Smith, & Bruns, 2006) pointed out that mobile learning facilitated by mobile technologies offered great flexibility to learners, in terms of community, autonomy, location and relationship. Communication can be completed through mobile technology synchronously or asynchronously, which offers great flexibilities for language learners particularly.

1.2.3. Mobile technology eases learning trajectories tracing

Learners can make good use of high-tech mobile facilities to record information in the context at any time. Taking pictures, generating audio files, texting and filming with mobile devices as well as some automatic context-aware collections promise sufficient documentation. Their activities of learning language could be recorded by using mobile devices to deliver materials, albeit materials with which the learner could interact rather than receive passively (Kukulska-Hulme & Shield, 2007). Learners' experiences and their learning contexts could be documented by these mobile devices for review, for sharing and for discussion later. Mobile Internet is a new trend to make distant synchronous discussion about documented experiences and trajectories. Lam's (2000) work has explored how the Internet provides new transnational contexts for immigrant youth's English identity development and language socialisation. The interactions via the Internet move learners away from a sense of alienation from the foreign language to a newfound sense of expressivity and solidarity. MALL is not only taken as an aid for acquisition of language in a "piece" of time, but encourages continuous engagement in linguistic activities in diverse contexts (Ros i Solé, 2009).

1.3. Mobile web 2.0

Web 2.0 technologies (e.g., blogs, wikis, and social bookmarking) allow users to do more than just retrieve information with high levels of interactivity among people, allowing them to contribute, create and modify content collaboratively, share results and discover new and related content through informal relationships with others (Low, 2006; Solomon & Schrum, 2007). Mobile 2.0 refers to services that integrate the social web with the core aspects of mobility – personal, localised, always-on and ever-present (Jaokar, 2006). Mobile devices are deployed in Mobile 2.0 such as smartphones and multimedia feature phones that are capable of delivering rich, interactive services, as well as being able to provide access to the full range of mobile consumer touchpoints including talking, texting, capturing, sending, listening and viewing.

Among those web 2.0 services, blogs are commonly used by individuals for social purposes, the media, and organisations (Thorne & Payne, 2005). Blogging opens up the possibility of regular peer assessment, helping learning anytime anywhere with collaboration, inclusiveness, flexibility and bringing more relevance to learners. Blogs afford self-expression, creativity, moving from knowledge consumer to knowledge producer and encouraging learners' authorship and engagement relevant to a larger, interactive community (Du & Wagner 2006; Kim, 2008; McIntosh, 2006; Sykes, Oskoz, & Thorne, 2008). Hanna and de Nooy (2003) believed that encouraging students to participate in non-educationally oriented online communities could develop awareness of appropriate genres of language use and patterns. Some linguists suggest blogs as social software can be used to enhance students' reading and writing, to increase their reflection both in their native language and the target language(s) (Ducate & Lomicka, 2005; Godwin-Jones, 2003; Salaberry, 2001). Blogs are receiving increasingly more attention in CALL research and second language instruction (e.g., Bloch, 2007; Ducate & Lomicka, 2005; Elola & Oskoz, 2008; Fidalgo-Eick, 2006; Sykes et al., 2008). Blogging through mobile devices, which is called mobile blogging or moblogging, has started to draw our attention.

The mobile Internet gives its contribution to learning as mobile devices can be used to capture situations and helps the contextualisation of the learning resource (Rosenbloom, 2006). Moblogs offer the potential to expound these benefits by removing time and place boundaries and adding authentic and personal visual content (Chinnery, 2006). Language learning can be enhanced by moblogging with easier and expanded interaction with other people and with the contexts in the real world.

The popular individual-centered moblogging activities can now be expanded to a group of people. Individuals in different geographical locations could apply what they get from one another to different dimensions of lives. If a mobile group blog is employed, individual mobile bloggers can collect and create their own contextual knowledge and share it with other members of a certain group. By exchanging stories or authentic experiences, members who are not in the same context, especially not in the same physical space, can probe deep comprehension about the real language use through the conveyance of context, which may be called "socialising the contexts". Learners would have open access to practical use of language in a real language context at the time when they are in the classroom or in a virtual world. Petersen, Chabert and Divitini (2006) described design considerations for the creation of a mobile community blog to support groups of language learners to promote contextual and sustainable learning, which is in line with Kukulska-Hulme and Shield, (2007). The mobile group blog as a mechanism to support language learning in a community is beneficial.

2. Case studies of second language context socialising

Our research is a trial of the application of mobile group blog in helping a group of Chinese students to get deep understandings of real language use in British culture by socialising the real context and exchanging contextual information. We recorded Chinese overseas students' adaptation in real British cultural environments by students' own contributions. Their experiences and contexts were delivered to remote students in China for better understanding of Englishness. Two studies were conducted: one in the UK for current overseas Chinese students, the other in China for prospective overseas students.

2.1. The mobile group blog

We designed and developed a mobile group blog, Nottsblog, by customising Wordpress 2.2 features, especially adding one plug-in for mobile devices. This web-based mobile application can be accessed from Internet-enabled mobile devices or PCs. The blog site is a collection of a group of international students' experiences and insights of Englishness in everyday life in the UK. There are four sections in the main web page: head bar, blog entry section, navigation and administration section, and blog description and help section. A blog entry contains the title and the content in the form of text and image. At the bottom of the entry is the date of blogging, the category to which this blog entry belongs, and the number of comments. Navigation and administration contains five key features: recent post, recent comments, categories, archives, and administration.

Recent post refers to the ten latest blog entries posted to the group blog. It lists the titles of these blog entries in reverse-chronological order. *Recent comments* refers to the five latest comments made by participants in reverse-chronological order, although it lists only the name of the person making the comment and the title of the blog entries. For the purpose of easier blog entry searching later, the *categories* entry lists the names of preset categories in alphabetical order: custom, conversation, events, life, buildings, food, shopping, traveling, and studies. The *archives* category gives archived blog entries by month to facilitate

Chapter 8

search. *Administration* provides the links to the registration and login webpage. Blog statement and help displays a brief description of what the blog is for and what could be posted, together with a link to the help pages (Figure 1).

Figure 1. The mobile group blog site

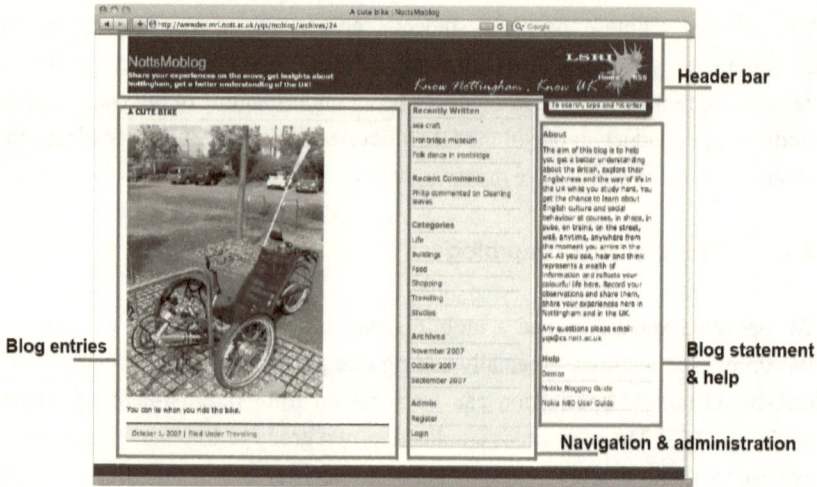

Figure 2. The interface of mobile blogging

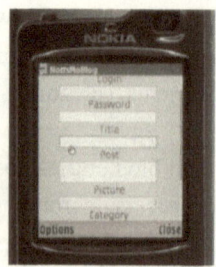

Figure 2 above shows the mobile interface through which users first login with their username and password. Every blogger can input the title and texts of their post in the textboxes, choosing pictures that had previously been taken and stored in the mobile device. Categories were preset by the researcher in the light of our pilot studies on overseas students' adaptation to the life in the UK (Shao, 2010). After categories and pictures are chosen, individual bloggers in this group can express what they see, what they experience and what they feel about their new life in the form of texts and images, in their favorite language straight to the mobile group blog site from mobile devices. All these blog entries were displayed in reverse-chronological order and visible for all bloggers.

2.2. Current overseas Chinese students in the UK

We first conducted a study for current overseas students in the UK. This study is not part of any institutional courses and was conducted informally in the real world in their everyday life. There was no curriculum and assessment syllabus for their contribution to the blog. Twelve newly arrived Chinese overseas students were recruited, aged from 19 to 25, who joined undergraduate or postgraduate programs of different subjects in the UK. All participants were from the Chinese Mainland and none had any experiences of mobile blogging before but all had their own personal blogs.

Each participant was loaned a Nokia N80 mobile phone for this study. They kept the Nokia phones for one month and were asked to do mobile group blogging as freely as they could, at any time and anywhere. Language learning was not emphasised in their activities and they were free to use their first or second language. They were encouraged to tell their own stories, feelings and capture any characteristics of British culture. All individual blog entries would be displayed in the blog site publicly.

They were also asked to read through other people's blog entries and to give their comments. The researcher observed their activities online and gave some advice to individual bloggers, acting as a member of the group particularly at the beginning, by giving a few examples of blog entries as semi-scaffoldings to the bloggers. Regular monitoring of the blog site revealed that some bloggers deviated from the original blog topic so messages were sent to pull them back. Log files were collected, pre and post interview and focus groups

Chapter 8

were conducted with all participants. They were asked about their experiences of blogging and their comments and suggestions for improving this mobile group blog system.

2.3. Prospective overseas students in China

The other one-day study was implemented in China. Twenty-three Chinese students of the Southwest University in Chongqing who intended to study abroad were recruited to be the mobile group blog readers. The purpose of this study was to find out how the contents on the group blog site contributed by mobloggers in the UK could benefit students in a completely different cultural and linguistic context. Thirteen participants were female and ten male. Ages ranged from 19 to 23.

Pre-reading focus groups and follow-up focus groups were conducted. Participants were then divided into six groups and asked to read through the group blog. Each group spent about thirty minutes on the reviews, during which time their conversations about the blog site were recorded by audio recorders. These students were then asked about their impressions of the blog, understandings about Britain and perceptions of using English.

3. Findings from the study in the UK

During the four weeks, 216 posts and 109 comments were submitted. The blog site received 1,126 hits. In this section, we list some findings of the mobile blogging activities. More findings are available in "mobile group blogging in learning" (Shao, 2010).

3.1. Time and space of moblogging

Figure 3 below reveals times when each moblogger submitted blog entries from their mobile phones during the study period of four weeks. These distributed moments for incidental observations, captures and collections of incidental happenings and contextual information also indicate they continued learning out of school time in informal settings frequently.

Figure 3. Frequency of mobile blogging

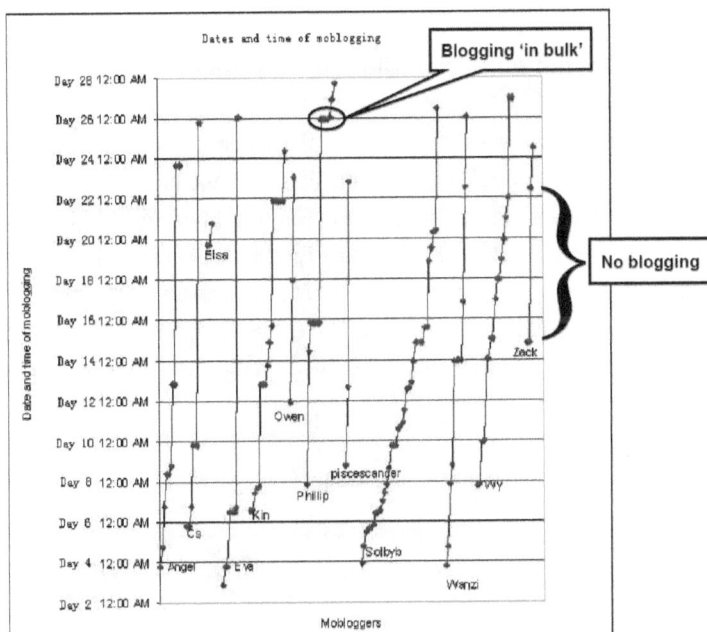

In Figure 3, the dots represent the time when blog entries were submitted and the lines between dots represent the duration when there was no moblogging activity. Those superimposed dots indicate bloggers posted several blog entries in bunches at one time. Figure 3 also implies that the majority of these participants did mobile blogging continuously though not regularly. Moblogging activity became intense in the second and third weeks. There is an interesting phenomenon that 'in bulk' moblogging often occurred in the evening. It was identified that 47% of bloggers posted blogs in the evening and during the night (after 7pm and before 2am); 39% blogged in the afternoon (after 12pm and before 7pm); and 14% in the morning (between 6am and 12pm). In the interviews, all participants claimed they often did moblogging in their dorm in the evening

Chapter 8

after classes. Although photos could be taken at any time, texts required time to type. They reported they also did moblogging on trains and buses, in the park, cafe and some public places. Participants submitted blogs only when they had enough time either strolling or sitting down. They did moblogging during their leisure time out of class.

3.2. Underlying shift from Chinese to English

A further phenomenon in the group blog was the unconscious shift in language use from mother tongue to English. Some students took the mobile group blogging as a process of storytelling, in Chinese or in English. Figure 4 and Figure 5 show that these texts were in Chinese with some English words included. The earlier blog entry in Figure 4 (posted October 12th) had many Chinese characters while the blog entry in Figure 5 (posted November 2nd) had only three Chinese characters. This may indicate the author's adaptation to language, a potential transition from Chinese to English.

Figure 4.   Blog example of mixed-language

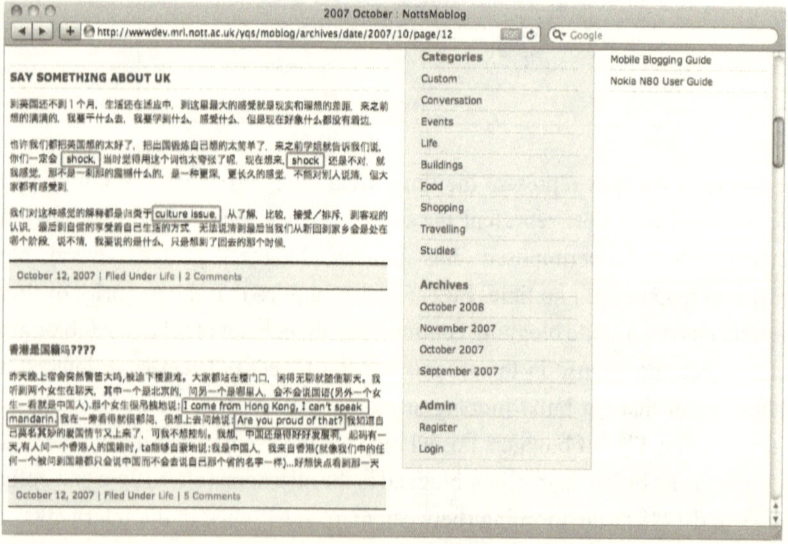

Figure 5.   Blog example of language transition

When we have a closer insight of their activities, in the first week, many blog entries were written in Chinese, but gradually we saw some English and Chinese mixed sentences by the end of the first week. Later, when more moblog entries were found, fewer and fewer blogs were written in Chinese. From the beginning of the third week, English texts started replacing Chinese texts, even for those who wrote traditional blogs using desktops/laptops.

In interviews and focus groups participants indicated that they had not been aware of this shift in language use. Some explained that they had started to adapt to life in Nottingham as language is one form of the adaptation, as stated in the following example:

> *Perhaps because now we have to write coursework in English.*
> *And everyday we have lectures in English, talking in English.*
> *We are gradually getting used to speaking, reading and*

Chapter 8

> *listening to English. Then unconsciously, we start writing blogs in English. (Wanzi, postgraduate, female)*

It can be assumed that speaking and writing more in English promoted their adjustment to new situations. They admitted their adaptation was spontaneous and was affected by the local culture and living environment.

3.3. Interactions in this mobile group blog community

The mobile group blog formed an online virtual community for the Chinese students, most of whom were previously unknown to one another. In this community these 'strangers' started conversation in contexts very similar to social life. Everything they shared and discussed was about what happened in everyday life, about their authentic collections and creations coming from the social contexts where they were currently in. Within the group blog, each participant shared their experiences, encouraged people who encountered problems, answered questions and discussed phenomena observed. They had communication through the mobile group blog, which afforded an online communicative context.

The findings of the interviews show that in this relative extended context, these overseas Chinese students found it comfortable and less stressful to talk about their authentic lives and true feelings. This mobile group blog therefore can easily record their real experiences, keep their trajectories in the real English culture and maintain these documents for later review or reflections. The following example shown in Figure 6 gives responses to a blog entry posted by Eva. Her blog conveys how she felt heart-broken about her uncle's death.

Three other people and the blog author were engaged in free interactions, expressing their experiences in everyday life either in Chinese or in English. The current overseas students studying in the UK in this group obviously owned a sense of belonging to a community. In this virtual community, they could have good conversations either synchronously on the move anytime with mobile devices or asynchronously with PCs.

Figure 6. Example of discussion through comments

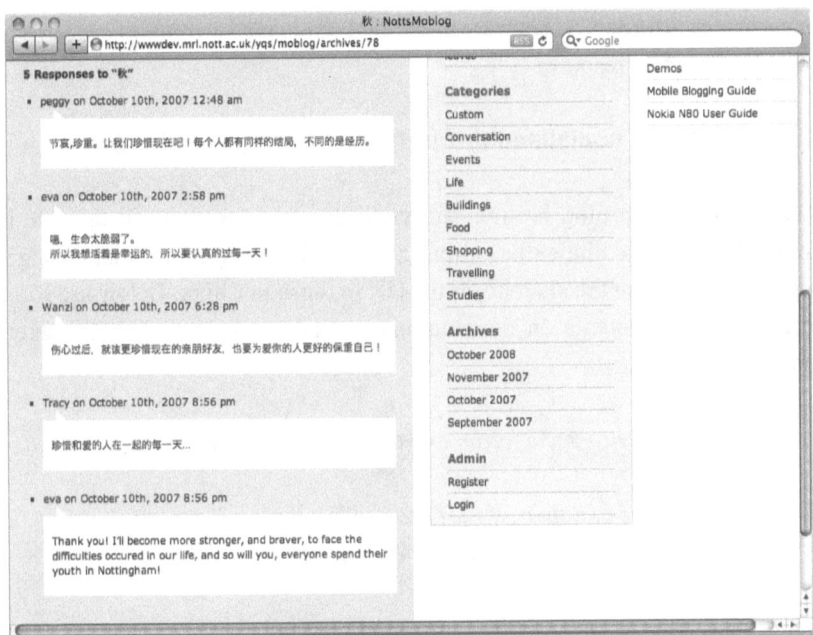

4. Findings from the study in China

Participants found that the information on the mobile group blog site supplemented traditional supports for understanding British life. The result of pre-reading conversation showed that they had some doubts and fear of language use and predicted some difficulties.

> *I guess there could be some barriers for me to get into the local community, such as language, culture, aloneness, new situations and so on. (Wei, postgraduate, female)*

It indicates that the prospective overseas students were quite aware and uncertain about the use of language in the target cultural contexts. They

Chapter 8

were not confident to apply what they learned in the classroom in China to the real target language context. The collection of authentic first-hand experiences afforded by learners in the real language surroundings seems to be a fundamental resource.

4.1. Context socialised through the mobile group blog

The mobile group blog brought the vivid contexts far away in the UK in front of them. The contextual information in the form of texts and images was delivered from the students in the UK to those in China. Below are some examples of comments on the studying abroad contexts that the bloggers stayed in.

> *Beautiful environment, clean and tidy. (Guo, undergraduate, female)*

> *We also have buildings of European styles, but not harmony with its environment. (Zhang, undergraduate, male)*

These blog readers far away in China could get an overall impression about the contexts they would be in, such as food, shopping, transportation, study and communication with local people. For example, Figure 7 illustrates how students in the UK handled their coursework. Students in China learned about the future learning context by reading this blog entry, which may not be easily imagined only through texts.

> *The coursework box looks interesting. The method of handing in coursework is special. (Bao, Undergraduate, female)*

More examples could be found on the mobile group blog site delivering information about contexts in the UK by the mobloggers in the UK to the readers in China in the second study. The authentic information collected and submitted by current overseas students in the UK provided contextual information for students in China to better understand about studying abroad, British culture and therefore promote their sense of learning English.

Figure 7. Blog entry of 'the coursework box'

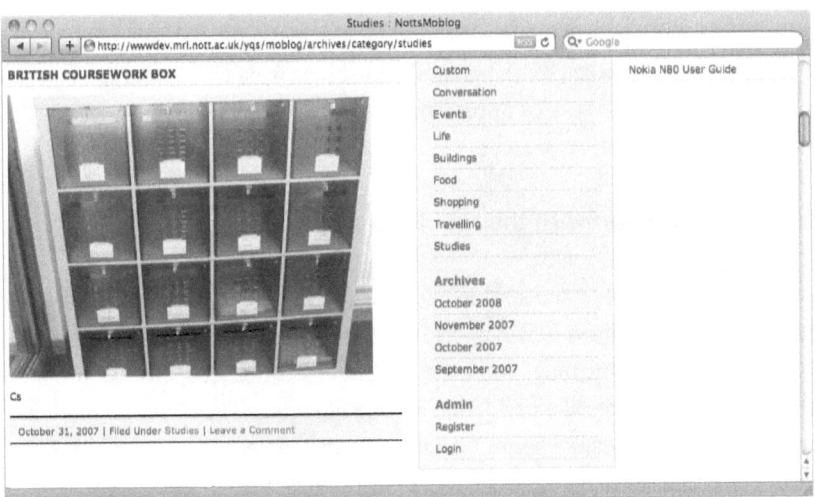

4.2. Language capability and confidence

For the prospective overseas students in China, language is also a barrier for some of them in understanding the contents of the blog site. Some participants complained about their difficulties in understanding English.

> *I am not good at English thus I can't understand some sentences, especially the name of some places they mentioned in the blog. Really don't know what they are talking about. Could you force them to write in Chinese? (Chen, postgraduate, male)*

It implied that compared to the students in China, the bloggers in the UK were much more confident to talk and write in English. From the quote above we can conclude that more contextual information was requested by these blog readers. Obviously, the lack of contextual information would hamper learners' understandings of the target contexts and the use of language. The missing contextual information obviously brought difficulties to the students in China to understand the communicative and social contexts.

Chapter 8

On the other hand, it would be reasonable to start the language transition from learners' mother tongue by joining in the online mobile community to develop their understanding despite their low proficiency in the English language. As we found in the study in the UK, the gradual transitions from Chinese to English also indicated an informal way of improving overseas students' language efficacy by using social software.

4.3. Interaction with the mobile bloggers

One solution to solve the problem of missing contextual information is to increase the interactions between the students in the UK and students in China via the mobile group blog. Students in China in this study asked for more bloggers in the UK to take part in the mobile blogging. They became motivated and enthusiastic to learn a second language in the context as bloggers do. Those bloggers' continuous engagement and contributions were in great demand.

> *It's better if we can join the group blog and have direct interactions with people who are now there. In this way we can have more doubts clarified and problems solved.*
>
> *Set up a big community and ask more people to join in, for more discussions.*

The overseas students' real trajectories of studying and living in the second language cultural contexts were good resources for second-language learners in their home country. They could also learn from the trajectories by observations on the blog site and interactions with those learners already in the target country.

5. Conclusion and recommendation

Successful language transition and promotion of second language efficacy were found as students in the UK submitted blog entries in Chinese and then in English. Students in China became more motivated and enthusiastic to learn English. The need raised for more communication within these two groups indicated the opportunities for learning a second language in a mobile online community, in and across the contexts in the physical and online world. The mobile group blog was found to be a feasible mechanism to assist informal language learning, especially keeping learning trajectories and socialisation of learning contexts. This could be verified from our research in the aspects approached below.

5.1. Mobile group blog forms an on-the-move online community

Students in the two studies were found actively engaged in the mobile group blogging. Students admitted they had the sense of belonging to the online community by sharing their experiences and having discussion with blog users. Although most participants stayed indoors to do their moblogs (Figure 3) or even submitted blogs in bulks and were still in the habit of writing blogs as a diary, about one-third of the participants tried blogging outdoors on the spot. The flexible submitting and getting information through the mobile group blog on-the-go brought the form of on-the-move online community. From the interviews, bloggers in the UK unfolded the desire of having local native speakers as experts, talking and learning more from them. In a further sense, scaling up this study to more international students would open up more beneficial interactions.

5.2. Mobile group blog as the carrier of learning trajectories

The mobile group blog not only records individual experiences in the real world, but also tracks their communications with other people on the mobile group blog community. Reflection could be done by both individual learner and the group of blog users. That means, individual mobloggers can do self-reflection on their own productions via their mobile devices any time anywhere and members in this group can do peer/group reflection on the community productions remotely. This mobile online community pushes learners back to the real world, searching and generating authentic artifacts and evidence through their own understanding of the real context, which could be shared instantly and globally (Shao, Deng, Crook, & Rodden, 2009).

5.3. Mobile group blog as the medium of context transition

Based on the interactions and communication among different roles in the mobile group blog community, the contexts of the overseas students in the UK were transferred to students in China for better understanding of English cultural environment. The mobile bloggers and their readers socialised the contexts, exchanging mutual learning contexts for their linguistic development remotely. By expressing and discussing about their respective own contexts, adding more cultural features in second language environments would help learners have better understanding of second language use and consequently improve their language efficacy.

5.4. Instant transnational communication

One of the limitations of this study is that we did not manage the real cross-national immediate communication within those students in the UK and in China. From the feedback of the students in China we can conclude that communication is strongly demanded and necessary. It is beneficial for second language learners in their home country to get useful authentic information about the target cultural contexts. By socialising the context, this cross-border community could benefit not only their present life but also their learning in the future.

We argue it would be more effective that learners in the home country can get immediate feedback and interactions with people in the second-language cultural context, to answer questions and remove doubts in good time. This is applicable either for adults or for adolescents learning second language informally in or out of school. For example, students in exchange programs studying in the target language country could play the role of mobloggers while those students in their own countries could learn through the mobile group blog site.

5.5. Scaffolding in mobile online community

In informal learning, there is a great risk that learners would get lost if they were put in a purely social context without any guidance. Learning will only be effective if the students are given educational scaffolding on "how to create a good post, what information to include in a good post, how to give feedback and respond to a feedback" (Huann, John, & Yuen, 2005, p. 6). In our research, the researcher acted as the facilitator and guide. Learners came to rely upon one another, as much or more than the guide or facilitator, in the production of messages, expression of their experiences and exchange of knowledge and contexts. The scaffolding could also be supported by senior learners or native speakers at times, producing authentic contexts and assistance for learning. Chances are that we promote this informal language learning to more structured and formal learning by establishing an adaptive-curriculum in this kind of mobile online community. We may have 'teacher-determined' topics at the very beginning and gradually hand over the control to learners themselves gearing their learning progress.

This research has taken only an initial step towards the application of the mobile group blog in assisting overseas study. This is small-scale mobile group blogging, where limited amount of information was generated. Further research or practices can include the exploration of application in informal learning, formal learning, or the transitions between formal and informal settings for language learning.

References

Atkinson, D. (2002). Toward a sociocognitive approach to second language acquisition. *The Modern Language Journal, 86*(4), 525-545. doi:10.1111/1540-4781.00159

Attewell, J., & Savill-Smith, C. (Eds.). (2003). *Learning with mobile devices: research and development. A book of papers.* London: Learning and skills development agency.

Bloch, J. (2007). Abdullah's blogging: a generation 1.5 student enters the blogosphere. *Language Learning & Technology, 11*(2), 128-141. Retrieved from http://llt.msu.edu/vol11num2/pdf/bloch.pdf

Burr, V. (1995). *An introduction to social constructionism.* London: Routledge.

Chalmers, M. (2004). A historical view of context. *Computer Supported Cooperative Work (CSCW), 13*(3-4), 223-247. doi:10.1007/s10606-004-2802-8

Chinnery, G. M. (2006). Going to the MALL: mobile assisted language learning (Emerging technology). *Language Learning & Technology, 10*(1), 9-16. Retrieved from http://llt.msu.edu/vol10num1/pdf/emerging.pdf

Cobcroft, R. S., Towers, S. J., Smith, J. E., & Bruns, A. (2006). Mobile learning in review: opportunities and challenges for learners, teachers, and institutions. In *Proceedings Online Learning and Teaching (OLT) conference 2006,* (pp. 21-30). Brisbane: Queensland University of Technology. Retrieved from http://eprints.qut.edu.au/5399/1/5399.pdf

Collentine, J., & Freed, B. F. (2004). Learning context and its effects on second language acquisition: introduction. *Studies in Second Language Acquisition, 26*(2), 153-171. doi:10.1017/S0272263104262015

Collins, T. G. (2008). *English class on the air: mobile language learning with cell phones.* Kaohsiung, Taiwan: Paper presented at the Fifth IEEE International Conference on Advanced Learning Technologies. Retrieved from http://doi.ieeecomputersociety.org/10.1109/ICALT.2005.137

Dias, J. (2002). Cell phones in the classroom. Boon or bane? *C@lling Japan, 10*(2), 16-21. Retrieved from http://jaltcall.org/cjo/10_2.pdf

Du, H. S., & Wagner, C. (2006). Weblog success: exploring the role of technology. *International Journal of Human-Computer Studies, 64*(9), 789-798. doi:10.1016/j.ijhcs.2006.04.002

Ducate, L. C., & Lomicka, L. L. (2005). Exploring the blogosphere: use of web logs in the foreign language classroom. *Foreign language annals, 38*(3), 410-421. doi:10.1111/j.1944-9720.2005.tb02227.x

Elola, I., & Oskoz, A. (2008). Blogging: fostering intercultural competence development in foreign language and study abroad contexts. *Foreign Language Annals, 41*(3), 454-477. doi:10.1111/j.1944-9720.2008.tb03307.x

Fidalgo-Eick, M. (2006). *Blogs in the foreign language classroom.* Paper presented at the annual conference of the Computer Assisted Language Instruction Consortium: Manoa, HI.

Godwin-Jones, R. (2003). Blogs and wikis: environments for on-line collaboration (Emerging technology). *Language Learning & Technology, 7*(2), 12-16. Retrieved from http://llt.msu.edu/vol7num2/pdf/emerging.pdf

Günther, S., Winkler, T., Ilgner, K., & Herczeg, M. (2008). Mobile learning with moles: a case study for enriching cognitive learning by collaborative learning in real world contexts. In J. Luca & E. Weippl (Eds.), *Proceedings of World Conference on Educational Multimedia, Hypermedia and Telecommunications 2008* (pp. 374-380). Chesapeake, VA: AACE. Retrieved from http://www.editlib.org/d/28422/proceeding_28422.pdf

Hanna, B. E., & de Nooy, J. (2003). A funny thing happened on the way to the forum: electronic discussion and foreign language learning. *Language Learning & Technology*, 7(1), 71-85. Retrieved from http://llt.msu.edu/vol7num1/pdf/hanna.pdf

Herron, C. (1994). An investigation of the effectiveness of using an advance organizer to introduce video in the foreign language classroom. *The Modern Language Journal*, 78(2), 190-198. Retrieved from http://www.jstor.org/stable/329009

Hirst, E. (2004). Diverse social contexts of a second-language classroom and the construction of identity. In K. M. Leander & M. Sheehy (Eds.), *Spatializing Literacy Research and Practice* (pp. 39-66). New York: Peter Lang.

Huann, T. Y., John, O. E., & Yuen, J. M. (2005). *Weblogs in education*. Singapore: Educational Technology Division, Ministry of Education. Retrieved from http://www.edublog.net/files/papers/weblogs in education.pdf

Hymes, D. H. (1972). *Reinventing anthropology*. New York: Random House.

Jaokar, A. (2006). Mobile web 2.0: web 2.0 and its impact on the mobility and digital convergence [Web log post]. Retrieved from http://opengardensblog.futuretext.com/archives/2005/12/mobile_web_20_w.html

Kelton, A. J. (2007). Second life: reaching into the virtual world for real-world learning. *Educause Center for Applied Research*, *17*, 1-13. Retrieved from http://www.educause.edu/ir/library/pdf/ERB0717.pdf

Kim, H. N. (2008). The phenomenon of blogs and theoretical model of blog use in educational contexts. *Computers & Education*, 51(3), 1342-1352. doi:10.1016/j.compedu.2007.12.005

Kramsch, C. (1993). *Context and culture in language teaching*. Oxford: Oxford University Press.

Kukulska-Hulme, A. (2006). Mobile language learning now and in the future. In P. Svensson (Ed.), *Från vision till praktik: språkutbildning och informationsteknik (From vision to practice: language learning and IT)* (pp. 295-310). Sweden: Swedish Net University (Nätuniversitetet). Retrieved from http://oro.open.ac.uk/9542/1/kukulska-hulme.pdf

Kukulska-Hulme, A., & Shield, L. (2007). *An overview of mobile assisted language learning: can mobile devices support collaborative practice in speaking and listening?* Paper presented at the EUROCALL 2007 Virtual strand. Retrieved from http://vsportal2007.googlepages.com/Kukulska_Hulme_and_Shield_2007.pdf

Kukulska-Hulme, A., & Shield, L. (2008). An overview of mobile assisted language learning: from content delivery to supported collaboration and interaction. *ReCALL, 20*(3), 271-289. doi:10.1017/S0958344008000335

Kukulska-Hulme, A., & Traxler, J. (Eds.). (2005). *Mobile learning: a handbook for educators and trainers.* New York: Taylor & Francis Inc.

Lam, W. S. E. (2000). L2 literacy and the design of the self: a case study of a teenager writing on the Internet. *TESOL Quarterly, 34*(3), 457-482. Retrieved from http://www.jstor.org/stable/3587739

Leander, K. M. (2001). "This is our freedom bus going home right now": producing and hybridizing space-time contexts in pedagogical discourse. *Journal of Literacy Research, 33*(4), 637-679. doi:10.1080/10862960109548128

Low, L. (2006). *Connections: social and mobile tools for enhancing learning.* Retrieved from http://kt.flexiblelearning.net.au/wp-content/uploads/2006/11/low.pdf

McIntosh, E. (2006). Learning logs to learning (b)logs - a great example [Web log post]. Retrieved from http://edu.blogs.com/edublogs/2006/01/learning_log_to.html

Mercer, N. (1992). Culture, context and the construction of knowledge in the classroom. In P. Light & G. Butterworth (Eds.), *Context and cognition: ways of learning and knowing* (pp. 28-46). Michigan: Harvester Wheatsheaf.

Meyer, B., & Bo-Kristensen, M. (2009). Designing location aware games for mobile language learning (Vol 2). In A. Méndez-Vilas, A. Solano Martín, J. A. Mesa González, & J. Mesa González (Eds.), *Research, Reflections and Innovations in Integrating ICT in Education* (pp. 1086-1090). Badajoz, Spain: Formatex. Retrieved from http://www.formatex.org/micte2009/book/1086-1090.pdf

Norbrook, H., & Scott, P. (2003). Motivation in mobile modern foreign language learning. In J. Attewell, G. Da Bormida, M. Sharples, & C. Savill-Smith (Eds.), *MLEARN 2003: learning with mobile devices.* London: Learning and Skills Development Agency.

Ogata, H., & Yano, Y. (2003). How ubiquitous computing can support language learning. *Computer and Information Science,* 1-6. Retrieved from http://goo.gl/kP8VG

Petersen, S. A., Chabert, G., & Divitini, M. (2006). Language learning: design considerations for mobile community blogs. Retrieved from http://goo.gl/i3W8T

Ros i Solé, C. (2009). The fleeting, the situated and the mundane: ethnographic approaches to mobile language learning (MALL). In G. Vavoula, N. Pachler, & A. Kukulska-Hulme (Eds.), *Researching mobile learning: frameworks, tools and research designs* (pp. 137-150). Oxford: Peter Lang.

Rosenbloom, S. (2006). Corners: in certain circles, two is a crowd. *The New York Time*. Retrieved from http://www.nytimes.com/2006/11/16/fashion/16space.html

Salaberry, M. R. (2001). The use of technology for second language learning and teaching: a retrospective. *The Modern Language Journal, 85*(1), 39-56. doi:10.1111/0026-7902.00096

Shao, Y. (2010). *Mobile Group blogging in learning: a case study of supporting cultural transition.* PhD thesis. University of Nottingham, Nottingham.

Shao, Y., Deng, H., Crook, C., & Rodden, T. (2009). *Learning cross the border towards a global mobile community: context-based, communicative and collaborative.* Florida: 8th World Conference on Mobile and contextual Learning.

Sharples, M. (2007). *Big issues in mobile learning: report of a workshop by the Kaleidoscope Network of Excellence Mobile Learning Initiative.* Nottingham: Learning Sciences Research Institute, University of Nottingham.

Smagorinsky, P., & Fly, P. K. (1993). The social environment of the classroom: a Vygotskian perspective on small group process. *Communication Education, 42*(2), 159-171. doi:10.1080/03634529309378922

Solomon, G., & Schrum, L. (2007). *Web 2.0: new tools, new schools.* Washington: International Society for Technology in Education.

Sykes, J. M., Oskoz, A., & Thorne, S. L. (2008). Web 2.0, synthetic immersive environments, and mobile resources for language education. *CALICO Journal, 25*(3), 528-546. Retrieved from https://calico.org/html/article_715.pdf

Thomas, S. (2005). *Pervasive, persuasive elearning: modeling the pervasive learning space.* Proceedings from the third IEEE International Conference on Pervasive Computing and Communications Workshops, Washington.

Thorne, S. L., & Payne, J. S. (2005). Evolutionary Trajectories, Internetmediated Expression, and Language Education. *CALICO Journal, 22*(3), 371-397. Retrieved from https://calico.org/html/article_137.pdf

Thornton, P., & Houser, C. (2005). Using mobile phones in English education in Japan. *Journal of Computer Assisted Learning, 21*(3), 217-228. doi:10.1111/j.1365-2729.2005.00129.x

Warschauer, M. (1999). *Electronic literacies: language, culture and power in online education.* Mahwah, NJ: Lawrence Erlbaum Associates.

Wertsch, J. V. (1991). *Voices of the mind: a sociocultural approach to mediated action.* Cambridge, Massachusetts: Harvard University Press.

Williams, M., & Burden, R. L. (1997). *Psychology for language teachers: a social constructivist approach.* Cambridge: Cambridge University Press.

Zhao, Y. (2003). Recent developments in technology and language learning: a literature review and meta-analysis. *CALICO Journal, 21*(1), 7-27. Retrieved from https://calico.org/html/article_279.pdf

Dynamically Assessing Written Language: To what Extent Do Learners of French Language Accept Mediation?

Sylvie Thouësny*

Abstract

In contrast to standardised assessment, dynamic assessment (DA) simultaneously combines teaching and assessment activities. The key difference between standardised and dynamic approaches lies in the fact that, in the latter, an expert is allowed to provide assistance to a novice during the assessment process. Mediation, whether in the form of interventions or in the form of negotiated interactions between mediators and learners, aims not only to help learners complete the task, but also to promote their cognitive development. Whilst an approach to dynamic assessment implies the mediator's participation, it is equally important to note the involvement of the learner during this process. However, the way in which learners contribute to dynamic assessment tends to be overlooked by researchers. This chapter examines a relatively small corpus of 14 language learners' written texts, who were asked to correct themselves with and without assistance by means of a computer-based application. It then investigates how learners responded to interventions, and how they negotiated mediation in terms of acceptance and refusal. Results not only show that learners' acceptance of mediation is unsystematic, but also demonstrate that learners may refuse and argue the mediation offered.

Keywords: dynamic assessment, interaction, intervention, mediation, written language, French as a foreign language.

---

*Dublin City University, Ireland. e-mail: sylvie.thouesny@icall-research.com

How to cite this chapter: Thouësny, S. (2011). Dynamically assessing written language: to what extent do learners of French language accept mediation? In S. Thouësny & L. Bradley (Eds.), *Second language teaching and learning with technology: views of emergent researchers* (pp. 169-188). Dublin: Research-publishing.net.

Chapter 9

1. Introduction

Although the term dynamic assessment originated in research investigating children's abnormal behaviours (Mathews, 1961) and is nowadays predominantly applied in areas such as learning disabilities or adults' language impairments (e.g., Navarro & Calero, 2009), other practitioners have started to widen the use of dynamic assessment practices to second language assessment and pedagogy (e.g., Ableeva, 2008; Erben, Ban, & Summers, 2008; Poehner, 2008). Dynamic assessment is commonly categorised depending on the type of "mediated assistance" provided to learners in order for them to attain their goal (Lantolf & Poehner, 2004, p. 54). For example, Daniel (1997) distinguishes two groups with different intervention processes: the first approach provides "standard interventions" and the second one "nonstandardised interventions" (p. 1041). While the former relates to the use of measures to determine the amount of prompts learners require to be able to provide a correct alternative, the latter refers to Feuerstein, Rand and Hoffman's (1979) idea of associating intervention with assessment (Daniel, 1997, p. 1041). Lantolf and Poehner (2004) refer to both approaches as "interventionist" and "interactionist", respectively (p. 54).

During an interventionist approach, teachers are "not free to respond to learners' needs [...] but must instead follow a highly scripted approach to mediation in which all prompts, hints, and leading questions have been arranged in a hierarchical manner" (Poehner, 2008, pp. 44-45). By contrast, mediated assistance between learners and teachers during an interactionist orientation is negotiated rather than established in advance, which is more in line with sociocultural theory (Lantolf & Poehner, 2004, p. 58). The learner's participation is then viewed as an active co-construction of knowledge between both the learner and the teacher (Poehner, 2008, p. 58).

Whilst an approach to dynamic assessment, either interventionist or interactionist, implies the participation of the mediator, the involvement of the learner during the process is equally as important. Yet, research seems to focus more on mediation techniques rather than on learners' participation and reciprocity (Van der Aalsvoort & Lidz, 2002). Poehner (2008) further points out that "learner reciprocity is critical to enhancing [...] interpretations of L2 learners' contributions during DA", and expands "the concept to include not only learners' responsiveness to mediation but also their requests for support and even their refusal of it" (p. 86).

Antón (2009), for instance, reports on the implementation of a dynamic assessment approach. Second language learners of Spanish were given twenty minutes to write an essay without assistance. The correction of their text was performed under the supervision of the teacher. Firstly, students self-edited their written text after which they were then given a dictionary and a grammar manual. Finally they were invited to interact with the examiner about concerns they might have about the composition of the text. According to Antón (2009), learners have the opportunity to revise what they think they do not know. However, and as stated by Skinner and Madden (2010), even if learners believe they need help, it is not certain that they will ask for it (p. 21). In the case of computer-based application, it is not because help is available to learners that they will use it (Fischer, 2007).

A computer-based dynamic assessment in line with interventionist approaches was designed and implemented for the purpose of this researcher's doctoral research (Thouësny, in progress). This chapter explores the learners' responses to interventions with regards to acceptance, refusal and negotiation of assistance when being dynamically assessed.

2. Method

2.1. Context of the study and participants

This study was conducted in a French language class at university level over the first semester of the 2008/2009 academic calendar. This class was composed of eighty-nine learners of French in their first year, and included twelve sessions of three hours a week. The module covered a project-based approach, which was to describe one typical week at the university from the students' point of view. It included text types such as the writing of a critical reflection on their own language learning experience, or wiki texts. Wikis, as mentioned by Warschauer (2010), are tools "for collaborative writing and collective knowledge development" (p.5). Within this class, the wiki naturally included texts written as a result of learners' collaboration, thus implying amongst other tasks peer-reviewing. However, all performances submitted for correction within this study were texts students had to write individually.

From the eighty-nine learners of French enrolled in the language course, nineteen students signed the consent form to participate in this study, and fourteen of them sent at least one text for correction. Almost all participants had English as their first language, except for one student whose native language was Portuguese. There were three males and eleven females, and the participants' age ranged from eighteen to twenty-four, except for one student who was fifty years old.

2.2. Participants' task

Learners were invited to review each of their texts via a web-based application and to provide alternatives to all forms that were marked as incorrect by the corrector. The assistance was given on a progressive scale varying from implicit to specific answers. While it is commonly assumed that if learners are able to produce a correct alternative with implicit assistance, which designates that they already have a certain control over their subject (Lantolf, 2009, p. 360), it could also be the case that producing a valid answer after the first level of assistance may result from a learner's guess. For this reason, students were asked to correct themselves three times consecutively and independently of what they may have proposed at previous levels of assistance.

2.3. Procedure

Learners' texts submitted for correction were manually annotated with the help of a computer-aided error annotation, and each incorrect form identified was linked to different levels of assistance going from implicit to explicit. The error type category used to annotate the learners' texts was adapted from (a) Mackey, Gass and McDonough (2000) with regard to morphosyntactic and lexical errors, (b) L'Haire (2007) with reference to syntax and punctuation, and (c) Granger (2003) with respect to grammar and typography. It includes the following domains: selection, syntax, morphosyntax, misspelling and typography, and each of these domains contained error types such as incorrect tense for selection, word addition for syntax, incorrect past participle agreement for morphosyntax, incorrect accent for spelling, or inappropriate space for typography.

The levels of assistance provided to learners were derived from Aljaafreh and Lantolf's (1994) regulatory scale. They are as follows:

- **Level 1.** The highlighted incorrect word, or group of words indicates that something is wrong, no further information is provided.

- **Level 2.** The error type is provided for each highlighted incorrect word or group of words, narrowing down the nature of the incorrect form.

- **Level 3.** Detailed explanations about the nature of the incorrect form is given to help the learner find the correct answer, yet without providing it.

- **Level 4.** The correct form is provided.

Each incorrect form is annotated with the editor tool in the following way:

incorrect form[errorType]{index@meta-linguistic feedback@correct form}.

The *incorrect form* sequence corresponds to the first level of assistance in the regulatory scale, where the incorrect form is solely highlighted. The [errorType] section coincides with the second level of assistance where only the error type of the incorrect form is issued. An index is given in order to make the sequence unique in the input text. The {_@meta-linguistic feedback} and *{_@correct form}* strings provide the information for the third and fourth levels of assistance, respectively. Information inside the curly brackets are separated with the @ sign, which is used afterwards as a splitting character when processing the string.

Students were then asked to review their written performance, and to re-submit their texts along with alternatives to their incorrect forms if they knew or thought they knew a correct replacement. For the first level of correction, learners had to correct all sequences marked as incorrect without any indication about the error type. For the second level of correction, they were provided with comments on the error type. For the third level of correction, they were provided with meta-linguistic feedback. The comments were visible with a mouse roll-over action on the incorrect forms. Finally, learners were offered the possibility to access correct alternatives to their ill-formed words that were proposed by the corrector.

3. Analysis

Accessing a feedback does not signify that the learner has read it. However, since learners had to move their cursor over the incorrect forms to display the annotation, and if the message was open sufficiently long, it was assumed that the learner had the intention to read it. To determine whether a feedback was accessed/read, the computer-based application (a) recorded the time at which any feedback pop-up was opened and closed, (b) computed the difference between both records, (c) calculated the time required to read the feedback, and (d) evaluated whether the access was sufficiently long for the feedback to be read.

The time required to read the feedback was determined depending on the amount of words included in the message and the speed rate at which learners read. While it is commonly assumed that the speed rate at which a native speaker reads is around 250 words per minute, Ziefle (1998) found that reading on a computer screen, as opposed to paper, slowed down the rate to 180 words per minute. Additionally, the author tested the reading rate on several display resolutions and found that there were no statistical differences between the various screen conditions. The only significant difference observed was between paper and computer screen. Following her findings, the speed rate adopted in this study was set up at 180 words per minute. The time in milliseconds required to read one word is thus equal to 333.33ms (60/180*1000).

Figure 1 below is a screen capture of a learner's report with regard to alternatives provided and whether or not they were correct. In addition, it shows whether the assistance was accessed.

Figure 1. Monitoring report

incorrect form	feedback	my correction	teacher's correction	Alternative validated?	Feedback read? How many times? Average time?
[francais]	misspelling	français	français	☑	☑ 1.46 seconds (1 time)
[les grammaires]	inappropriate word choice	la grammaire	les exercices de grammaire	☒	☑ 1.53 seconds (1 time)
[était]	subject verb agreement	-	étaient	☒	☑ 3.86 seconds (1 time)
[rencontrerai]	misspelling	recontrerai	rencontrerai	☒	☑ 1.35 seconds (3 times)
[apres]	incorrect or missing accent	après	après	☑	☒ Not read!
[heures!]	missing or inappropriate space	heures !	heures !	☑	☑ 2.64 seconds (1 time)
[bientot]	incorrect or missing accent	bientôt	bientôt !	☑	☒ Not read!

For instance, the incorrect word *était (was)* –fourth row– was accessed once for 3.86 seconds. In fact, the feedback was accessed twice; the other access lasted 21 milliseconds. Since the feedback message includes three words, i.e., *subject verb agreement*, the time required to read this message is calculated to be at least 999 milliseconds. As a result, the access that lasted 21 milliseconds was not considered long enough to ensure the reading of the message

Results

The corpus includes in total 2,118 incorrect sequences, for which 4,236 annotations were given at levels two and three of the regulatory scale. From these 4,236 annotations, 47.01% (N=1994) of them were not accessed, which implies that they were not read. Figure 2 provides an overview of the learners' behaviour with regard to feedback access. In addition, the diagram displays the amount of alternatives provided with and without assistance, and whether these alternatives were correct.

Figure 2. Overview of feedback access

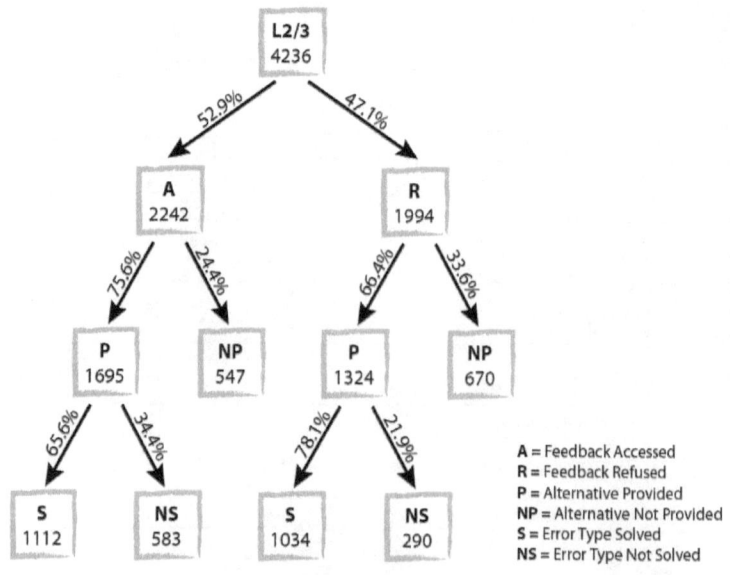

Breaking down the analysis, Table 1 below provides the percentage of feedback each student did not access, and outlines different behaviours in terms of acceptance and refusal of assistance. For instance, student #2 opened 80.1% of all her feedback (19.9% were not read), whereas student #6 did not read 86.5% of the feedback provided to her.

Table 1. Percentage of feedback not read per student

Student	Amount of feedback provided (levels 2 and 3)	Percentage of feedback not read
#2	1614	19.9%
#6	148	86.5%
#7	272	47.4%
#9	44	6.8%
#10	312	52.6%
#11	156	75.6%
#12	74	36.5%
#13	150	58.7%
#14	120	33.3%
#15	98	54.1%
#16	192	55.7%
#17	914	78.4%
#18	64	53.1%
#19	78	83.3%

Mediation is considered as *refused* when learners did not access the assistance made available to them at the different stages of their correction task. Additionally, mediation is also regarded as refused when learners proposed alternatives which were identical in all respect to their initial incorrect forms, whether the assistance was accessed or not. Alternately, accessing the assistance presupposes that learners *accepted* it. The fact that they disagreed with the assistance indicates that they *negotiated* the content.

3.1. Refusing the assistance

In the event of learners' refusal with regard to feedback access, that is, where learners did not open the pop-up windows that included the error type or meta-linguistic feedback, learners could either provide alternatives or leave the fields blank. Altogether students did not propose any alternatives to 33.6% of all incorrect forms for which the feedback was not accessed/ read. Breaking down the analysis per student, Figure 3 below illustrates the percentage of incorrect forms that were not attempted when the assistance was not accessed.

Figure 3. Percentage of incorrect forms not attempted when feedback is not read

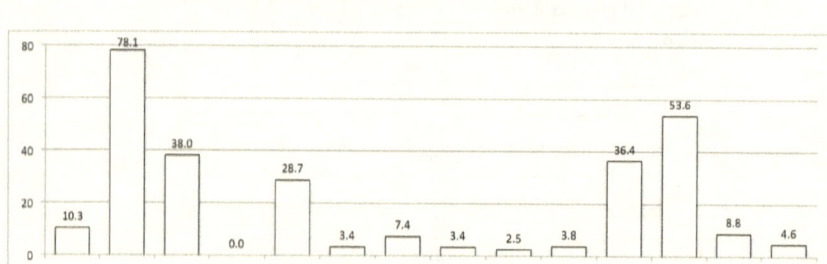

While student #6 scored rather weakly in terms of engagement with 78.1% of incorrect forms left without any replacement, the other students generally proposed alternatives to their incorrect forms despite the fact that they did not access the assistance. For example, student #14 did not provide any alternatives to 2.5% of all her incorrect forms for which no feedback was read, which implies that 97.5% of her incorrect forms were attempted, whether successful or not.

As mentioned above, students altogether proposed alternatives to 66.4% of all incorrect forms for which the feedback was not read. The percentage of correct alternatives when assistance is not accessed is illustrated in Figure 4 below.

Figure 4. Percentage of correct alternatives without seeking assistance

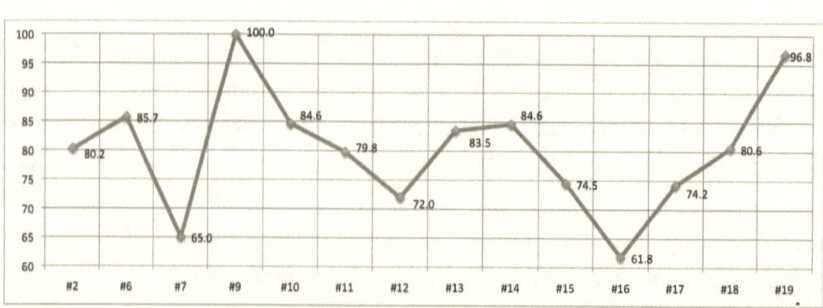

While student #16 was slightly over confident with 61.8% of success when editing herself, students #9 and #19 were able to successfully correct their incorrect sequences for which no assistance was required, 100% and 96.5%, respectively. For most students, the percentage of success in correcting themselves without assistance is higher than 70%.

Another form of refusal relates to situations where learners reproduced their initial incorrect forms after either accessing the assistance or skipping it. Table 2 below lists the percentage of alternatives that were rewritten exactly as the incorrect sequences at all three levels of assistance.

Table 2. Percentage of incorrect sequences rewritten as such

Level of assistance	Amount of alternatives provided	Incorrect sequence reproduced as such
1	1372	45 (3.27%)
2	1478	13 (0.87%)
3	1541	11 (0.71%)

The percentage of sequences rewritten as such is higher at level one (3.27%) than at levels two and three, 0.87% and 0.71%, respectively. The decrease at levels two and three is due to the fact that learners were able to edit themselves after reading the assistance. What is interesting to note, however, is the figure of 0.87% and 0.71% of incorrect forms that were reproduced at levels two and three, especially after being provided with assistance. For example, Table 3 displays the alternatives that were identically rewritten as the incorrect forms by student #2.

Table 3. Examples of alternatives rewritten as the incorrect sequences

Level of assistance	Feedback accessed	Incorrect sequence reproduced as such by student #2
1	NA	[informathique], [À], [amusée], [mes], [contribuons], [de]
2	1 time	[informathique]
3	2 times	[informathique]

The word *informathique (computing)* was incorrectly rewritten at all levels, although the feedback was read at least once at levels two and three. Rewriting the incorrect sequence certainly signifies more than merely not knowing how to correct the highlighted words, otherwise student #2 would have rewritten with the same orthography the 23 incorrect forms she left without any replacements at level one, the 16 incorrect forms she left blank at level two, and the 12 incorrect forms for which she did not enter a correction at level three. Mostly, when students did not know how to self-edit themselves or did not understand the feedback, they left the field blank as was advised during the training session.

3.2. Accepting the assistance

Accepting the assistance designates that the feedback was opened long enough to be read. Table 4 shows that of the 2,242 feedback comments that were accessed, learners suggested alternatives to 1,695 incorrect forms (75.6%).

Table 4. Alternatives provided after reading the feedback

Amount of alternatives provided		Amount of alternatives not provided	
1695	75.6%	547	24.4%

The analysis of whether an alternative was provided after reading the feedback shows varying percentages when splitting the data per error category. Figure 5 displays the percentage of all alternatives provided in selection, syntax, morphosyntax, misspelling, and typography, and Figure 6 shows the percentage of correct alternatives provided within these categories.

Figure 5. Alternatives provided after reading the feedback per error category

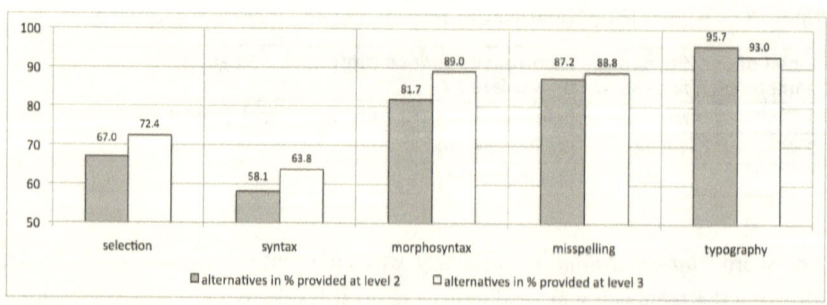

Figure 6. Correct alternatives provided after reading the feedback, per error category

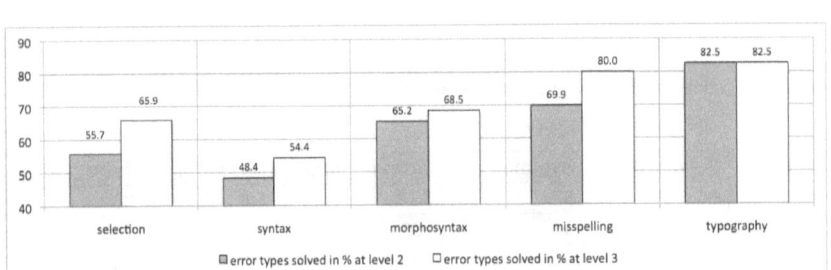

Learners tend to have less difficulties in proposing alternatives to incorrect sequences related to morphosyntax, typography and misspelling. However, when the focus is on syntax, learners seem to be more challenged. While the participants provided 95.7% of alternatives at level two in typographic error types, 82.5% of them were resolved. With regard to syntactic incorrect forms, learners are inclined to correct themselves more often with a *word omission* error type than a *word addition* error type. For example, the following sequence marked as *word omission* –the preposition is missing– **besoin une... (need one...)* was appropriately corrected by student #2 as *besoin d'une*. The following sequence marked as *word addition* –the preposition *de* is added– **position de sociale* was edited by the same student as **position de la sociale*, where a correct answer would have been *position sociale (social position)*.

In general terms, it may be advanced that learners tend to have more difficulties in providing correct alternatives after accessing the assistance for selection and syntactic error types than morphosyntactic, misspelling and typographic categories. However, when looking at the distribution of correct alternatives per student, the conclusion to be drawn is to some extent different, as illustrated in Table 5 below. Student #19, for instance, does not struggle with any of the error types, since she achieved 100% of correct alternatives in all five error categories after accessing the assistance at level three. Syntax is not an issue for student #9, nor student #13, who performed 100% correctly. As for students #6 and #12, they could not correct themselves even with a full explanation about the incorrect forms in the syntax feedback. This table below demonstrates that one individual may have issues in one category and skills in another, which may not correspond to the group average.

Table 5. Percentage of correct replacement provided at level 3 per student per error category

Student	Selection	Syntax	Morphosyntax	Misspelling	Typography
#2	64.1	57	70.8	76.8	88
#6	100	3	100	3	100
#7	75	66.7	20	87.5	100
#9	100	100	100	80	100
#10	71.4	66.7	72.7	92.9	50
#11	83.3	75	3	100	0
#12	55.6	20	100	0	100
#13	100	100	50	90.9	0
#14	81.8	40	50	83.3	50
#15	71.4	33.3	3	50	0
#16	60	40	100	3	3
#17	50	20	50	80	100
#18	33.3	50	0	100	100
#19	100	100	100	100	100

3.3. Negotiating the assistance

While the computer-based application used to collect the data was not originally designed for negotiation, student #14 discussed (literally) the content of one feedback. The incorrect sequence marked as *not understandable* in terms of word meaning is as follows:

> Je commence chaque jour avec [des céréales] *d'être polarisé sur mon jour*.
> *(I always start my day with cereals in order to be physically and morally fit for the day)*

The participant attempted an unfruitful alternative at level one, i.e., without assistance, *à être polarisé sur mon jour*. Then, the learner accessed the feedback at level two twice with an average time of 15 seconds each, yet without providing any alternatives. At level three, the learner accessed the metalinguistic annotations three times with an average time of 11 seconds for each reading, and tried to reformulate the sequence differently *d'être en forme*. After the self-editing task, the student came to the corrector and said that her semiotic intention was misunderstood. This interesting comment led to a conversation in French about the meaning of the whole sentence, and the meaning of the word *polariser (polarise)* in this context. The participant added that she was tempted to argue during the self-editing task, and wished to write (in English) the reasons for which she thought her formulation was correct. Yet, the learner did not take the liberty to do so, since she said the guidelines were to enter alternatives or to leave the field blank if she had no clue how to edit the incorrect sequence. In this case, the learner did not reproduce her original sequence as a form of objection, rather, she left the field blank.

4. Discussion

The aim of this chapter was to address the learners' contribution to dynamic assessment and to investigate how learners responded to assistance when correcting their texts written in the French language. The assistance offered to learners was displayed on request, as opposed to being systematically given with each incorrect form. As Clarebout and Elen (2006) suggested, the use of such tools should presuppose "that learners are good judges of their learning needs" (p390). The results not only show that a large part of annotations (47.01%) were never accessed, but also established that learners' refusal to read feedback was not to be interpreted as a definitive refusal of engagement. Although the feedback was not read, most students tried to correct themselves, suggesting that they were willing to take turns in the interaction process. They proposed replacements to 66.4% of their incorrect forms from which 78.1% were correct. Despite the fact that learners could have rejected the assistance on account of several factors "that play important role in the success of online test", such as user friendliness or interface design (Nordin, Arshad, Razak, & Jusoff, 2010, p. 62), it may equally be the case that if learners did not seek help when proposing alternatives, it was because they did not need it.

Chapter 9

The fact that some learners reproduce their incorrect forms when correcting themselves even after consulting the assistance could be more than just a misunderstanding of the feedback read; learners might have internalised a misconception which could be interpreted as an example of fossilisation (Selinker & Lamendella, 1979). Although the term *fossilisation* is often acknowledged as lacking a unified definition (Han, 2004), it is generally understood as a cessation in language learning, which could be for instance permanent (Selinker & Lamendella, 1981, p. 217), backsliding (Selinker, 1972), or long lasting (Ellis, 1999). Yet, the synchronic analysis undertaken within this study does not allow to confirm whether these incorrect forms rewritten as such were indeed internalised misconceptions. A longitudinal study would be more appropriate to investigate whether language development had stopped.

Since stimulated recalls were not organised after the self-editing task, the reasons for not providing any alternatives when the assistance was not accessed (33.6%) are not straightforward. As a first explanation, it might be the case that learners were more interested by the final correction and decided to skip some of the incorrect forms along with their feedback so as to attain the final level of correction faster. In that case, learners might be characterised as *browsers*; they "browse through the exercises, sometimes requesting the answer without providing any input" (Heift, 2002, p. 301). Secondly, given the fact that a comprehensive error annotation was adopted, learners may have felt overwhelmed by the amount of highlighted incorrect forms to be corrected (Ferris, 2002), and thus decided to skip some of them in order to lighten the burden of correcting themselves. Finally, learners may have thought that they would not be able to self-edit a particular incorrect form even with feedback, so there were no point in reading the assistance.

In addition to focusing on learners' refusal of assistance, this chapter investigated the extent to which learners accepted and negotiated help. Generally, alternatives were proposed after learners accessed the assistance (75.6%). Reasons for which the learners left the field blank after reading the feedback might be that they did not understand the message, or that the message was not adapted to their incorrect forms, or simply that they did not know how to correct themselves even after being provided with help. Furthermore, not entering alternatives after reading the feedback has been shown to be a form of negotiation with learner #14. She would have argued the content of the message at the time of the self-editing task, but did not as the guidelines were to enter an alternative only if she knew one. This example of negotiation cannot be generalised but it certainly opens the door to the possibility of integrating learner's interactions as opposed to interventions in computer-based dynamic assessment targeting written language.

5. Limitations and future work

While learners provided an alternative for most of the incorrect forms for which they read the feedback, a probable explanation of not suggesting any replacement after accessing assistance could be due to a misunderstanding of the message read. Given that learners seemed to be familiar with the linguistic terms when addressing them orally in class, and given that most of the participants had an introductory course in linguistics, it was assumed that they would understand the terminology used. Yet, they seemed to have experienced difficulties in comprehending certain meta-linguistic feedback. Student #7, for instance, wrote the following words in the wrong order *je suis enregistrée me*; the correct formulation would be *je me suis enregistrée (I have signed up)*. The learner edited herself at level one without assistance and at level two without reading the error type, which indicates that she had a good sense of how to make it correct. After reading the meta-linguistic feedback for 15 seconds at level three, she was not able to provide a correct alternative. Learners' ability to interpret the message might have been overestimated in some occasions, as it seems some of them may have struggled with terms describing specific aspects of the language, such as *auxiliary* or *direct object*. Lee (1997) finds that teachers often used "a wider range of metalinguistic terms than students could understand" (p. 471). Consequently, future research should adjust more precisely the level of meta-linguistic annotation to each individual so as to ensure a proper understanding of the feedback itself.

From a human-computer interaction perspective, Bahr and Ford (2011) very recently have established that pop-up windows might be "annoying and frustrating" for participants (p. 781). As a result, it may be relevant to investigate other means of dispensing feedback when implementing computer-based language learning (CALL) applications, and more specifically computer-based dynamic assessment, so as to ensure a more sustained engagement from learners. As noted by Heift (2010), "even the best team of CALL software designers cannot always anticipate the ways in which learners will use a CALL system" (p. 445). Identifying learners' behaviour with regard to refusal or acceptance of feedback may assist students and teachers alike in reframing the type of assistance that is required in order for learners to self-edit their incorrect forms.

Continuing on from this research, and taking a pedagogical perspective into account, future research should be directed towards the self-editing task, where it was demonstrated that the mediation may have in some occasions not been adapted to the learners' need or comprehension. As Poehner (2005) noted, the advantage of dynamic assessment "lies in the timeliness of the mediation" (p. 148), which is not without challenges when the assistance is provided through the means of a computer-based dynamic assessment application. A future and extremely ambitious direction may include research at the level of negotiated interactions, as opposed to interventions, between a computer and a learner.

References

Ableeva, R. (2008). *Listening comprehension in foreign language instruction. (CALPER professional development document 0810)*. University Park, PA: Center for Advanced Language Proficiency Education and Research Publications. Retrieved from http://calper.la.psu.edu/publication.php?page=pdd6

Aljaafreh, A., & Lantolf, J. P. (1994). Negative feedback as regulation and second language learning in the zone of proximal development. *The Modern Language Journal, 78*(4), 465-483. doi:10.2307/328585

Antón, M. (2009). Dynamic assessment of advanced second language learners. *Foreign Language Annals, 42*(3), 576-598. doi:10.1111/j.1944-9720.2009.01030.x

Bahr, G. S., & Ford, R. A. (2011). How and why pop-ups don't work: pop-up prompted eye movements, user affect and decision making. *Computers in Human Behavior, 27*(2), 776-783. doi:10.1016/j.chb.2010.10.030

Clarebout, G., & Elen, J. (2006). Tool use in computer-based learning environments: towards a research framework. *Computers in Human Behavior, 22*(3), 389-411. doi:10.1016/j.chb.2004.09.007

Daniel, M. H. (1997). Intelligence testing: status and trends. *American Psychologist, 52*(10), 1038-1045. doi:10.1037/0003-066X.52.10.1038

Ellis, R. (1999). Item versus system learning: explaining free variation. *Applied Linguistics, 20*(4), 460-480. doi:10.1093/applin/20.4.460

Erben, T., Ban, R., & Summers, R. (2008). Changing examination structures within a college of education: the application of dynamic assessment in pre-service ESOL endorsement courses in Florida. In J. P. Lantolf & M. E. Poehner (Eds.), *Sociocultural theory and the teaching of second languages* (pp. 87-114). London: Equinox Publishing Ltd.

Ferris, D. R. (2002). *Treatment of error in second language student writing.* Ann Harbour: University of Michigan Press.

Feuerstein, R., Rand, Y., & Hoffman, M. B. (1979). *The dynamic assessment of retarded performers: the learning potential assessment device, theory, instruments, and techniques.* Baltimore: University Park Press.

Fischer, R. (2007). How do we know what students are actually doing? Monitoring students' behavior in CALL. *Computer Assisted Language Learning, 20*(5), 409-442. doi:10.1080/09588220701746013

Granger, S. (2003). Error-tagged learner corpora and CALL: a promising synergy. *CALICO Journal, 20(3),* 465-480. Retrieved from https://calico.org/html/article_289.pdf

Han, Z. (2004). *Fossilization in adult second language acquisition.* Clevedon, England: Multilingual Matters.

Heift, T. (2002). Learner control and error correction in ICALL: browsers, peekers, and adamants. *CALICO Journal, 19*(2), 295-313. Retrieved from https://calico.org/html/article_428.pdf

Heift, T. (2010). Developing an intelligent language tutor. *CALICO Journal, 27*(3), 443-459. Retrieved from https://calico.org/page.php?id=5

L'Haire, S. (2007). FipsOrtho: a spell checker for learners of French. *ReCALL, 19*(2), 137-161. doi:10.1017/S0958344007000420

Lantolf, J. P. (2009). Dynamic assessment: the dialectic integration of instruction and assessment. *Language Teaching, 42*(3), 355-368. doi:10.1017/S0261444808005569

Lantolf, J. P., & Poehner, M. E. (2004). Dynamic assessment of L2 development: bringing the past into the future. *Journal of Applied Linguistics, 1*(1), 49. doi:10.1558/japl.1.1.49.55872

Lee, I. (1997). ESL learners' performance in error correction in writing: some implications for teaching. *System, 25*(4), 465-477. doi:10.1016/S0346-251X(97)00045-6

Mackey, A., Gass, S., & McDonough, K. (2000). How do learners perceive interactional feedback? *Studies in Second Language Acquisition, 22*(4), 471-497.

Mathews, W. M. (1961). Study of the abnormal child: special session, 1960 (President W. Mason Mathews, Chairman, introducing Professor Alexander Romanovich Luria). *American Journal of Orthopsychiatry, 31*(1), 1–16. doi:10.1111/j.1939-0025.1961.tb02104.x

Navarro, E., & Calero, M. D. (2009). Estimation of cognitive plasticity in old adults using dynamic assessment techniques. *Journal of Cognitive Education and Psychology, 8*(1), 38-51.

Nordin, N. M., Arshad, S. R., Razak, N. A., & Jusoff, K. (2010). The Validation and development of electronic language test. *Studies in Literature and Language, 1*(1), 62-68. Retrieved from http://www.cscanada.net/index.php/sll/article/download/1242/1934

Poehner, M. E. (2005). *Dynamic assessment of oral proficiency among advanced L2 learners of French.* Doctor of Philosophy. The Pennsylvania State University, State College.

Poehner, M. E. (2008). *Dynamic assessment: a Vygotskian approach to understanding and promoting L2 development.* Milton Keynes: Springer.

Selinker, L. (1972). Interlanguage. *IRAL - International Review of Applied Linguistics in Language Teaching, 10*(3), 209-232.

Selinker, L., & Lamendella, J. T. (1979). The role of extrinsic feedback in interlanguage fossilization. *Language Learning, 29*(2), 363-376. doi:10.1111/j.1467-1770.1979.tb01075.x

Selinker, L., & Lamendella, J. T. (1981). Updating the interlanguage hypothesis. *Studies in Second Language Acquisition, 3*(2), 201-220. doi:10.1017/S0272263100004186

Skinner, B., & Madden, M. C. (2010). Help seeking in English language learning. *ELT Journal, 64*(1), 21-31. doi:10.1093/elt/ccp019

Thouësny, S. (in progress). *Modeling second language learners' interlanguage and its variability: a computer-based dynamic assessment approach to distinguishing between errors and mistakes.* Ph.D. Dublin City University, Dublin.

Van der Aalsvoort, G. M., & Lidz, C. S. (2002). Reciprocity in dynamic assessment in classrooms: taking contextual influences on individual learning into account. In G. M. Van der Aalsvoort, W. C. M. Riesing, & A. J. J. M. Ruijssenaars (Eds.), *Learning potential assessment and cognitive training* (pp. 111-146). Amsterdam: Elsevier.

Warschauer, M. (2010). Invited commentary: new tools for teaching writing. *Language Learning & Technology, 14*(1), 3-8. Retrieved from http://llt.msu.edu/vol14num1/commentary.pdf

Ziefle, M. (1998). Effects of display resolution on visual performance. *Human Factors, 40*(4), 554-568. doi:10.1518/001872098779649355

Computer-Mediated Negotiated Interactions: How is Meaning Negotiated in Discussion Boards, Text Chat and Videoconferencing?

Cédric Sarré*

Abstract

Despite the amount of published research on the use of text-based computer-mediated communication (CMC) in second language acquisition (SLA), very little attention has been paid to voice-based CMC (audioconferencing and videoconferencing) and to how it compares with the better known text-based CMC modes. This chapter investigates and compares the potential of three different CMC modes (discussion board, text chat and videoconferencing) to foster negotiated interactions (negotiation of meaning routines and negative feedback), as well as the influence of task type on such interactions. From the analysis of the interactions generated by the completion of meaning-focused tasks as part of an online module of English for specific purposes (ESP) aimed at first year Master's Degree Biology students (French non native speakers (NNSs) of English), this study demonstrates that closed tasks fostered more negotiation work than open tasks, and that all three CMC modes gave rise to negotiation of meaning. However, significant differences were highlighted between the three CMC modes under study: overall, videoconferencing was conducive to a lot more negotiation of meaning than the other two CMC modes, and discussion board interactions did not generate any corrective feedback.

Keywords: negotiation of meaning, negative feedback, CMC, text chat, discussion board, videoconferencing, meaning-focused tasks.

*Centre Interdisciplinaire de Recherche sur les Mobilités (CIRTAI). Université du Havre, France. Laboratoire Ligérien de Linguistique (LLL). Université d'Orléans, France. e-mail: cedric.sarre@univ-orleans.fr

How to cite this chapter: Sarré, C. (2011). Computer-mediated negotiated interactions: how is meaning negotiated in discussion boards, text chat and videoconferencing? In S. Thouësny & L. Bradley (Eds.), *Second language teaching and learning with technology: views of emergent researchers* (pp. 189-210). Dublin: Research-publishing.net.

Chapter 10

1. Introduction

As was noted by Henri and Lundgren-Cayrol (2001), distance learning courses are often limited to individual learning situations and therefore lacking in connectivity between learners (p. 5). This criticism has, however, slowly been tackled by the growing use of information and communication technology (ICT) to enable such interactions to take place in what has become known as computer-mediated communication. CMC encompasses a wide range of activities such as sending e-mails, posting topics on a discussion board, chatting or talking to someone on the internet, and can thus be either synchronous (taking place in real time) or asynchronous, text-based (when communication occurs through the written medium) or voice-based, and one-to-one (one person communicates with another person) or one-to-many. Since the early 1990s, growing interest has been shown in CMC for language learning and teaching in the field of second language acquisition, which has now become a field of research in itself known as network-based language teaching (NBLT). Indeed, as CMC supports interaction, it has potential for interlanguage development (Kelm, 1996). If most published research in the field of NBLT originally dealt with the use of discussion boards, more varied modes of CMC for language learning and teaching are now being investigated, even though text-based CMC (especially text chat) still prevails. Research on voice-based CMC for language learning, however, remains confidential. The aim of this chapter is to fill part of this gap by examining the impact three different CMC modes (discussion board, text chat and desktop videoconferencing) can have on the type of interaction learners engage in, as interaction is believed to be beneficial to interlanguage development.

1.1. Interaction in SLA

The potential of interaction to interlanguage development has given rise to much published research (Gass, 1997; Gass, Mackey, & Pica, 1998; Long, 1983, 1996; Pica, 1994; Py, 1990). Building on Krashen's (1981) input hypothesis, which claims that learners acquire a second language (L2) when they are able to understand the input they are exposed to, these researchers put forward the idea that interaction can be considered as an essential source of comprehensible input. However,

Long's (1983) interaction hypothesis takes Krashen's (1981) theory one step further as it states that exposure to comprehensible input is not enough to ensure acquisition and that it should be complemented by social interaction. Indeed, Long (1983) considers interaction between learners as the best type of input for language acquisition as it gives learners exposure to more accessible input thanks to all the adjustments their interlocutors are able to make on their request. In this way, a more competent speaker will be able to provide a more comprehensible input to his less competent interlocutor and thus help their interlanguage develop. These adjustments to the interaction, which occur whenever one of the interlocutors experiences problems to understand what is being said and which increase input comprehensibility, are termed negotiation of meaning (Pica, 1994).

1.2. Negotiation of meaning

Negotiation of meaning is claimed to play an important part in SLA as it is supposed to offer a connection between input, internal learner capacities and output in productive ways (Long, 1996). In other words, being engaged in interpersonal interaction during which comprehension problems that can be negotiated arise supports acquisition (Ellis, 1999, p. 4). Pica (1994) showed that negotiation routines give rise to a lot more input modification than any other part of the interaction between learners. The first attempt at modeling negotiation routines was made by Varonis and Gass (1985) who designed a four-phase model: first, a trigger (which can be lexis-based, grammar-based, syntax-based or content-based) sets off the negotiation routine. Phase two consists of a signal from the interlocutor aimed at showing their non-comprehension. This signal can take the form of a clarification request, a confirmation check or a comprehension check (Long, 1983). The next phase is the response to the signal, which can be a self-repetition, a paraphrase or an incorporation (Long, 1983). The last phase –which is optional– is the reaction to the response given, its objective being to signal the end of the negotiation routine and to show that the interactants are ready to resume their conversation.

In addition to his original theory, Long (1996) later claimed that negotiation of meaning can also contribute to L2 acquisition through negative feedback:

this form of corrective feedback that learners receive from their interlocutors, and the opportunities to repair their own utterances that stem from it, are also suggested to be facilitative to interlanguage development. Negative feedback can either be explicit (explicit correction by the interlocutor, question asked by the interlocutor to prompt correction) or implicit (recast, i.e., implicit correction of the speaker's utterance by repeating it in its correct form), and can also give rise to self-correction. It is beneficial to L2 acquisition as it encourages learners to focus on form while completing a learning task.

1.3. Focus on form and meaning-focused tasks

Long (1983) emphasises the importance for learners to focus on form while they are processing meaning, which is one of the possible outcomes of negotiation of meaning as learners' attention can temporarily shift from meaning to form as comprehension problems arise (Long & Robinson, 1998). Focus on form through negotiation of meaning occurs during the completion of a meaning-focused task as negotiation of meaning and modified output are claimed to be more prevalent in goal-oriented tasks than in casual conversation (Pellettieri, 2000). According to Ellis' (2003) typology, tasks can be either open or closed. Open tasks include opinion gap tasks, a good example of which could be a debate. Problem-solving tasks can be either open or closed tasks, depending on how contrived they are. Following Pica, Kanagy and Falodun (1993) who claimed that closed tasks are likely to give rise to more negotiation of meaning, Pellettieri (2000) thus recommends to set up goal-oriented tasks with a limited number of possible outcomes to encourage negotiation of meaning.

1.4. Research questions

This chapter is based on previously published research on negotiated interaction through CMC and aims at exploring potential differences and similarities in the use of negotiation of meaning routines and negative feedback between three modes of CMC: asynchronous text-based CMC (discussion board), synchronous text-based CMC (chat) and synchronous voice-based CMC (desktop videoconferencing). It reports on a study we carried out as part of an action-research project whose starting point was a problem identified in the field: the interactional competence –which we see as the "fifth element", following Kramsch (1986) and He and Young (1998)– in English of a group of French Master's degree students specialising in biology was considered to be under-developed compared to the other four skills (written and oral comprehension, written and oral production). Consequently, the solution envisaged was to set up an online English for specific purposes course following the action-oriented approach encouraged by the Common European Framework (CEF) for languages and thus promoting interactions (more appropriately termed "co-actions" in Puren, 2002) between learners. This was thought to be a way of giving learners more opportunities to interact in English about subject-specific topics outside the English classroom. Indeed, the main objective of the course was to help students develop their interactional competence through computer-mediated collaborative work, with the technical support of the experimental virtual learning environment called CLADUO (Centre de Langues A Distance de l'Université d'Orléans). Negotiation of meaning is an important component of interactional competence (Kramsch, 1986) and was thus the focus of part of our research project. This chapter aims at answering the following research questions:

1. Does negotiation of meaning take place in all three CMC modes?

2. Which types of negotiation of meaning occur in the three different CMC modes?

3. Which types of negotiation of meaning occur during completion of the two different task types?

2. Method

2.1. Context of the study

This study was conducted in 2008 with a whole class of first year Master's degree students specialising in biology at a French university (Université d'Orléans).

As part of their course requirements, all students had to follow a 55h English class consisting of:

- 24h-face-to-face class aiming at developing their skills in oral scientific English with a view to making subject-specific presentations in English;

- 6h mini-conference during which all students had to present a paper in English based on a review article;

- 25h English module online (estimated time) following the CEF's action-oriented approach aiming at developing all five skills, with a strong emphasis on collaborative work and interactional competence development.

All three elements of the class were assessed on a continuous assessment basis. This chapter only reports on the research carried out about the online part of the class.

2.2. Participants

Between January and April 2008, 15 groups of four non native speakers of English took part in the class. They were all biology majors enrolled on a Master's degree programme. Prior to their participation in the English class, a computerised test in English was administered to all students using DIALANG, a language diagnosis system developed by several European higher education institutions and based on the CEF's common levels (A1 to C2). In written comprehension, over a third of the students were assessed at levels A (A1: 7%, A2: 29%), over half were B levels (B1: 33% and B2: 23%), and the remaining 8% were C levels (C1: 7% and C2: 1%). As for listening comprehension results, they showed that just under three quarters of the students were levels A (A1: 39% and A2: 33%), while the other quarter was mostly B levels (B1: 20%, B2: 5%). As they were clearly more discriminating than the reading comprehension results, the listening comprehension results of the test were used to organise students in mixed-ability groups of four students with a view to ensuring that less competent students would make the most of peer scaffolding, hence setting the stage for potential negotiated interactions.

The students were split into three meta-groups according to the CMC mode they had to use to complete the collaborative tasks: a chat group, a videoconferencing group and a discussion board group. Four groups of four students were assigned to each meta-group (that is 16 students for each CMC mode), which makes a total of 48 participants.

2.3. Tasks

The online part of the class was organised around five different subject-specific scenarios (as shown in Table 1) whose main characteristics were as follows:

- they were composed of several macro-tasks (corresponding to Ellis's (2003) definition of tasks as "real-world activities", that is meaning-focused tasks) and micro-tasks (as termed by Guichon (2006) and described by Bertin, Gravé and Narcy-Combes (2010) as language-oriented tasks meant to fill language and communication gaps, that is, form-focused tasks);

- learners were put in realistic situations and were given a main mission to complete;

- the outcome of each scenario was a written language product that all the previous micro-tasks were geared towards completing;

- the different tasks were either individual or collaborative (though the final written production was always an individual task);

- the different tasks were organised in six parts: background and objectives, getting started, reading time, listening time, sharing time and writing time;

- the input (written and oral) that was provided to learners was progressively more complex throughout the different scenarios, as was the type of written production they were expected to complete;

- two types of collaborative tasks were set up: problem-solving (with a limited number of possible solutions) and opinion gap tasks (with more possible outcomes); all collaborative tasks were meaning-focused.

Table 1. Scenario characteristics

	Scenario 1	Scenario 2	Scenario 3	Scenario 4	Scenario 5
Topic	Studies and careers in biological sciences	Safety in the biology lab	The genetics of cancer	Phytore-mediation	GM food
Written input	Text from the American ministry of labor	Scientific article	Biology university textbook	Scientific article	Scientific abstracts from different articles
Oral input	Interviews of biological scientists	Specialised video	Specialised video	Specialised video	Conference presentation extract
Collaborative task 1	Opinion gap (CT1)	Individual	Opinion gap (CT4)	Opinion gap (CT6)	Opinion gap (CT8)
Collaborative task 2	Decision-making (CT2)	Problem-solving (CT3)	Decision-making (CT5)	Problem-solving (CT7)	Decision-making (CT9)
Outcome (written language product)	A brochure	A poster	Course material	A guide for the general public	A brochure

2.4. Equipment and materials

The online module was based on the technical support of Dokeos, a courseware management system (CMS) which was carefully selected after assessing over 40 different open-source CMSs (Sarré, 2008). The virtual learning environment thus set up included, among other tools, a chat tool and a discussion board. As no desktop videoconferencing tool was included in the CMS, an external application (Flashmeeting, developed for the British Open University by the Knowledge Media Institute (KMI)) was also selected to complement existing CMC tools. For research and feedback purposes, all three CMC tools made it possible for the tutor to have access to learners' interactions after they had taken place, which is fairly standard in the case of discussion boards, but not so much so for the other two modes of CMC (the chat tool automatically created a log file of the interactions, and Flashmeeting automatically recorded the videoconferencing sessions which could then be played back using the integrated playback function). The videoconferencing sessions then had to be recorded using Camstudio, open-source screen recording software, which captured the sessions in a video file (avi) for easier data processing. All tools were internet-based and did not require any set up procedure by students as most of them are JAVA applications.

2.5. Procedure

All 12 groups had to complete the five scenarios over a ten-week period, each scenario needing to be completed in no more than two weeks. The six collaborative tasks (three open tasks: CT4, CT6 and CT8, and three closed tasks: CT3, CT5 and CT7) gave rise to interactions in all 12 groups. It was decided not to use data from the first scenario in order to give students time to adapt to the virtual learning environment and format of the scenarios. No instruction was given as to how long interactions had to be, the main objective being to complete the task effectively (although videoconferencing sessions were limited to 30 minutes each).

The data collected included 24 chat log files (text files), 24 discussion board files (the discussions were copied from the webpage and pasted in a text file) and 24 video files (corresponding to the 24 videoconferencing sessions). The video files were transcribed, time-aligned and annotated using EXMARaLDA Partitur Editor, a tool originally designed for the transcription and annotation of spoken language. What makes EXMARaLDA different from most other transcription tools is that it can also be used for the annotation of written language (imported from text files), thus making it possible to research different data types with the same tool. Chat log files and discussion board files were also imported in EXMARaLDA Partitur Editor and annotated.

Following Long (1983), Varonis and Gass (1985) and Pellettieri (2000), negotiation routines were annotated as shown in Table 2.

Chapter 10

Table 2. Annotation of negotiation routines

Phase	Tag	Description
TRIGGER	TLEX	Lexical trigger
	TSYNT	Syntactic trigger
	TCONT	Content-related trigger
SIGNAL	SCR	Clarification request *(What does that mean?)*
	SCC	Confirmation check *(Did you mean that…?)*
	SST	Statement of non-understanding *(I didn't get that.)*
RESPONSE	RMIN	Minimal response *(Yes/No.)*
	RSR	Self-repetition
	RPAR	Paraphrase *(with lexical elaboration)*
	RSC	Self-correction
	RCOMPC	Comprehension check *(Is it ok?)*
REACTION	REAC	Reaction to response

Following the annotation scheme, all negotiation work was annotated on a specific speaker-dependent tier (coded [NOM] for Negotiation Of Meaning), while a separate speaker-dependent tier was devoted to the verbal data itself (coded [v]), as shown in Figure 1.

Figure 1. Example of annotated data

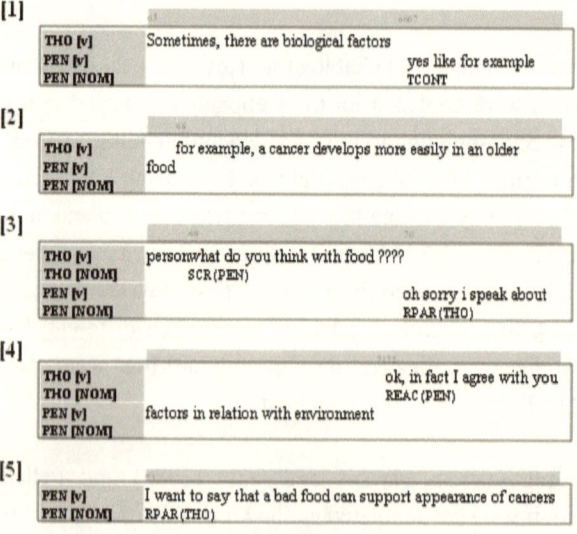

As for negative feedback (Long, 1996), it was annotated using the scheme shown in Table 3.

Table 3. Annotation of negative feedback

Tag	Description
EXCO	**Explicit correction:** The interlocutor explicitly corrects the speaker's mistake *(It's not X, it's Y.)*.
QUES	**Question:** The interlocutor prompts the speaker to self-correct with a question *(Could you say that again?)*.
RECA	**Recast:** The interlocutor corrects the speaker's mistake by repeating the utterance in its correct form.
INC	**Incorporation:** The speaker repeats his/her utterance in its correct form following interlocutor's feedback.
SELCO	**Self-correction:** The speaker corrects his/her own mistakes without prompting from his/her interlocutor.

All negotiation of meaning routines and negative feedback were annotated on a speaker-assigned tier that was separate to the orthographic transcription tier. EXAKT, EXMARaLDA's analysis and concordancing tool, was then used to count and analyse tagged negotiation work and negative feedback.

3. Results and discussion

3.1. Global results

The very first conclusion that can be drawn from the analysis of the data collected is the fact that the completion of meaning-focused tasks through computer-mediated communication does foster negotiated interactions. This result is evidenced in Table 4 and Table 5, and is in line with previous studies on text chat (Pellettieri, 2000; Shekary & Tahririan, 2006; Smith, 2003), on audioconferencing (Jepson, 2005) and, more recently, on videoconferencing (Zhao & Angelova, 2010). No such study has been found on discussion boards.

Table 4. Negotiation of meaning routines

Phase	Tag	Number
TRIGGER	TLEX	13
	TSYNT	7
	TCONT	30
	TOTAL	50
SIGNAL	SCR	15
	SCC	15
	SST	28
	TOTAL	58
RESPONSE	RMIN	0
	RSR	5
	RPAR	34
	RSC	3
	RCOMPC	3
	TOTAL	45
REACTION	REAC	17

Our data shows that most negotiation routines were triggered by content-related problems (30 such triggers were counted), while very few were triggered by syntactic problems (7 in total), which can be explained by the fact that syntax has a low communicative load and thus does not foster much negotiation (Pellettieri, 2000). It should also be noted that lexical triggers, which seem to be the main cause of negotiation routines in text chat (Pellettieri, 2000), were present but not as the main type of trigger in our mixed-CMC-mode data. However, the variety of trigger types tends to show that learners engaged in negotiation work on both form (lexis, syntax) and meaning (content), as illustrated in examples 1 to 3 (Table 5 below). It should be noted that triggers were always clearly identified as being either lexical, syntactic or content-related. Although combined trigger types (i.e., a lexical trigger combined with a syntactic trigger, for example) would not be a problem in the annotation process, no such combined triggers were found in our data.

Example 1, in Table 5, shows a lexical trigger (the word *greenhouse*), followed by a clarification request from the interlocutor (FAN, on lines 6 and 7), the response to which is a paraphrase that explains what a greenhouse is (CAR, on lines 10 and

11). In example 2, it seems to be CHR's syntactically deficient sentence (line 3) which calls for a non-understanding signal from her interlocutor (CAR, on lines 6 and 7), who then repeats her question and self-corrects her mistake (line 10). In example 3, LAU signals her non-understanding with a clarification request (on lines 5 and 6), but the problem cannot be attributed to either lexis, or syntax. This time, the trigger is content-related, as LAU does not understand why MAM thinks that the biosafety level of the laboratory they are carrying out their training period in should be reassessed in the near future. MAM then explains (on lines 7 to 11) that a recent incident that occurred in the lab (a man walking in a corridor carrying dangerous cell cultures with no specific protection dropped them on the floor and sprayed them onto someone who happened to be in the corridor at that time) is the reason why she thinks the biosafety level should be reassessed. LAU then reacts to the response and shows comprehension.

Table 5. Examples 1, 2 and 3

	Example 1: TLEX		Example 2: TSYNT		Example 3: TCONT
1	CAR: Euh, moreover we	1	CHR: The last question	1	MAM: So, in a few months,
2	have to play safe and euh	2	is what do you think can	2	we will determine a new
3	perhaps build a greenhouse	3	be done the correct racial	3	biosafety level. Do you
4	in order to suppress the risk	4	disparity in the survival	4	agree?
5	of contamination by plants.	5	and treatment of cancer?	5	LAU: Can you explain,
6	FAN: Sorry, CAR, could	6	CAR: Sorry CHR, could	6	please?
7	you repeat please?	7	you repeat?	7	MAM: Yes, a mistake like
8	CAR: I said that euh we	8	CHR: Yes euh, what do	8	this should not occur. When
9	should perhaps build a	9	you think can be done	9	a man walks in a corridor
10	greenhouse. Euh it's a place	10	the = to correct racial	10	with dangerous cultures, I
11	where we put plants.	11	disparity in the survival	11	think there is a big problem.
		12	and treatment of cancer?	12	LAU: Ah, yes, OK, I
				13	understand.

Concerning the nature of signals, our data demonstrates that all three types were used by learners, the most commonly used one being statements of non-understanding (SST). Confirmation checks (SCC) and clarification requests (SCR, as illustrated in examples 1 to 3) were equally used. It should be noted that the difference between the number of signals and the number of triggers (there are more signals than triggers) can be accounted for by the fact that different signals can be attributed to the same trigger (Table 6, example 4) and that signals produced by different speakers can also be attributed to the same trigger (Table 6, example 5).

Table 6. Examples 4 and 5

Example 4	Example 5
1 FAN: So, let's continue with the 2 last question. What measures 3 should be taken on a long term 4 basis? 5 LAU: Euh, in fact I don't really 6 understand the question. Can you 7 help me? It seems that we have to 8 take measures to avoid this 9 problem in the future?	1 CHR: Yes, euh, what do you think 2 can be done the = to correct racial 3 disparity in the survival and 4 treatment of cancer? 5 LAU: Euh, for me, euh. I don't know 6 what to say about that because in fact 7 I don't really understand the 8 problem. So, I don't know. 9 CHR: Yes, I totally agree with you. 10 I don't understand too.

In example 4, LAU signals her non-understanding by successively using a statement (on lines 5 and 6), a clarification request (on lines 6 and 7) and a confirmation check (on lines 7 to 9). In example 5, we can see that the same content-based trigger (the question asked by CHR on lines 1 to 4) can give rise to signals from both LAU, who uses a statement on lines 7 and 8, and CHR herself, who also uses a statement (line 10).

As for responses to signals, they are mainly paraphrases (34 such responses were used), as illustrated in example 1 above. Very few self-repetitions, self-corrections (as illustrated in example 2 above) and comprehension checks were found in our data. Occurrences of negative feedback were more modest, as shown in Table 7, with the exception of unprompted self-corrections (SELCO).

Table 7. Negative feedback

Tag	Number
EXCO	1
QUES	0
RECA	6
INC	0
SELCO	112
TOTAL	119

Table 8 shows that only one occurrence of explicit correction was noted (example 6), very few recasts (example 7) were produced (6 in total), and no incorporation could be found, while over a hundred self-corrections occurred (example 8).

In addition, no occurrence of question was noted: this can be explained by the very pedagogical nature of such feedback which is not naturally used by NNSs communicating with each other (Long & Sato, 1983).

Table 8. Examples 6, 7 and 8

Example 6: EXCO		Example 7: RECA		Example 8: SELCO	
1	NAB: Euh, it's good to	1	GAE: Moreover, we need	1	LAU: I agree with you.
2	think to ameliorate always	2	a washer and bottled	2	Cancer begin by qualitative
3	boats and euh maritime	3	water because imagine if	3	and quantitative
4	transport in order to evitate	4	a solution arrives in your	4	modifications of genes.
5	euh...	5	eyes. Euh, it's very	5	Sorry, cancer begins.
6	NAO: Euh, excuse me. It's	6	dangerous.		
7	not ameliorate but improve	7	NEL: Euh, GAE, it's true		
8	and not evitate but to avoid.	8	that an eyewash or a		
		9	shower would be a first		
		10	step.		

In example 6, NAO explicitly corrects NAB's mistakes (on lines 6 to 8), whereas in example 7, NEL implicitly corrects GAE's utterances with a recast of the word *eyewash* (on line 8) inappropriately called a *washer* by GAE on line 2. Example 8 shows LAU self-correcting a grammar mistake (on line 5) without any prompting from her interlocutors. Generally speaking, we can say that the more explicit the correction technique is, the more threatening for the speaker's face it becomes: learners thus prefer to use self-initiated, self-completed repairs because they are less face-threatening acts than explicit repairs of an interlocutor's utterances (Schegloff, Jefferson, & Sacks, 1977).

3.2. Results per task type

The distribution of negotiation routines and negative feedback among the two different task types is clearly irregular, as shown in Table 9 below. With the exception of the optional phase (phase 4 – Reaction to response), negotiation routine phases are consistently more numerous in interactions produced during the completion of closed tasks, the total number of all four phases being 50% higher in such tasks than in open tasks. The same conclusion can be drawn from the analysis of the distribution of negative feedback: all three types of negative feedback are consistently more numerous during the completion of closed

Chapter 10

tasks than that of open tasks. These results corroborate findings from previous research both in traditional settings (Pica et al., 1993) and network-based settings (Pellettieri, 2000): meaning-focused closed tasks, namely tasks with a limited number of possible outcomes, completed through CMC are conducive to a lot more negotiation of meaning and corrective feedback than open tasks. Research question number three has thus been answered.

Table 9. Negotiation routines and negative feedback per task type

	Type	Open tasks	Closed tasks
NEGOTIATION ROUTINES	Trigger	19	31
	Signal	22	36
	Response	17	28
	Reaction	10	7
	TOTAL	68	102
NEGATIVE FEEDBACK	Explicit correction	0	1
	Recast	2	4
	Self-correction	51	61
	TOTAL	53	66

3.3. Results per CMC mode

The analysis of the distribution of negotiation routines among the three CMC modes under study shows significant differences, as displayed in Table 10. As the amount of output produced during interaction was considerably different between the three modes (both in total number of words and in number of turns), the proportion of negotiated turns has been calculated and included in the table, in addition to raw numbers, for the sake of comparison. These results are in line with Zhao and Angelova's (2010) recent findings: overall, videoconferencing was conducive to a lot more negotiation of meaning than text chat. However, despite the low raw number of negotiation phases found in discussion boards, the proportion of negotiated turns in discussion board interactions is also superior to that found in text chat. Still, the small raw number of routine phases generated in discussion board interactions is probably due to their asynchronous nature, which means that a reply can occur several days after the original post was first written, thus not really encouraging question/answer moves as they could take a long time to be completed.

Table 10. Negotiation routines per CMC mode

Phase	Tag	Text chat		Videoconferencing		Discussion board	
		Number	% of turns	Number	% of turns	Number	% of turns
Trigger	TLEX	3	0,1%	9	1%	1	0,5%
	TSYNT	0	-	6	0,6%	1	0,5%
	TCONT	12	0,5%	16	1,8%	2	0,9%
	TOTAL	15	0,6%	31	3,4%	4	1,9%
Signal	SCR	8	0,3%	4	0,4%	3	1,5%
	SCC	3	0,1%	10	1,1%	2	0,9%
	SST	6	0,3%	21	2,3%	1	0,5%
	TOTAL	17	0,7%	35	3,8%	6	2,9%
Re-sponse	RSR	0	-	5	0,5%	0	-
	RPAR	12	0,5%	18	2%	4	1,9%
	RSC	2	0,1%	1	0,1%	0	-
	RCOM-PC	0	-	3	0,3%	0	-
	TOTAL	14	0,6%	27	2,9%	4	1,9%
Reaction	REAC	8	0,3%	9	1%	0	-

If we now take a closer look at the nature of the triggers, we can see that no syntactic trigger was found in text chat: this can be explained by the fact that text chat interaction generates shorter turns (9 words per turn on average, versus 55 for videoconferencing sessions and 130 for discussion board interactions), which means less complex sentences, thus greatly limiting potential syntactic problems. Content-related triggers were the most numerous trigger types found in our data.

The most widely used signal type in both synchronous CMC modes is statements of non-understanding: this could be explained by the fact that statements are less syntactically complex (i.e., easier to formulate for NNSs) than both other types (clarification requests and comprehension checks) which are questions, thus considered to be more difficult to formulate on the spot by many learners. Not surprisingly though, this is not the case in discussion board interactions which generate more clarification requests and comprehension checks than statements. This could be due to the fact that asynchronous contributions can be more easily thought out, making it easier for learners to produce more complex utterances.

A closer analysis of response types shows that self-repetitions (RSR) and comprehension checks (RCOMPC) are absent from both text chat and discussion board interactions, but not from videoconferencing sessions, which is consistent with Jepson's (2005) findings about audioconference and text chat. Self-repetition seems fairly unnecessary in text chat and discussion board interactions since interactants still have access to their interlocutors' previous contributions, which could explain why no such response could be found in these two CMC modes. As for comprehension checks, they are sometimes considered to be too pedagogical (Long & Sato, 1983) to be used naturally by learners. Finally, the most widely used response type is paraphrases, possibly because this is seen as being the most effective way of making oneself understood.

The distribution of negative feedback among the three CMC modes is displayed in Table 11.

Table 11. Negative feedback per CMC mode

Tag	Text chat		Videoconferencing		Discussion board	
	Number	% of turns	Number	% of turns	Number	% of turns
EXCO	0	-	1	0,1%	0	-
RECA	2	0,08%	4	0,4%	0	-
SELCO	59	2,6%	53	5,8%	0	-
TOTAL	61	2,7%	58	6,4%	0	-

As was the case for negotiation routines, videoconferencing generated more negative feedback (in proportion of turns) than the other two CMC modes, even if text chat globally gave rise to more negative feedback in raw number. The fact that more occurrences of self-correction were found in text chat and videoconferencing is not surprising though: due to their asynchronous nature, discussion board interactions can be carefully thought out and checked for language, which is not the case in text chat and videoconferencing sessions. It is thus suggested that the nature itself of discussion board interaction is accountable for the total absence of negative feedback, as synchrony seems to be required to foster all types of negative feedback, namely explicit correction, recasts and self-correction.

4. Conclusion

The analysis of our data has demonstrated that negotiation work occurs using all three CMC modes, thus providing an answer to research question number one. However, it has also shown that the distribution of negotiation routines and negative feedback among these modes is significantly different, thus answering question number two: videoconferencing sessions contained more negotiated turns (negotiation routines and negative feedback) than both text chat and discussion board interactions. In terms of negotiation routines, our data has also demonstrated that discussion board interactions contain a higher proportion of negotiated turns than text chat. Nevertheless, it should also be noted that discussion board interactions generated no negative feedback at all, which counterbalances their superiority in terms of negotiation routines.

From a more qualitative point of view, our study reports differences in the routine and negative feedback types generated with the three different CMC modes. It supports previous research findings about the importance of task type as regards the quantity of negotiation work generated (Pellettieri, 2000): closed tasks were shown to foster more negotiation of meaning (routines and negative feedback) than open tasks.

Our study also contributes to the discussion of the potential benefits of CMC-negotiated interactions to interlanguage development. Although our objective was to better characterise and compare negotiation work in text chat, videoconferencing sessions and discussion board interactions, our results should not be generalised to other settings without great caution as many variables could have influenced our findings. For example, Flashmeeting, the desktop videoconferencing tool used, does not allow for multiple speakers to talk at the same time: a queuing system enabling interactants to ask for the floor has to be used. Our results might have been slightly different if the videoconferencing system had given different speakers the opportunity to talk at the same time, thus making interactions even more synchronous (for those who want the floor but have to wait their turn) than they were with Flashmeeting.

More empirical research is needed to explore the potential of CMC for negotiation of meaning between NNSs, especially the role of videoconferencing, which remains very uncommon in such research, and its potential differences and similarities with audioconferencing (voice chat).

References

Bertin, J.-C., Gravé, P., & Narcy-Combes, J.-P. (2010). *Second-language distance learning and teaching: theoretical perspectives and didactic ergonomics.* Hershey: IGI Global.

Ellis, R. (1999). *Learning a second language through interaction.* Amsterdam: John Benjamins.

Ellis, R. (2003). *Task-based language learning and teaching.* Oxford: Oxford University Press.

Gass, S. M. (1997). *Input, interaction, and the second language learner.* Mahwah: Lawrence Erlbaum Associates.

Gass, S. M., Mackey, A., & Pica, T. (1998). The role of input and interaction in second language acquisition. *The Modern Language Journal, 82*(3), 299-307. Retrieved from http://www.jstor.org/stable/329456

Guichon, N. (2006). *Langues et TICE: méthodologie de conception multimédia.* Paris: Ophrys.

He, A., & Young, R. (1998). Language proficiency interviews: a discourse approach. In R. Young & A. He (Eds.), *Talking and testing: discourse approaches to the assessment of oral proficiency* (pp. 1-24). Amsterdam: John Benjamins.

Henri, F., & Lundgren-Cayrol, K. (2001). *Apprentissage collaboratif à distance.* Sainte Foy: Presses de l'Université du Québec.

Jepson, K. (2005). Conversations – and negotiated interactions – in text and voice chat rooms. *Language Learning & Technology, 9*(3), 79-98. Retrieved from http://llt.msu.edu/vol9num3/pdf/jepson.pdf

Kelm, O. (1996). The application of computer networking in foreign language education: Focusing on principles of second language acquisition. In M. Warschauer (Ed.), *Telecollaboration in Foreign Language Learning* (pp. 19-28). Honolulu: University of Hawai'i Press.

Kramsch, C. (1986). From language proficiency to interactional competence. *The Modern Language Journal, 70*(4), 366-372. Retrieved from http://www.jstor.org/stable/326815

Krashen, S. D. (1981). *Second language acquisition and second language learning*. Oxford: Pergamon.

Long, M. H. (1983). Native speaker/non-native speaker conversation and the negotiation of comprehensible input. *Applied Linguistics*, *4*(2), 126-141. doi:10.1093/applin/4.2.126

Long, M. H. (1996). The role of the linguistic environment in second language acquisition. In W. C. Ritchie & T. K. Bhatia (Eds.), *Handbook of second language acquisition*. San Diego: Academic Press Inc.

Long, M. H., & Robinson, P. (1998). Focus on form: theory, research and practice. In C. Doughty & J. Williams (Eds.), *Focus on form in classroom second language acquisition* (pp. 15-41). Cambridge: Cambridge University Press.

Long, M. H., & Sato, C. J. (1983). Classroom foreigner talk discourse: forms and functions of teachers' questions. In H. W. Seliger & M. H. Long (Eds.), *Classroom-oriented research in second languages* (pp. 268-285). Rowley: Newbury House.

Pellettieri, J. (2000). Negotiation in cyberspace: The role of chatting in the development of grammatical competence. In M. Warschauer & R. Kern (Eds.), *Network-based language teaching: concepts and practice* (pp. 59-86). Cambridge: Cambridge University Press.

Pica, T. (1994). Research on negotiation: what does it reveal about second-language learning conditions, processes, and outcomes? *Language Learning*, *44*(3), 493-527. doi:10.1111/j.1467-1770.1994.tb01115.x

Pica, T., Kanagy, R., & Falodun, J. (1993). Choosing and using communication tasks for second language instruction. In G. Crookes & S. Gass (Eds.), *Tasks and language learning: integrating theory and practice* (pp. 9-34). Clevedon: Multilingual Matters.

Puren, C. (2002). Perspectives actionnelles et perspectives culturelles en didactique des langues-cultures : vers une perspective co-actionnelle-co-culturelle. *Les Langues Modernes*, *96*(3), 55-71.

Py, B. (1990). Les stratégies d'acquisition en situation d'interaction. *Acquisition et utilisation d'une langue étrangère – L'approche cognitive. Le français dans le monde, numéro spécial*, 81-88.

Sarré, C. (2008). Les plates-formes de téléformation dans l'enseignement-apprentissage des langues : pour un choix raisonné. *Les Cahiers de l'APLIUT*, *XXVII*(3), 48-69.

Schegloff, E. A., Jefferson, G., & Sacks, H. (1977). The preference for self-correction in the organization of repair in conversation. *Language*, *53*(2), 361-382. Retrieved from http://www.jstor.org/stable/413107

Shekary, M., & Tahririan, M. H. (2006). Negotiation of meaning and noticing in text-based online chat. *The Modern Language Journal*, *90*(4), 557-573. Retrieved from http://www.jstor.org/stable/4127043

Smith, B. (2003). Computer–mediated negotiated interaction: an expanded model. *The Modern Language Journal*, *87*(1), 38-57. doi:10.1111/1540-4781.00177

Varonis, E. M., & Gass, S. M. (1985). Non-native/non-native conversations: a model for negotiation of meaning. *Applied Linguistics*, *6*(1), 71-90. doi:10.1093/applin/6.1.71

Zhao, Y., & Angelova, M. (2010). Negotiation of meaning between non-native speakers in text-based chat and videoconferencing. *US-China Education Review*, *7*(5), 12-26. Retrieved from http://goo.gl/XmwkZ

Websites

CAMSTUDIO: http://camstudio.org
CLADUO: http://www.departementdeslangues.com/claduo
DIALANG: http://www.dialang.org
DOKEOS: http://www.dokeos.com
EXMARaLDA: http://www.exmaralda.org
FLASHMEETING: http://flashmeeting.open.ac.uk

Name Index

A

Ableeva, Rumia 170, 186
Abrams, Zsuzsana I. 125, 138
Ackermann, Edith 85, 90
Adell, Jordi 17, 27
Alderson, J. Charles 48, 67
Aljaafreh, Ali 173, 186
Anderson, Terry 78, 90
Angelova, Maria 199, 204, 210
Antón, Marta 171, 186
Arshad, Shahrul Ridzuan 183, 188
Atkinson, Dwight 144, 163
Attewell, Jill 144, 163
Attwell, Graham 16, 22, 25

B

Bachman, Lyle F. 49, 52, 67
Bahr, G. Susanne 185, 186
Bailey, S. M. 31, 41
Bannan, B. 77, 91
Ban, Ruth 170, 187
Barab, Sasha A. 10, 25
Beauvois, Margaret H. 125, 139
Belz, Julie A. 97, 99, 115, 120, 127, 139
Benson, Philip 22, 25
Bertin, Jean-Claude 195, 208
Blin, Françoise iv
Bloch, Joel 148, 163
Bo-Kristensen, Mads 145, 166
Boulton, Alex 36, 37, 41
Bradley, Barbara 19, 27
Bradley, Linda iv, xi, 1, 5, 95
Brown, Ann L. 77, 91
Brown, Gillian 50, 67

Brown, H. Douglas 125, 139
Brown, John 119, 120
Brown, John Seely 76, 91
Brown, Sally 46, 67
Bruns, Axel 146, 164
Bucholtz, Mary 3, 7
Buck, Gary 48, 52, 53, 54, 65, 67
Burden, Robert L. 144, 168
Burns, Hugh L. Jr. 2, 7
Burr, Vivien 144, 164

C

Calero, Maria Dolores 170, 188
Carter, Ronald 50, 67
Chabert, George 148, 166
Chalmers, Matthew 144, 164
Chalon, René 76, 91
Chapelle, Carol A. 139
Chinnery, George M. 148, 164
Clarebout, Geraldine 183, 187
Cobcroft, Rachel S. 146, 164
Collentine, Joseph 144, 164
Collins, Allan 76, 91
Collins, Timothy G. 146, 164
Colpaert, Josef 40, 41
Conole, Gráinne 96, 120
Cornell, Paul 13, 26
Crook, Charles 162, 167

D

Daniel, Mark H. 170, 187
David, Bertrand 76, 91
Davidson, Fred 48, 68
Davies, Graham 3, 7

211

Name Index

Davis, Boyd 126, 139
Deci, Edward L. 22, 26
Deng, Hui 162, 167
de Nooy, Juliana 126, 139, 140, 147, 165
Dewaele, Jean-Marc 125, 126, 134, 135, 139
Dewey, Martin 97, 108, 120
Dias, Joseph 146, 164
Dickinson, Leslie 22, 26
Dippold, Doris 96, 120
Divitini, Monica 148, 166
Dokter, Duco 40, 41
Donato, Richard 104, 120
Douglas, Dan 57, 68
Downes, Stephen 13, 26
Drexler, Wendy 18, 19, 26
Ducate, Lara C. 98, 109, 120, 148, 164
Dudeney, Gavin 50, 68
Duguid, Paul 76, 91, 119, 120
Du, Helen S. 147, 164

E

Elen, Jan 183, 187
Ellis, Rod 184, 187, 191, 192, 195, 208
Elola, Idoia 148, 164
Erben, Tony 170, 187

F

Falodun, Joseph 192, 209
Felix, Uschi 13, 26
Ferguson, Gibson 52, 68
Ferris, Dana R. 184, 187
Feuerstein, Reuven 170, 187

Fidalgo-Eick, Maria 148, 164
Fischer, Robert 171, 187
Fly, Pamela K. 144, 167
Ford, Richard A. 185, 186
Fowley, Cathy viii
Freed, Barbara F. 144, 164
Fulcher, Glenn 48, 68

G

Garrett, Nina 1, 7
Gass, Susan 173, 188
Gass, Susan M. 190, 191, 197, 208, 210
Gee, James Paul 14, 22, 26, 96, 120
Gilmore, Alex 50, 68
Gimeno-Sanz, Ana iv, xi, 52, 58, 60, 62, 63, 68, 69
Gitsaki, Christina 49, 69
Glasner, Angela 46, 67
Godwin-Jones, Robert 148, 164
Grabe, William 48, 68
Granger, Sylviane 173, 187
Gravé, Patrick 195, 208
Gray, William S. 48, 68
Guichon, Nicolas 195, 208
Günther, Silke 145, 165
Gustafsson, Magnus 95
Guth, Sarah 18, 19, 26

H

Hale, Constance 51, 68
Hamp-Lyons, Liz 51, 68
Hanna, Barbara E. 126, 139, 147, 165
Hannafin, Michael J. 77, 93
Han, Seungyeon 2, 7

Name Index

Han, ZhaoHong 184, 187
Harel, Idit 85, 93
Hawisher, Gail E. 2, 7
He, Agnes 193, 208
Healey, Deborah 15, 27
Heift, Trude 31, 40, 41, 42, 184, 186, 187
Hémard, Dominique 40, 42
Henri, France 190, 208
Herczeg, Michael 145, 165
Hernández-Ramos, Pedro 2, 7
Herron, Carol 144, 165
Higgins, John 40, 42
Hill, Janette R. 2, 3, 7
Hinkel, Eli 126, 139
Hirst, Elizabeth 145, 165
Hoffman, Mildred B. 170, 187
Holland, V. Mellissa 41, 42
Horai, Tomoko 55, 69
Hourigan, Tríona 116, 121
Houser, Chris 146, 167
Hoven, Debra 55, 69, 76, 88, 91
Howard, Martin 126, 140
Huann, Tan Yuh 163, 165
Hubbard, Philip 2, 7
Huffaker, David 117, 120
Huhta, Ari 27
Hymes, Dell H. 56, 57, 69, 144, 165

I

Ilgner, Kai 145, 165

J

Jacobs, Joanne 117, 122
Jager, Sake 41, 42

Jaokar, Ajit 147, 165
Jefferson, Gail 203, 209
Jepson, Kevin 199, 206, 208
John, Ow Eu 163, 165
Johns, Tim 41, 42
Julien, R. 30, 42
Juntunen, Merja 17, 26
Jusoff, Kamaruzaman 183, 188

K

Kanagy, Ruth 192, 209
Kelley, Loretta 2, 3, 8
Kelm, Orlando 190, 208
Kelton, A. J. 145, 165
Kenning, Marie-Madeleine 15, 26
Keränen, Anna 27
Kim, Hyung Nam 147, 165
King, Alison 84, 91
Kinginger, Celeste 127, 139
Knobel, Michele 10, 12, 25, 26
Koller, Thomas 41, 42
Kramsch, Claire 83, 86, 89, 91, 97, 99,
    100, 115, 118, 120, 121, 145, 165,
    193, 208
Krashen, Stephen D. 190, 191, 209
Kukulska-Hulme, Agnes v, 73, 77, 91,
    144, 145, 146, 148, 165, 166

L

Laakkonen, Ilona vi, 4, 9, 17, 26
Lafford, Barbara A. 86, 91
Lamendella, John T. 184, 188
Lam, Wan Shun Eva 147, 166
Lankshear, Colin 10, 12, 25, 26

213

Name Index

Lantolf, James P. 75, 92, 104, 117, 121, 128, 140, 170, 172, 173, 186, 187
Larsen-Freeman, Diane 83, 89, 92
Laurillard, Diana 77, 92
Lave, Jean 10, 26, 76, 92
Leander, Kevin M. 145, 166
Lee, Icy 185, 187
Lee, Lina 96, 97, 105, 121, 136, 137, 140
Lee, Mark 23, 27
Levy, Mike 2, 7, 15, 26, 41, 42, 49, 54, 55, 69, 96, 121
L'Haire, Sébastien 173, 187
Liaw, Meei-Ling v
Lidz, Carol S. 171, 188
Lindström, Berner 95
Lomicka, Lara L. 96, 98, 109, 120, 121, 148, 164
Long, Michael H. 190, 191, 192, 197, 199, 203, 206, 209
Lonsdale, Peter 73, 92
Lord, Gillian 96, 98, 121
Low, Leonard 147, 166
Lundgren-Cayrol, Karin 190, 208
Luoma, Sari 55, 56, 57, 69
Luukka, Minna-Riitta 12, 27
Lyster, Roy 125, 140

M

Macario de Siqueira, José 5, 45
Macário de Siqueira, José vi
MacFarlane, Alina 126, 140
Mackey, Alison 173, 188, 190, 208
Madden, Mary Catherine 171, 188
Magnan, Sally Sieloff 128, 140
Makarova, V. 30, 42
Martínez-Sáez, Antonio viii, 5, 45, 63, 67, 69
Mathews, W. Mason 170, 188
McCarthy, Michael 50, 67
McDonough, Kim 173, 188
McGarr, Oliver 85, 92
McIntosh, Ewan 147, 166
McKenney, Susan 90, 92
McLoughlin, Catherine 23, 27
Mercer, Neil 144, 166
Messick, Samuel 46, 65, 69
Meyer, Bente 145, 166
Miller Nelson, Laurie 2, 7
Mortensen, Torill Elvira 116, 118, 121
Mougeon, Raymond 126, 140
Müller-Hartmann, Andreas 98, 121
Murray, Liam 116, 121
Mwanza-Simwami, Daisy 77, 92

N

Nadasdi, Terry 126, 140
Nagata, Noriko 41, 42
Naismith, Laura 73, 77, 92
Narcy-Combes, Jean-Paul 195, 208
Navarro, Elena 170, 188
Nerbonne, John 32, 40, 41, 42
Ní Chiaráin, Neasa x
Nieveen, Nienke 90, 92
Norbrook, Hamisch 146, 166
Nordin, Norazah Mohd 183, 188
Nunan, David 41, 42

Name Index

O

O'Dowd, Robert 97, 98, 99, 100, 121
Ogata, Hiroaki 145, 166
Oskoz, Ana 12, 27, 147, 148, 164, 167
O'Sullivan, Barry 55, 69
Oxford, Rebecca L. 33, 35, 42

P

Pachler, Norbert 73, 75, 92
Palalas, Agnieszka vii, 5, 71, 72, 83, 88, 91, 93
Palmer, Adrian S. 49, 52, 67
Papert, Seymour 85, 93
Paulussen, Hans v
Payne, J. Scott 125, 140, 147, 167
Pelletier, Luc G. 22, 26
Pellettieri, Jill 192, 197, 199, 200, 204, 207, 209
Peña-López, Ismael 17, 27
Pennycook, Alaistair 41, 42
Petersen, Sobah Abbas 148, 166
Pettit, John 73
Pica, Teresa 190, 191, 192, 204, 208, 209
Plomp, Tjeerd 77, 93
Poehner, Matthew E. 170, 171, 186, 187, 188
Pöyhönen, Sari 27
Puren, Christian 193, 209
Purves, A. C. 51, 69
Py, Bernard 190, 209

R

Rand, Ya'acov 170, 187
Razak, Norizan Abdul 183, 188
Read, John 47, 69
Reagan, Vera 126, 139
Reeves, Thomas C. 2, 8
Rehner, Katherine 126, 129, 136, 140
Reinking, David 19, 27
Rheinhardt, Jonathon 10, 27
Richards, J. C. 31, 43
Ringstaff, Cathy 2, 3, 8
Ritchie, Mathy vii, 6, 123
Robinson, Peter 192, 209
Rodden, Tom 162, 167
Rodgers, Theodore S. 31, 43
Roithmeier, Waltraud 126, 140
Rosenbloom, Stephanie 148, 167
Ros i Solé, Christina 147, 167
Rost, Michael 85, 93
Roth, Wolff-Michael 10, 25
Ryan, Richard M. 22, 26
Rystedt, Hans 95

S

Sacks, Harvey 203, 209
Salaberry, M. Rafael 148, 167
Sarré, Cédric vii, 6, 189, 196, 209
Sato, Charlene J. 203, 206, 209
Savignon, Sandra J. 126, 140
Savill-Smith, Carol 144, 163
Sax, Kelly 126, 141
Schegloff, Emanuel A. 203, 209
Schmenk, Barbara 41, 43
Schrum, Lynne 13, 27, 147, 167
Schulze, Mathias 31, 40, 42, 43
Schürcks-Grozeva, Lily 40, 41
Scott, Paul 146, 166

215

Name Index

Selfe, Cynthia L. 2, 7
Selinker, Larry 184, 188
Sevilla-Pavón, Ana ix, 5, 45, 63, 67, 69
Sfard, Anna 12, 27
Shao, Yinjuan viii, 6, 143, 152, 162, 167
Sharples, Mike 73, 76, 77, 83, 92, 93, 145, 167
Shekary, M. 199, 210
Shield, Lesley 73, 146, 148, 166
Siemens, George 14, 27
Skinner, Barbara 171, 188
Smagorinsky, Peter 144, 167
Smith, Bryan 199, 210
Smith, Judith E. 146, 164
Smit, Petra 40, 41
Solomon, Gwen 13, 27, 147, 167
Söter, A. 51, 69
Stockwell, Glenn 2, 7, 15, 26, 49, 54, 55, 69
Summers, Robert 170, 187
Swain, Merrill 125, 126, 141
Sykes, Julie M. 12, 14, 27, 147, 148, 167

T

Taalas, Peppi v, 27
Tahririan, M. H. 199, 210
Takala, S. 51, 69
Tarnanen, Mirja 27
Tarone, Elaine 125, 126, 141
Taylor, Josie 76, 93
Taylor, Richard 49, 69
Thiede, Ralf 126, 139
Thomas, Siobhan 146, 167

Thorne, Steven L. 10, 12, 27, 75, 93, 97, 98, 99, 100, 103, 104, 113, 117, 121, 141, 147, 167
Thornton, Patricia 146, 167
Thouësny, Sylvie iv, xi, 1, 6, 169, 171, 188
Towers, Stephen J. 146, 164
Traxler, John 144, 166

U

Uzum, Baburhan 126, 141

V

Vähäpassi, A. 51, 69
Vallerand, Robert J. 22, 26
Van den Akker, Jan 90, 92
Van der Aalsvoort, Geerdina M. 171, 188
Van Essen, Arthur 41, 42
Van Harmelen, M. 16, 27
Van Lier, Leo 86, 93
Varonis, Evangeline M. 191, 197, 210
Vavoula, Giasemi 73, 76, 92, 93
Vygotsky, Lev Semenovich 76, 93, 97, 121

W

Wagner, Christian 147, 164
Wang, Feng 77, 93
Ward, Monica vi
Ware, Paige D. 97, 99, 100, 115, 118, 121
Warschauer, Mark 15, 22, 27, 98, 122, 125, 141, 146, 168, 172, 188
Wegerif, Rupert 119, 122
Weigle, Sarah Cushing 51, 52, 69

Weinstein, Nina 94
Weir, Cyril 55, 69
Wenger, Etienne 14, 28, 76, 92
Wertsch, James V. 144, 168
Wheeler, Steve 17, 21, 28
White, Cynthia 33, 35, 42, 43
Whiteside, Anne 97, 120
Whitney, Paul J. 125, 140
Wiley, David 2, 7
Williams, Jeremy B. 117, 122
Williams, Marion 144, 168
Winkler, Thomas 145, 165
Wood, Peter viii, 5, 29, 30, 35, 40, 42, 43

Y

Yano, Yoneo 145, 166
Yin, Chuantao 76, 91
Young, Richard 193, 208
Yuen, Jeanne Marie 163, 165
Yule, George 50, 67

Z

Zhao, Ying 199, 204, 210
Zhao, Yong 145, 168
Ziefle, Martina 174, 188

www.ingramcontent.com/pod-product-compliance
Lightning Source LLC
Chambersburg PA
CBHW022006160426
43197CB00007B/306